THE BEGINNING

OF WISDOM

A COMPILATION OF SELECTED STATEMENTS FROM THE AVATAR OF THE KALI AGE, BHAGAVAN SRI SATYA SAI BABA.

**COMPILED BY
JACK SCHRAMM**

A compilation of wisdom from the kali yuga (age) avatar,
Bhagavan Sri Sathya Sai Baba

__INTRODUCTION:__

Enclosed in these pages are selected statements from the Avatar of the Kali age, **Bhagavan Sri Sathya Sai Baba**. This book is a brief sampling of some of his wisdom.

The statements included in this book were selected from Sai Baba's many lectures and discourses. These specific selections will make it easier for the American reader to readily grasp the point of the statements. Statements with references to ancient Sanskrit, ancient Indian deities, etc. were purposely not used in this book. This book, The Beginning of Wisdom, will not require anything beyond the English language for comprehension; there are many books which include all of his statements which you may wish to place on your reading list (sources are listed at the at the end of the book).

Why should we value Sai Baba's statements? The statements themselves answer this question in a way unique for each person. Since you have not read this book as yet, I believe that the first question to answer is: What is an Avatar?

A brief definition for "Avatar" would be: __Divinity apparently born and existing as a human person, but in reality remaining as the limitless divine__. Sai Baba has demonstrated, time and time again, that he is indeed an Avatar (for the uninitiated souls, I suggest you read any one of many books on his life. I think that a good place for Americans to start would be "Sai Baba, Avatar", by Howard Murphet). To go into his many "ways" and "miracles" is not part of the scope of this book.

Many people alive right now recently had the opportunity to experience a true Avatar in human form. Unfortunately, Sai Baba left his body in 2011. I am of the understanding that the last Avatar to appear before Sai Baba was Krishna, approximately 5,800 years ago; and before that it was Rama, about 21,000 years ago.

Why has an Avatar come to the earth now? Sai Baba answers that in his statement found in "The Breath of Sai", by Grace T. McMartin:

"Man has become the bond-slave of lower instincts and desires, He is unable to distinguish between the low urges of lust and the elevating urge of Love. Love is the first step on the road that leads to Divine Grace. But man wallows in lust for physical comfort and pleasure; he is haunted by that nefarious companion of lust, called anger. When lust is frustrated, anger overtakes him and he becomes bestial and even demonic. When lust envelops the heart of man, truth, justice, compassion and peace flee from it. The world degenerates into a snake pit, and God comes to rescue mankind from its doom.

The Avatar comes to reveal man to himself, to restore to him his birthright of inner bliss. He does not come to found a new creed, to breed a new faction, to instill a new God. If such happens, it is the consequence of the evil in man. The Avatar comes as Man in order to demonstrate that Man is Divine, in order to be within reach of Man. The human mind cannot grasp the Absolute, attributeless Principle; it is abstract and beyond the reach of speech, mind and intellect. Fire is inherent in the match-stick but it is only when it is struck as a flame that we can benefit by it. The Formless has to manifest as Form: the Formless has to appear with Form. Then only can man listen, learn, understand, follow and be saved, through the Bliss of that experience. He lights the flame of Realization in each; and the age-old ignorance is destroyed in an instant."

It is my sincere desire that this book may be the beginning of your journey on the noble path of wisdom.

A SPECIAL THANKS TO MY FRIEND BARBARA HENDERSON FOR ALL OF THE HELP AND INPUT THAT WAS REQUIRED FOR THE COMPLETION OF THIS BOOK.

<u>FORWARD</u>

I have made an attempt to compile the statements into categories so this book could be used as a reference once it has been read through. The categories in which the statements have been placed are not precise; so it might be difficult to find a particular statement that one would want to reread. You will quickly see early on, that all statements could easily fit under the "Wisdom" category, and many would fit well into two or three categories.

I have compiled this group of statements for the benefit of all who will read, but especially for my fellow Americans. It is my belief that many Americans are caught in the "cycle of births and deaths", not the slightest bit aware that their lives do not reflect even a beginning thought towards the "goal of life". Entrenched in materialism and many desires, perhaps this book will come to them "just at the right time" when their life is not flowing as they would like it to, and the feeling that a review of life's direction is in order.

It is my belief that this book can serve as a guiding light towards new directions and answers to the age old questions like, "Why am I here?", and "Are there wiser choices that I could make with my life at this time?" Presently, I have found Sai Baba's great words of wisdom to be the highest source for answers to life's many questions.

Come.......it is time now for you to see for yourself, just what I am talking about..........

TABLE OF CONTENTS

THE AVATAR

0001: The Lord incarnates as Man to help man comprehend that which apparently cannot be understood and to enable him to attain that which is seemingly unattainable. By this, however, the Lord who is Infinite, Immutable and Immanent, does not suffer any diminution. Neither is He, though embodied in a human form, influenced by the taints and blemishes that normally affect a human being.
Summer Showers, 1979, p. 88

0002: Avatars do not come in unique form. The reason is all the creatures in the world carry out their specific functions. Animals, birds, insects, ants and mosquitoes do not deviate from their respective roles in leading their lives. But, man alone has forgotten his duties. Birds obey "reason and season". Man alone behaves without regard to "reason and season". Hence the Avatar has come in human form to reform man who has gone astray. Thus it is declared that "God comes in human form". If God comes in any other form, say a bird, it will be driven away. Man will take no notice of it. If the Avatar comes in the form of a buffalo, it will be driven away with a stick.
Sanathana Sarathi, September, 1996, p. 244

0003: There are various reasons for the advent of the Divine in human form. For the human being, his past Karma (action) is the cause of birth. The circumstances of each one's birth depend on his past actions. Man is bound by the consequences of his actions. It may be asked, "what is the karma that accounts for the advent of Avatars"? For Divine incarnations karma is not the cause. The evil deeds of the wicked and the good deeds and yearning of the righteous are responsible for the advent of Avatars.
Sathya Sai Speaks. Volume VI, p. 333

0004: God takes human form when the Godliness that is inherent in man is submerged: when the moral code and the spiritual discipline that have been prescribed by the experiences of Godly seekers are neglected; when man slides into beast from which he rose and becomes a terror to brother man.
Gems of Wisdom, Avatar, p. 293

0005: The Avatar behaves in a human way so that mankind can feel kinship, but rises to superhuman heights so that mankind can also aspire to those heights.
Sathya Sai Speaks; Volume IV, p. 41

0006: When the Divine comes down as Avatar, it is only for one purpose. You recognize only the momentary results of the advent. But you should note that the Divine comes as Avatar only to teach mankind the truth about love. "Oh man, it is because you lack love and are filled with selfishness that the world is plunged in

So much conflict and chaos. It is only when you develop love and the spirit of sacrifice that you will realize the divinity that is in the human." The man who has no spirit of sacrifice will be a prey to all ills. A man without love is a living corpse. It is love and sacrifice which makes man Divine.

Sathya Sai Speaks; Volume X, p. 229

0007: When Dharma (code of conduct) is distorted and man undermines his earthly career, forgetting the high purpose for which he has come, the Lord incarnates and leads him along the correct path. That is to say HE comes as MAN, to restore the principles and re-establish the practice of Dharma.

Gems of Wisdom, Avatar, p. 296

0008: I am determined to correct you only after informing you of my credentials. That is why I am now then announcing my nature by means of miracles, that is, acts which are beyond human capacity and human understanding. Not that I am anxious to show my powers. The object is to draw you closer to me, to cement your hearts to me.   *Sathya Sai Speaks; Volume II, p. 118*

0009: In the past ages, Avatars rid the world of evil by destroying the few fanatics and monstrously cruel persons. But, today fanaticism and felony reign in every heart. The number of evil men is legion; no one is free from that discredit; all are wicked to some extent or other. Therefore, everyone needs correction, everyone has to be educated and guided into the right path.

Sathya Sai Speaks; Volume IV, p. 3

0010: To elevate man, to raise the level of His consciousness, He has to incarnate as man. He has to speak to them in their own style and language. He has to teach them the methods that they can adopt and practice. Birds and beasts need no Divine Incarnation to guide them, for they have no inclination to stray away from their dharma (code of right conduct). Man alone forgets or ignores the goal of life.

The Avatar behaves in a human way so mankind can feel kinship, but rises to super-human heights so that mankind can aspire to those heights.

Gems of Wisdom, Why is God not seen? p. 348

0011: I always speak of dharma (code of right conduct), for I have come to reestablish it. I have no other work here. You should not infer that dharma is declining only in India, because all the Avatars you know took birth here; the Avatar has to take shape in the place where dharma originated and where it is still studied and valued. The rest of the world is but the branches of this tree. For Me this is no native land or foreign land. All humanity has to be brought back to the path of dharma.   *Gems of Wisdom, Sai Baba's Mission, p. 424*

0012: For this Sai has come in order to achieve the supreme task of uniting the entire mankind as one family through the bone of brotherhood, of affixing and illuminating the Atma Reality of each being, in order to reveal the Divine which is the basis on which the entire cosmos rests and of instructing all, recognizing the common Divine heritage, that binds man to man so that man can rid himself of the animal, and rise into the Divine which is his goal.

Gems of Wisdom, Sai Baba's Mission, p. 428

0013: Some objects Swami creates in just the same way that he created the material universe. Other objects, such as watches are brought from existing supplies. There are no invisible beings helping Swami bring things. His Sankalpa, his Divine Will, will bring the object in a moment. Swami is everywhere. His creations belong to the natural unlimited power of God and are in no sense the product of yogic powers as the yogis or of magic as with magicians. The power is in no way contrived or developed, but is natural only.

Gems of Wisdom, How the Divine Acts, p. 441

0014: The Divine does not make the descent as an Avatar without a purpose. The purpose is to enable Nature to fulfill its role. To be born as human beings is a rare blessing. The Avatar instructs humanity how to redeem human existence.

Sanathana Sarathi, September 1997, p. 230

0015: If I had come among you as Marayana with four arms holding the conch, the wheel, the mace and the lotus, you would have kept me in a museum and charged a fee for those who seek darshan. If I had come as a mere man, you would not have respected my teaching and followed it for your own good. So I have to be in this human form with superhuman wisdom and powers.

Sathya Sai Baba, God as man

0016: This human form is one in which every divine entity, every divine principle, that is to say all the forms and names ascribed to God by man are manifest . . . why do you waste your time and energy trying to explain Me? Can a fish measure Me, you will only fail. Try rather to discover your own measure. Then you will succeed better in discovering My measure.   *Sathya Sai Baba, God as man*

0017: My life is my message. Eons come and go. But the Eternal Verities Sathya (Truth) and Dharma (Righteousness) remain valid for all ages. Whenever Truth and Righteousness decline, the Divine comes down in human form to show mankind the way of Sathya and Dharma and to help them realize the Divine Source from which they have come.   *Sanathana Sarathi, July 1997, p. 178*

0018: The role of every Avatar (Incarnation of the Divine) is to establish the way of Truth and Righteousness, banish all that is evil, false and unrighteous in the world, and help to manifest the divinity in mankind.
Sanathana Sarathi, June 1996, p. 155

0019: Whenever ashanti (absence of peace) overwhelms the world, the Lord will incarnate in human form to establish the modes of earning prashanti (tranquillity) and to reeducate the human community in the paths of peace. At the present time, strife and discord have robbed the family, the school, the community, the society, the villages, the cities and the state, of peace and amity.
Sathya Sai Speaks, Volume IV, p. 150

0020: Man has become the bond-slave of lower instincts and desires. He is unable to distinguish between the low urges of lust and the elevating urge of Love. Love is the first step on the road that leads to Divine Grace. But man wallows in lust for physical comfort and pleasure; he is hounded by that nefarious companion of lust, called anger. When lust is frustrated, anger overtakes him and he becomes bestial and even demonic. When lust envelops the heart of man, truth, justice, compassion and peace flee form it. The world degenerates into a snake pit, and God comes to rescue mankind from its doom.

    The Avatar comes to reveal man to himself, to restore to him his birthright of inner Bliss. He does not come to found a new creed, to breed a new faction, to instill a new God. If such happens, it is the consequence of the evil in man. The Avatar comes as Man in order to demonstrate that Man is Divine, in order to be within reach of Man. The human mind cannot grasp the Absolute, Attributeless Principle; it is Abstract and beyond the reach of Speech, Mind and Intellect. Fire is inherent in the match-stick but it is only when it is struck as a flame that we can benefit by it. The Formless has to manifest as Form: the Formless has to appear with Form. Then only can man listen, learn, understand, follow and be saved, through the Bliss of that experience. He lights the flame of Realization on each; and the age-old ignorance is destroyed in an instant.
Baba, The Breath of Sai, p. 305

THE BODY

0021: A man regards his visible body as real and the invisible Spirit as unreal. He does not realize that the invisible is the cause of his pleasure and pain. "Let no one imagine that beauty, youth and vitality will last for ever. Old age is looming ahead and will bring on its train of miseries" (Telugu Poem)
Sanathana Sarathi, September, 1996, p. 24

0022: You have earned this human body by the accumulated merit of many lives as inferior beings (animals, beasts, reptiles, etc.) and it is indeed a great pity if you were to fritter away this precious opportunity in activities that are natural only to those inferior beings.   *Sathya Sai Speaks, Volume V, p. 4*

0023: The human body is the most wondrous machine in the world. It has a bewildering multiplicity of limbs, organs, veins, nerves and cells which co-operate to maintain it under varied conditions. If any one of these rebels or refuses to rescue another, the body is bound to suffer. So too, a society, community, or nation can be safe, secure and happy only when the individuals comprising it are mutually helpful and bound together in skillful and sincere service. Every generation has to receive education and training in such intelligent cooperation and service, or else, the world has to face confusion and chaos.
                Gems of Wisdom, The Teacher and Tomorrow, p.192

0024: The body by its nature is perishable. But the Dehi (the Indwelling Spirit) is undying. Through the IMPERMANENT body, the eternal spirit has to be experienced. Men are immersed in seeking the passing pleasures of the senses forgetting the lasting bliss to be derived from the spirit. People should realize that true happiness can be got only by union with God.
                Sanathana Sarathi, September, 1996, p. 241

0025: It is nature that induces the belief that you are the body. This identification has led to an inordinate degree of attention to the body and consequently to worry and misery.   *Gems of Wisdom, Spiritual Quality is Essential, p. 279*

0026: You will be subject to the duality's of pleasure and pain, joy and sorrow, good and evil as long as you identify yourself with the perishable and mutable physical body.   *Summer Showers, 1979, p. 26*

0027: Of the five sensory organs, the tongue is the most important. It has a dual role to play, unlike the eye, the ear, the nose and the skin which have only the single functions of seeing, hearing, smelling and touching, respectively. The tongue has not only the capacity to taste, but also the power of speech. The tongue has tremendous alertness and forbearance as is shown by its survival in the midst of thirty-six sharp teeth which may inadvertently bite it at any time. Besides, it displays enormous self-respect and does not leave its abode, the mouth, even under the most difficult circumstances! The wound caused by a slip of the foot may be healed by medication; on the other hand, the damage caused by a slip of the tongue may be irreparable. That is why the tongue must be carefully controlled at all times.   *Summer Showers, 1979, p. 152*

0028: Treat the body as an instrument for realizing the Divine by engaging yourselves in sacred activities. Then humanity will blossom into Divinity. Contemplation on the Divine is the only way to achieve this. Continuous contemplation leads to God-Realization, and then you become God, Himself.
Divine Discourse on Gurupurnima Day, 7/26/91

0029: So long as life is present, we are to some extent enjoying and appreciating the bodily relationship of either a mother or a father or a brother or a sister or a wife and so on. But once life has fled, then we will realize that all the relationships which we were enjoying were only bodily relationships and have no value. That anything that has been permanent is true only in respect of the Divine soul that is contained in the body and not the body itself, becomes very clear. Therefore, the one who is a true relation to us, the one who is a true friend to us, the one who is a true guide to us, can only be God and none other. All relationships are like passing clouds which come and go. The permanent and eternal truth of God should be your ultimate aim. Other things which look like truths are not permanent truths. They are not eternal truths. You should give them up. You should fill your hearts with "prema" (love). That is the only way in which you can reach the eternal truth of God. You should work with a determination to fill your hearts with prema and reach this goal.
Gems of Wisdom, Where is God?, p. 340

0030: Try to prevent the five sins that the body commits: killing, adultery, theft, drinking intoxicants, and the eating of the flesh.
　　　A man is judged by the nature of his actions; if they are good, then he, too is a good man, and if they are bad, then he too is considered a bad or wicked man. Mans' qualities and actions are interdependent.
Gems of Wisdom, Serve ever, Hurt Never, p. 402

0031: The realization of the Atma is impeded by envy, malice and jealously which are caused by attachment to the perishable physical body.
Summer Showers, 1979, p. 27

0032: Consider the relationship between the body and God. The hands, the eyes, the ears, the mouth and the nose are organs in the body; all these are limbs of the body. The body is a limb of society. Society is a limb of Nature. Nature is a limb of the Divine. This is the integral relationship between the human body and God. The indweller in the body and God are one. The body is a moving temple. Without the indwelling spirit, the body is only a corpse fit to be burnt or buried.
Sanathana Sarathi, May 1995, p. 134

0033: Trees bear fruits, rivers carry water, cows yield milk, not for their own sake

but for the sake of others. Equally, the body is given to man for helping others.
Sanathana Sarathi, May 1996, p. 123

0034: Treat the body as a chariot wherein God is installed and is being taken in procession. To avoid a breakdown, be vigilant on the following points:

1. Fast one day in a week.
2. Sit down for a meal only when acute hunger overtakes you.
     Do not eat at fixed times; wait for the call of hunger before reloading the stomach.
3. Carry out your personal work and do not depend on servants.
     Hard work
     will keep you fit.
4. Keeping the mind fixed on God and pure ideas will ensure good health.
5. Keep the eye, ear, tongue, hands, and feet under restraint.
6. Use the body as a boat to cross the ocean of life with devotion and detachment as the two oars.
7. Do not worry about the health at all times.
8. Be in sun, let its rays fall on the body; that will help you to be healthy.

Three things will enable man to lead a proper life; all begin with the letter "W": **Work**- stands for good sacred work for promoting the prosperity of the country. **Worship**- should be done with a pure mind. **Wisdom**- is the superior knowledge and man should aspire for acquiring it with devotion.
Sathya Sai Speaks, Volume X, p. 278

0035: The one who is immersed in body consciousness is a prey to all kinds of troubles and worries. It should be realized that the body is only an instrument and is bound to perish some time or other. When death is bound to follow birth, why worry about it?   *Sanathana Sarathi, August 1997, p. 200*

0036: The body is a house taken on rent by man. We know how the owner of the house persecutes the tenant in order to compel him to vacate it when the rent is not paid, or when the payment is delayed, or when the tenant does not maintain the house with care and when he damages it through negligence or sheer wantonness. Therefore, it is our duty to keep the body in good trim and avoid the wrath of the owner. The owner will certainly appreciate a considerate, courteous and cooperative tenant. In truth God is the owner of the house in which we live as He owns the body. The tenant can win the owner's love and respect by means of his own goodness.

The body is for realizing Godness, which is total goodness. But, the body is not itself goodness or Godness: it is an instrument that breaks down every moment and that is rebuilt, every moment getting weaker in the process. The fathe says proudly, "My son is growing fast," but really, his life is ebbing fast. The body is valuable only on account of its use in realizing God. The human body is not an ordinary thing. It is like the temple of God. In this sacred and divine temple the human body, the effulgent self is living. Like every river flows to join the sea, human life must also flow to join its ultimate destination, to the Ocean of Divinity.

Baba, The Breath of Sai, p. 228

0037: In every human being, divinity is present in the form of Atma. In order that we may understand the sacred Atma that is present in our body, we should regard our body as simply a container for the Atma.

Summer Showers in Brindivan, 1977, p. 99

0038: The body that has been given to us for the search of truth is being used for inferior objectives. Truly, we have to search for and find a precious stone in dust. A precious stone cannot be found on the top of a tree. In the same manner, the pearls of wisdom can be found only by searching for them in the human body which is just dust. Dust thou art and to dust thou shalt return.

Summer Showers in Brindivan, 1977, p. 248

0039: Everyone should try to convert the body into a flute for the Divine to make His music flow through it. The body should be made a fit instrument for such music. Then it becomes a means of service to others. The best way to love God is to love all, serve all. You must learn even to love your enemy. A kind word even to an enemy may eliminate his hatred. It is through love that man should refine his nature.

Sanathana Sarathi; October, 1997, p. 263

0040: The body, the sense organs, the mind and the intellect are the instruments for a human being. Only the person who understands the secret of these instruments will be able to comprehend the Atmic Principle.

If a man cannot understand the vesture he is wearing, how can he understand the mystery of the Infinite Indwelling Spirit?

First comes the body. It is called "deha" because its ultimate destiny is cremation. The body is burnt after the life goes out of it. The body may be judged by its form, but it is in fact a receptacle for all kinds of garbage and is subject to numerous ills of the flesh.

The body at the beginning is a lump of flesh (as fetus). Then it acquires an attractive form. Youth confers on it special charm. In old age it develops deformities.

The body is consumed by the fire of worry when a man is alive or is burnt on the funeral pyre when he is dead.

Sanathana Sarathi, November 1997, p. 287

0041: However great a scholar may be, however profound his knowledge of the scriptures, he has to learn all about the body because it brings with it the consequences of the previous lives of the individual. The body is the basic instrument for all actions in this life and for the acquisition of all knowledge and skills. Everyone at the time of birth brings with him a necklace from the Creator made up of the results of his good and bad actions in past lives.

Everyone can reap only the fruits of what he sows. Only good actions can produce good results. Your happiness or sorrow is related to the nature of your actions.   *Sanathana Sarathi, November 1997, p. 287*

0042: You are considering the bodies which are different in form as different from you. To do so is "sin". You must only see the Atma in all. There are many bulbs of different shapes and sizes here in this hall. But the electric current that makes them shine is only one. The "Atnathathva", the principle of Atma, is the one current that activates all the bodies which are like bulbs of different hues and shapes.   *Sanathana Sarathi, June 1995, p. 165*

0043: In ordinary life people regard the body as permanent and for the sake of its pleasures undertake all kinds of efforts. This is a sign of ignorance. A body without a mind is as useless as a school without a teacher and a temple without a deity. The body should be regarded as an instrument for right living.
                    Sanathana Sarathi, January 1995, p. 1

0044: People speak about Moksha (liberation). What is it from which they have to be liberated? Is it from family, wealth or position? No. Liberation is from the sense of identification with the body. The body is only an instrument and not your true self. The body is a gift from God. It does not belong to you, but you have to protect it as an instrument given to you. Everything belongs to God. You have to treat it as a trust and not as your private property. It is therefore, your duty to make right use of the body and senses given to you.
                    Sanathana Sarathi, December 1995, p. 320

0045: Just as the body is the house you live in, the world is the body of God.
                    Sathya Sai Speaks, Volume IV, p. 18

0046: The body is impermanent. But it is the abode of the indwelling Spirit. It is a shrine and when it moves, the Divine moves with it. Hence, the body should be cared for in the same way in which an iron safe which is of little value in itself, is safe-guarded for the sake of valuables kept in it.

What is it that binds man to the illusory world? It is not family or property. These can be given up when one wishes to do so. But what are most difficult to renounce are attachment and hatred. As long as these are dominant in man, he cannot realize his true self. And as long as man remains unaware of his true self, he is in bondage. For man in bondage, there is no freedom from suffering or worry.   *Sanathana Sarathi, March 1996, back cover*

0047: The body in not a mass of flesh and bone; it is a medium for manthras (sacred words or formulae) which save when they are meditated upon. It is a sacred instrument earned after long ages of struggle, equipped with reason and emotion, capable of being used for deliverance from grief and evil. Honour it as such; keep it in good condition, so that it might serve that high purpose; maintain it even more carefully than these brick houses; and, always preserve the conviction that it is an instrument and nothing more. Use it for just the purpose for which it has been designed and given.   *Sathya Sai Speaks, Volume IV, p. 17*

CHARACTER

0048: A virtuous character is the lamp which illumines the path to peace and joy. This is the teaching of Sages who had the welfare of humanity at heart and who bore the rigors of asceticism to discover the key.

Which do you cleanse more in a drinking vessel? The interior or exterior? Inner cleanliness should be your first aim.

Purify your feelings and impulses; do not worry that others are not doing it. Each man carries his destiny in his own hands. You will not be bound because others are not free. You should strive for your salvation at your own pace from where you started when you were born into this chance. Earn yourself, for yourself. Two people may have equal plots of land, but they reap different quantities of grain depending on the skill and attention they bestow and the quality of the soil, the seeds and the manure they use.

Thoughts automatically give rise to actions. Actions in turn produce habits, and habits, then, form man's character. It is the character which decides our destiny- for good or bad.   *Gems of Wisdom, Character, p. 224*

0049: The crisis of character which is at the root of all the troubles everywhere, has come about as a result of the neglect of this aspect in education. Wisdom thrives when man is afraid of vice and sin and is attached to the Divine.
     Sathya Sai Speaks, Volume X, p. 3

0050: You do not lose much if a finger is so damaged that it needs to be cut off. The body can still function and be a fit instrument. Even if you lose a limb, you can function and benefit with the help of your faculties. But if you lose your character, then everything is lost.   *Sathya Sai Speaks, Volume X, p. 129*

0051: You cannot be fresh and feeling fine, wearing a washed vest under an unwashed shirt; or an unwashed vest under a washed shirt. Both have to be clean, to provide the sense of tingling joy. So too outer and inner cleanliness is but a reflection of the inner achievement. There is a strange glow on the face of guileless person. Inner cleanliness has its own soap and water- the soap of strong faith and the water of constant practice.

Gems of Wisdom, Morality, p. 227

0052: Morality is virtuous character. These are the very foundations of progress, the very basic needs. They grow in the realm of the spirit. But today the spirit is neglected, physical and animal needs are catered to. They are accepted as the ends of living: all efforts are directed to these.

Sathya Sai Speaks, Volume VII, p. 336

0053: Good conduct, good qualities, good character alone constitutes our real treasure. But man today has given up these three and is busy seeking worldly goods and is imagining that he is leading a pious life. God cannot be attained through such delusions. Man today is trying to master every kind of knowledge, but is unable to discover his own true nature.

Gems of Wisdom, Wealth, p. 227

0054: There are educational institutions in the farthest corners of every land, but it is a pity that peace of mind has become very rare. Why has peace remained out of reach in spite of the plethora of gadgets and contrivances that offer man comfort and pleasure?

The fault lies in human conduct, which runs along evil lines. When man thinks, speaks and acts along virtuous lines, his conscience will be clean and he will have inner peace. Knowledge is power, it is said; but virtue is peace. The world reveres, even today, great men and women who have lives exemplary lives of virtue. Jesus, Mohammed, Zoroaster, Buddha, Sankaracharya, Madhacacharya, Ramanujacharya and others were able to command the loyalty and adoration of people solely on account of the purity of their conduct and actions. They have become immortal residents in the heart of mankind. Scholarship cannot confer this high historic ascendancy. Mastery of books may help you to expound or exhibit dialectical skill, but what really is the width and depth of your experience; and just examine how conceited you have become! Man must saturate his daily life in truthful speech, virtuous acts and holy thoughts.

Sathya Sai Speaks, Volume X, p. 267

0055: If you say that the world is not a bed of roses but is a place of misery, the fault lies in you, the inhabitants. It is character that marks the life of a good individual.

Sanathana Sarathi, August 1997, p. 204

0056: To remove the chaos and violence prevailing in society you have to become Karmayogis and devote all your knowledge, ability and energies to the transformation of Society. It is not wealth that is important. Character alone counts. Sensual pleasures (Bhoga) can only lead to disease (Roga), Sacrifice (Thyaga) leads to Yoga (Communion with the Divine). Discipline is vital.
Gems of Wisdom, Service, p. 158

0057: For human life, virtue confers beauty. Without virtue, life ceases to be beautiful. Virtue implies conduct which evokes the approbation of others. It must be exemplary and confer delight on others. It should not cause harm to others or appear ludicrous. It should bring a good name.
Sanathana Sarathi, August 1994, p. 218

0058: The sapling has to be tended very carefully, so that it could grow into a mighty tree in the right manner and serve the people well. To whatever country you may belong, cultivation of character is essential at any point of time. There is no such thing as American character, Russian character and so on. Character is common to the entire humanity. There is only one caste, the caste of Humanity, one language, the language of the Heart and one Religion, the Religion of Love. Whichever country you may hail from, whatever language you speak and whichever faith you follow, you should maintain sterling human character.
Sanathana Sarathi, August 1997, p. 203

0059: Man's bad or good fortune is related to his thoughts. Sowing the seed of thoughts, man reaps the fruit known as Karma (deeds). Sowing the seed of Karma, man reaps the fruit of character (Seela). From character, one reaps the fruit of good fortune. Thus fortune is based on character, which is based on good practices arising out of good deeds based on good practices arising out of good deeds and good thoughts. Thus according to the development of good thoughts, one's good fortune will also grow.   *Sanathana Sarathi, January 1995, p. 2*

0060: When one's wealth is lost, it can be acquired again. If one's friend is lost, another can be got. It the wife passes, one can marry again. If land is lost, it can be acquired again. But if time is lost it cannot be got back.

In this vast cosmos and among the myriad species, man is the highest and noblest being. He is sublime. He is full of good traits. If a man loses these attributes of humanness, they cannot be easily regained. Young men and women! The prosperity and well being of the world depend on the conduct of the youth. Only when their conduct is good, the world can have an ideal future.
Sanathana Sarathi, July 1997, p. 171

0061: There are two qualities in man; one is the animal nature; the other is humanness. Unfortunately man is forfeiting his humanness by falling a prey to the six enemies: lust, anger, greed, envy and others, and misusing his God-given talents. He thereby degrades himself to the level of the animal. On the other hand, man should use his mind, status, and talents to become virtuous, pursue the path of righteousness and strive to raise himself from the human to the Divine. All things in the world should be used properly, and not misused. A knife can be used for cutting vegetables or another's throat. How a knife is used depends on the man using it. His mental state should be in proper condition. A man's conduct is related to his thoughts and feelings. The heart is inherently pure. But one's thoughts can pollute it or keep it pure. One can make or mar his destiny by his thoughts and actions. *Sanathana Sarathi, July 1997, p. 171*

0062: Today everywhere the world is haunted by suffering, unrest, disorder and agitations. Any country filled with noble beings is bound to be peaceful and happy. What is the reason for the sad plight of a country? It is the absence of men and women of high character. To protect a country it is not so important to have arms and missiles and atom bombs. It is most essential to have men and women of great virtue. *Sanathana Sarathi, July 1997, p. 172*

0063: The end of wisdom is freedom; the end of culture is perfection; the end of knowledge is love; the end of education is character.
Sanathana Sarathi, December 1993, p. 335

0064: Truth endows one's life with sweetness. Loving words sweeten life. Let your speech be always sweet, whatever the circumstances. Just as sugarcane has to go through crushing and other processes before you can get candy from it, the body has to go through certain ordeals to manifest its sweet nature. These are termed Samakaras: the good thoughts, good feelings and good actions which bring about refinement. Love is essential for this refinement. Hence, love is the means to realize the nectarine sweetness of life.
Sanathana Sarathi, August 1994, p. 218

0065: The control of the senses is itself a form of sacrifice which leads to Immortality. Sacrifice of wealth of possessions is no sacrifice at all. It is the sacrifice of the senses (the desires caused by them) which is the highest sacrifice. *Sanathana Sarathi, April 1994, p. 89*

0066: In the spiritual field, man is enjoined at the very outset to know himself. He should not be a slave of the senses. Nor should he follow others like sheep. "Be a ship and not sheep". A ship serves to carry others and cross the Ocean.
Sanathana Sarathi, April 1995, p. 98

0067: Some say that knowledge is valuable, but character is more valuable than knowledge. One may be a learned scholar, one may hold high positions of authority, one may be very wealthy or be an eminent scientist, but if one has no character, all the other acquisitions are of no use at all.

Sanathana Sarathi, May 1994, p. 113

DEATH

0068: How sad it is that this human life, precious as an invaluable diamond that cannot be priced at all, has been cheapened to the standard of a worn-out worthless coin! There is no use repenting after wasting time without profit, without meditating on God, or practicing any spiritual discipline to realize Him.

What is the use in planning a well, when the house has caught fire? When is it to be dug? When will water become available? When is the fire to be extinguished? It is an impossible task! If at the very start, there was a well ready, how helpful it would be on such critical occasions! Beginning to contemplate on God during the last moments is like beginning to dig the well. So, if from now on, one equips himself by the contemplation of God off and on, it will stand him in good stead when the end approaches. Start today the spiritual discipline that has to be done tomorrow! Start now the Spiritual discipline that has to be done today! One does not know what is in store the next moment. Therefore, there should be no delay in engaging one-self in the spiritual discipline that has to be done. But people in their foolishness continue to postpone in a world from which, today or tomorrow, they are bound to depart.

Therefore, awake soon. Try to know the essence of everything, the eternal Truth. Try to experience the Love which is the Over-self itself. Discriminate at every turn, accepting what is true and discarding the rest. Instead of getting enslaved to the evanescent and the false and wasting precious time in their pursuits, dedicate every minute to the discovery of Truth, the contemplation of the everlasting, ever-true Lord. Such dedication is the real function of the soul. The spending of time in illusory appetites, on the other hand, is the drag of the world. One should not fall a victim to the poisonous attractions of worldly luxuries, or the wiles of seductive beauty. One day, all these fascinating scenes will vanish as a story unfolded in dream!

Baba, The Breath of Sai, p. 167

0069: You have been born for one purpose; to die. That is to say, to kill the "I". If Delusion dies, you become the Absolute, or rather, you know that you are the Absolute. All the literature, all the effort, all the Sacrifice, all the Teaching is just to hold a mirror before you, so that you may see Yourself.

Baba, The Breath of Sai, p. 171

0070: The play is His, the role is His, the lines are written by Him. He directs, He designs the dress and decoration, the gesture and the tone, the entrance and exit. You have to act well the part and receive His approbation when the curtain falls.   *Sathya Sai Speaks, Volume IV, p. 33*

0071: Death will not leave off anyone, whatever he be. It continues to threaten all. If is another's turn today, it is your tomorrow. Look at the blossoms in the garden! When the gardener plucks the flowers, the buds exult that tomorrow is their turn to be gathered into his hands and their faces are full of joy when they unfold in that hope. Do they feel any sadness? Do their faces drop? Are they any less bright? No. The moment they know that the next day it is their turn, they make themselves ready with great gusto and excitement. So also, one must be ready on the path of Spiritual discipline, enthusiastically remembering the name of the Lord, without worrying and feeling sad. That one's turn is to go, because someone died today. The body is like a tube of glass. Inside it the mind is ever changeful and restless. Seeing its antics, death keeps laughing.
                    Baba, The Breath of Sai, p. 166

0072: Man commits the great fault of identifying himself with the body. He has accumulated a variety of things for the upkeep and comfort of the body. Even when the body becomes weak and decrepit with age, he attempts to bolster it up, by some means or other. But, how long can death be postponed? When Yama's (Death) warrant comes, each has to depart. Before Death, position, pride and power, all vanish. Realizing this, strive day and night, with purity of body and mind and spirit, to realize the Higher Self, by the service of all living beings.
                    Baba, The Breath of Sai, p. 165

0073: Man alone has the chance to liberate himself from the wheel of birth and death, through the most pleasant means, that of serving God. But, as a result of ignorance or what is worse, perversity, he lets the opportunity slip from his hands, and suffers grief and pain, fear and anxiety, ad infinitum. By escaping from the clutches of the fascination exercised by material objects and physical pleasures, man can succeed in his efforts to liberate himself. He has traveled long enough on the wrong road; it is time now to turn back and move steadily towards the goal. The love that he has cultivated for man and things has to be sublimated into pure, divine worship.   *Baba, The Breath of Sai, p. 136*

0074: Life is eternally stalked by Death. But, yet, man does not tolerate the very mention of the word "Death". It is deemed inauspicious to hear that word. However insufferable the word, every living thing is every moment proceeding nearer and nearer that event. Intent on a journey and having purchased a ticket for the same, if you enter a train, whether you sit quiet or lie down or read or meditate, the train takes you willy-nilly to the destination. So too, each living thing has at birth received a ticket to Death and has come on a journey. So, whatever

your struggles and safeguards and precautions, the place has to be reached some day. Whatever is uncertain; Death is certain. It is impossible to change that Law.
Baba, The Breath of Sai, p. 183

0075: The individual who is eternal and immortal is born again and again as a transitory mortal. Just as a person discards old clothes and wears new ones, the dweller in the body discards one body and dons another. The body is to the individual what the clothes are to the body. It is the body that decays and dies, not the individualized Soul. Awaken to the inevitable cycle of birth and death, of senility and disease, of grief and evil and other signs of the temporariness of this created worl d and life in it. Though people see these things happening to them aswell as others they do not investigate the reasons for these and the methods of escaping from them. That is the greatest mystery, the wonder.

Whatever is born is destined also to die. But, today human beings want to find a reason for death but they are not wanting to know the reason for birth. We always ask why and how one has died but we do not ask why one is born. As we do not know the cause of one's death, we also do not know the cause of one's birth. For superficial purposes, we think that one has died because of accident or of sickness. This is not so. For death, birth alone is responsible. If we recognize that birth is the reason for death, we will not feel sorry for death. Of all the fears of man, the fear of death is the fiercest as well as the most foolish. For none can escape death having committed the error of birth. To get rid of the wheel of births and death, awareness of the undying unborn Self which is one's Reality is the only method available to man.

One must realize in this body itself the Eternal Truth, and the relationship between man and that Truth, before death takes its toll.
Baba, The Breath of Sai, p. 161

0076: Yama, or the God of Death is described as dragging his victims to his abode by means of the rope. Well, you manufacture the rope yourself and have it ready round your neck; he has only to take hold of the rope and pull you along! It is a three stranded rope, the strands being Egoism, Sense-attachment and Desire. The God of Death is called Time. He is as omnipresent and omnipotent as Time. He does not run a rope factory to drag into his home all the millions who die. The dying person has the rope already spun and twisted round his neck. He has only to come and pull! Man spins the rope by every act of his, done with egoism, self interest, an eye on the beneficial consequences, the fruits, give a little more length, a stronger twist to that rope.
Baba, The Breath of Sai, p. 184

0077: God has given man a hundred years of life and plenty of work to fill the year with; but you fritter the time away in playful games, in founding and fostering a family; and awake to the fact on not preparing for death only when Death knocks at the door. Then, you feverishly pray for a little more extension of the span of life in order to fulfill the task for which you have been sent.

You have no time for reciting the Name of the Lord or meditating on His Form, which is within you! Alas! You have time for the club, for a game of cards, for the film show, for wayside chats, for all kinds of trivialities but no time for a little quiet, for a simple item like worship. It is a false excuse, this, the want of time. No. Face the truth and proceed toward the Truth.

Take the tonic to strengthen the spirit, the tonic of the Repetition of the Name of the Lord, the tonic of meditating on the Glory of God in the silence of the heart.

The heart has the precious treasure of Bliss, but man does not know the key to open the lock; that key is the repetition of the Name of the Lord, with a pure heart. Purify the heart with the four instruments: Truth, Righteousness, Peace and Love.   *Baba, The Breath of Sai, p. 171*

0078: Everything that is born must die; everything that is constructed will disintegrate. But you can escape death, by not being born again. When you know that you are the limitless Self, you are no longer subjected to the limitation of birth. That is the secret.

To cross safely to flood of "Birth-death continuum" the bridge called Steadfastness of discipline of an unflinching kind is essential. It must be a sturdy safe bridge, or else you will fall into the raging waters and be drawn into the sea, infested with sharks: Lust and Anger.

Everyone of you has in possession a ticket for liberation, from the cycle of birth and death.

Those who are endowed with the knowledge of the Self as their basic truth do cross the ocean of birth and death and without doubt attain liberation.

Birth is the consequence of Desire. Death is the consequence of time.   *Baba, The Breath of Sai, p. 254*

0079: Therefore, from tomorrow, keep always before the eye of memory, death which is inevitable, and engage yourself in the journey of life, get immersed in the Lord's Name, with good wishes for all, with strict adherence to truth, seeking always the company of the good, and with the mind always fixed on the Lord. Live avoiding evil deeds, and hateful and harmful thoughts, and do not get attached to the World. If you live thus, your last moment will be pure, sweet and blessed.   *Baba, The Breath of Sai, p. 173*

0080: Trees are helpful even when they become dead and dry serving as firewood. Trees are the best example of the attitude of sacrifice. They are the greatest teachers of the quality of sacrifice. But human beings, who get all the benefit from trees, are not having the same spirit of sacrifice. They are attached to their bodies and spend their energy and time to provide comforts for the body.

How long will the body last? It is a bundle of diseases, a repository of filth and foul excreta. It cannot help one to cross the ocean of life (samsaara). It is subject to changes such as childhood, adolescence, youth, adulthood, old age and finally death. One does not know when, where and how death will occur. Man neglects his rightful duty and relies on this transient body, behaving like a beast. He does not make any effort to realize that in the changing body there is the changeless and eternal Atma (Spirit). This Divinity is the same in all beings and changeless through all the stages of life.   *Sanathana Sarathi, May 1994, p. 123*

0081: Birth and death are incidental to the body alone. Your Self has neither birth nor death. What is born (the body), dies.

Death relates to the body and not to the Atma. The Atma is eternal. It is the truth. You have to acquire this awareness to experience lasting bliss. To experience permanent bliss, one has to develop firm faith in God.

Sanathana Sarathi, October 1996, p. 255

0082: It does not matter how long each one lives, everyone must leave his body sometime or other. It is very necessary that so long as we live in this body, we use the available time for understanding God. It is necessary to find the means for ultimately merging with God. We do not know when we are going to leave this body. The body is made up of matter and it will die. Our ancients have said that the limit for human life is a hundred years but we cannot believe this. We do not know whether death will come in young age or in old age, in middle age or in the adolescence, or whether it will come in water, air or land, in the village or in the forest.

One thing is true and that is death is certain. If you are a wise man, you should strive to understand yourself while you are alive. Without knowing who you are and without realizing the nature of your true self, whatever you may do in your life and whatever you may have achieved, you would have wasted your time and you would not have spent your life in a useful and purposeful manner.

You are spending all your time, reading newspapers that come from different parts of the world, and you are anxiously waiting to get news about some individuals from various parts of the world. But you are not anxious to find out what news comes from within your own heart. This news is the most important news.

This world is like a newspaper. You can read a newspaper from beginning to end only once, but no one reads the same newspaper again and again day after day. Similarly, we have come into this world and we have seen the newspaper of this world once. We should not attempt to see the same newspaper again. A newspaper of today is a wastepaper of tomorrow. In this way, if we subject our life to the repeating cycle of birth and death, we will be turning our life into a wastepaper. Therefore, we should not agree to see this world again and again. We should make up our mind and strive to see the Divine which is really the paper of taste.   *Summer Showers in Brindavan, 1973, p. 31*

0083: No one can be isolated from the steam of life. Each one is a part and parcel of society. One should make an attempt to merge with the omnipresent. By being in this world one gets a chance to progress spiritually. Therefore, man feels some obligation arising from his social conscience towards society. It is well known however that when one leaves this world, one has to leave everything. Even a blade of grass cannot be carried when one dies. Even Sri Rama and Sri Krishna were not able to take anything with them when they gave up their mortal bodies. Such great beings, however, leave behind some sacred ideals for prosterity. The good actions and spiritual maturity of such beings is remembered for all times.   *Summer Showers in Brindavan, 1973, p. 177*

DESIRE

0084: There is no penance superior to peace (of mind). Every individual, every family, every society, every nation seeks peace in all possible ways. Every man should strive in every way to achieve peace as the most desirable objective.

There is no greater happiness than contentment. Man is perpetually in quest of happiness. But what is the happiness he seeks? Worldly happiness, transient pleasures? These cannot confer true happiness.

Why has man lost this happiness? Because man is afflicted with insatiable desires. These desires are the cause of various maladies. It is only by limiting desires and thereby eliminating the diseases arising from them that man can secure peace.   *Sanathana Sarathi, March, 1997, p. 57*

0085: Of course, man cannot eliminate all desires from his mind. The ancient scriptures (Vedas) lay down four goals before man: Righteousness, Wealth, Desire and Liberation (Dharma, Artha, Kama and Moksha).

Since the first and last are difficult to attain without detachment and deprivation of sensual pleasures, man has given them up as impractical and is struggling in all lands and climes with the middle two- Wealth and Desire. All the misery and fear of life can be traced to this dire mistake. What has to be done is to take the four as two inseparable pairs, Dharma-Artha and Kama-Moksha. That is to say, earn wealth through righteousness and use wealth for the promotion of righteousness, and let Liberation be your only desire.

Sathya Sai Speaks, Volume X, p. 70

0086: In the economic sphere, when human desires are governed by righteousness, a divine impulse will arise in man. When the quest for wealth and the concern for sensuous pleasures are based on righteousness, the mind will spontaneously turn towards God.   *Sanathana Sarathi, March, 1997, p. 58*

0087: Students should have firm faith in God and minimize their desires. You must treat with contempt sensuous pleasures. Whenever any worldly desires arise in the mind, treat them as garbage that should be thrown only. By this means, students will enter on the path of purity. Then the Divine will welcome you and fill you with bliss. There is no greater goal, no higher destiny.

Sanathana Sarathi, September, 1996, p. 248

0088: To experience God you have to apply the heat of the fire of spiritual knowledge to the heart filled with love. You must come near to God and become dear to Him through your love. When that happens desires disappear.

Sanathana Sarathi, September, 1996, p. 240

0089: After a heavy meal, food becomes uninteresting. Once satiated, the thing desired becomes disgusting. *Gems of Wisdom, Desires, p. 72*

0090: Lord Krishna stresses in the Bhagavad Geeta that absolute purity of the heart is an essential requisite for treading the path of sacrifice. What is sacrifice? What is it that one must give up? Is it the transient wealth one has? Does sacrifice mean the giving up of one's wife and children? Nay, these are but matters that relate to the environment conditioning man's external life. Sacrifice means giving up one's desires (kama), anger (krodha) and greed or extreme miserliness (lobha). Man generally identifies himself with the "Anatma"(non-Atma) without realizing his true nature. The reflection of the sky in a pot of water disappears the moment you pour out the water. Likewise, when you recognize the temporal nature of all that is non-Atma and attribute their ephemeral existence to worldly desires, and give them up, you get closer to the Atma. Unless you sacrifice desire, anger and greed or miserliness, you cannot attain divinity.

Desire impels you to go against the established code of social behavior even at the cost of losing your honor and reputation. It makes you get immersed in selfishness and disregard your duty to society and God. It raises its ugly hood in every aspect of your life and turns you into a demon.

Anger destroys your intelligence and warps your judgment. The angry man forfeits success in all his endeavors and invites societal censure. He brings dishonor to himself, to his friends and relations desert him. He is led to sin and thereby ruins his life. *Summer Showers, 1979, p. 70*

0091: Man reaches out to fulfill a new desire the moment one is realized. Man today is chasing the temporary, short duration pleasures instead of seeking the Eternal, the Lasting, the Source and the Substance. Desire multiplies desires.

Gems of Wisdom, Desires, p. 72

0092: What is grief? It is merely a reaction to the loss of something gained or the failure to gain something desired. Therefore, the only way to escape grief and sorrow is to conquer desire for the illusory.

Gems of Wisdom, Happiness, p. 164

0093: Mind is like a clear mirror, but it is made impure by our desires.
Summer Showers in Brindavan, 1973, p. 108

0094: The happiness in life will be in inverse proportion to your desires. In the journey of life, as in a railway journey, the less luggage (desires) you carry, the greater the comfort. *Gems of Wisdom, Happiness, p. 165*

0095: By chanting the Lord's name, desires can be reduced, while legitimate wishes get fulfilled. *Sanathana Sarathi, February 1995, p.36*

0096: The greater the desires, the less the happiness you will experience. Promote the sense of contentment. The discontented man loses everything; only the contented man can experience real joy.
Gems of Wisdom, Happiness, p. 165

0097: What is the root of worry? Wants: and the efforts to fulfill them, and the fear of not succeeding to the extent desired. Reduce wants and you reduce worry.
Gems of Wisdom, Suffering, p. 174

0098: What meaning is there in acquiring millions? A contented man is happier than a millionaire. The poorest man in the world is the one who has insatiable desires. *Sanathana Sarathi, April, 1997, p. 94*

0099: Conquering desire, a man becomes happy. Life is a long journey. Desires are the luggage you carry. The less the luggage the greater the comfort during the journey. Man has to discriminate between necessities and luxuries and confine his desires to what is essential.   *Sanathana Sarathi, May 1996, p. 126*

0100: For a tree to grow and provide fruit and shade, there are three essential things- Wind, Rain, and Earth. More than these three, the seed is of even greater importance; without the seed, a tree can never grow. In the same manner, it is in accordance with the Desire of the Lord that man is created in this world. Man comes into this world as if he comes from a seed. In the case of every man, the desire that creates him is like a seed. So long as the desires are in man, it is not possible for him to escape being born. *Gems of Wisdom, Spiritual Level, p. 265*

0101: Man should realize that there should be no excessive indulgence in any desire, whether it be food or other necessities. This is the lesson we have to learn from our ancients, who practiced self-restraint in every aspect of life. In the ancient days you did not have the kind of education that is imparted today. They

did not secure high degrees; but they led a life of purity and integrity.
Sanathana Sarathi, November 1997, p. 288

0102: Man is born out of desire, lives on desire, and passes out by desire. His life is based on desires (thoughts) which control his actions. Hence, man's destiny is determined by his thoughts. *Gems of Wisdom, Avatar, p. 296*

0103: Put a ceiling on desires. First rule is: don't waste money, the misuse of money is evil. Second rule is" don't waste time, time is God; time wasted is life wasted. Third rule is: don't waste food. Fourth rule is: don't waste energy.
Gems of Wisdom, Discipline, p. 411

0104: Man today is weighed down by the overwhelming burden of desires. Spiritual progress is directly related to the reduction of desires. God's grace goes with human effort. *Sanathana Sarathi, November 1997, p. 303*

0105: So long as man is puffed up with pride, none, not even his wife and children will love him. One should shed his ego and arrogance, if he wants to be loved by others. One has to suffer grief and misery as long as he is prone to anger. It is only when he gives up anger he can be happy. So long as one goes on multiplying his desires, he will continue to be in want. When he controls his desires, man attains prosperity, Greed makes a man unhappy and miserable, only when greed and miserliness are given up one can have as enjoyable and peaceful life. *Sanathana Sarathi, August 1997, p. 210*

0106: We say often we have no "Saanthi" or peace. Why? Because you are multiplying your desires. One who is bereft of desires is peaceful. You must breed only good thoughts and progress forward transcending all thoughts and reaching a state of ending the mind which is but a conglomeration of thoughts. Desire is like the luggage during a journey. If you have less luggage, travel will be more comfortable. So also in life's journey you should restrict your desires which burden you. *Sanathana Sarathi, August 1997, p. 216*

0107: One is very fortunate to get a human birth but because we are filling such a human life with various material desires, we are filling our life with sorrow. If we have no desires, we cannot get sorrow at all, and there can be no one more happy, than one who has no desires. All this sorrow is our own creation. Worry has no form at all. It is simply your own creation. The form of worry is nothing. Our own desires are responsible for our sorrow. You should keep illusory troubles at a distance and lead a happy life. *Baba, The Breath of Sai, p. 281*

0108: People today are totally immersed in self-interest; multiplying desires without limit, they are becoming demonic beings. They are not content with having what they need for essential purposes. They wish to accumulate enormously for the future. They are filled with worries and discontent. Thereby they forfeit their happiness here and in the hereafter. Birds and beasts are content to live on what they can get. Man alone is afflicted with insatiable desires. Birds and animals have no desire to hoard or to exploit others. But man is a prey to these vises. He forgets his natural qualities and behaves worse than animals. When these tendencies are given up, the inherent divinity in man will manifest itself.   *Sanathana Sarathi; October, 1997, back cover*

0109: If you analyze the difference between God and man you will find that life plus desire is man, and life minus desire is God. Confine your desires to primary necessities for sustaining life such as food, clothing and shelter. When you have excessive desire you become restless. Whatever the nature of your work, if you dedicate it as an offering to God, you will have no worry at all.
Sanathana Sarathi, May, 1993, p. 125

0110: "Kaamam hithwaa nisswaarthavaan bhavanthi" (By conquering desire, one becomes unselfish). As long as one is overwhelmed by desires, one cannot be contented. He loses control over his senses. He is intoxicated with insatiable desires. But there should be a limit to them. Limitless desires can result only in ruin. Prosperity will elude him. The moment man is able to control his desires, all things will come to him of their own accord.
Sanathana Sarathi; October, 1997, p. 261

0111: Your great resolve should be: I shall ever maintain harmony in thought, word and action. The spiritual path is easy to follow, all you have to do is to cast off your desires. The road ahead is smooth and straight, and there is a charioteer waiting to guide you.   *Sanathana Sarathi, June 1994, p. 154*

0112: The more desires are controlled, the more blissful one will be.
Sanathana Sarathi, December 1995, p. 320

0113: When the will-power is weak, even when one sits in meditation he cannot steady his mind and it will only be a waste of time. One should reduce desires toprogress in spiritual sadhana (discipline).   *Sanathana Sarathi, January 1994*

0114: The organs and the mind always wish to look at and concern themselves with the external objects. The mind develops sensuous desires by looking at such external objects. As a result of these desires, the mind becomes impure.
Summer Showers in Brindavan, 1973, p. 50

0115: No man filled with greed, fear and anger can achieve anything in this world. Greed comes first. Excessive desires degrade man. You cannot give up desires entirely. But there should be a limit to them. When they exceed the limits, a man goes astray. Desires are dreadfully dangerous. Today's enemy may become tomorrow's friend and vice versa. But desires are perpetual enemies. They haunt man ceaselessly. The Gita declares desire as the eternal enemy of man; hence, desire has to be kept under control.   *Sanathana Sarathi, May 1995, p. 122*

0116: The Divine Atma, which dwells in the heart of every human being, is not recognized by man because it is covered by the clouds of desire. The splendor of the sun is revealed when a wind drives away the clouds that hide the sun. Likewise, when the wind of love blows away the clouds of desire in the heart, the ego ("I -ness") and possessiveness (sense of "mine") are driven out and the effulgence of the Atma within is revealed in all its glory, Man has to restrain the feelings of "I" and "Mine". Uncontrolled desire can bring down anyone, even deities presiding over human destiny. However intelligent, scholarly or powerful a man may be, he may succumb to desires. Hence everyone has to be vigilant in controlling desires.   *Sanathana Sarathi, May 1995, p. 123*

DIVINE GRACE

0117: If you win the Grace of God, even the decrees of the adverse effect of karmas can be overcome.   *Gems of Wisdom, Protection of God, p. 361*

0118: The most desirable form of wealth is the Grace of God. He will guard you, even as the eye lids guard the eye. Do not doubt this.
          Sathya Sai Speaks; Volume IV, p. 190

0119: God's Grace is the greatest wealth. To consider the amassing of money, gold or other material objects as symbols of wealth and social prestige is incorrect. The goal of life, instead should be the acquisition of the divine wealth of God's Grace.   *Summer Showers; 1979, p. 152*

0120: God gives everything; whatever we get is his Grace. You have no right to judge whether what you get is good or bad.
          Gems of Wisdom, Where is God?, p. 339

0121: Individual effort and Divine Grace are both interdependent. Without effort, there will be no conferment of Grace. Without Grace, there can be no gain from the effort. To win that Grace, you need have only Faith and Virtue.

Sathya Sai Speaks; Volume V, p. 188

0122: The chief duty of man is investigation into truth. Truth can be won only through dedication and devotion, and they are dependent on the grace of God, which is showered on hearts saturated with love.

Sathya Sai Speaks, Volume VI, p. 1

0123: Do your duty and God's grace will follow. Pray from the depth of your heart for the well-being of all people.   *Sanathana Sarathi, February 1997, p. 33*

0124: It is essential to see the unity that underlies the apparent diversity. When more and more people recognize this unity, most of the world's problems will get solved. All social conflicts will end when people learn to see the one Divine in all beings. It is the hatred born of divisive feelings which is the cause of deadly discord in society. The Atmic Principle is the means of liberation. Self control is the means to secure divine grace.   *Sanathana Sarathi, March, 1997, p. 68*

0125: God is no stony-hearted despot. He is compassion. He draws you near and grants you consolation and courage.

God's grace is like insurance; it will help you in your time of need without any limit.

The word Kaalam (time) is derived from Kaa + Alam. This means that God, embodiment of Time, is the one who rewards people according to their deserts. God does not submit to worldly offerings, worldly authority or worldly power. HE responds only to spiritual aspirations.

Some say that the Lord punishes some and favors others. Let Me tell you, the Lord does neither. He is like the electric current that rotates the fan and makes one's life comfortable; it also operates the electric chair and makes one's life shorter. The Lord's Grace is like the wind that blows. Roll up your sails and the boat hardly moves; unfurl them, it moves faster and faster. It is like light; one person does good in its illumination, another executes an evil plan with its help.

Gems of Wisdom, Why is God not seen? p. 347

0126: The wealth you earn is not true wealth! True wealth is the Grace of God.

Gems of Wisdom, Wealth, p. 228

0127: The effulgent Sun can be seen only with his own light. Similarly, only by the grace of the Divine can one obtain a vision of the Divine. No skill, intellectual effort or scholarship is required to experience the Divine. Just as clouds may obscure the Sun, the clouds of egoism, attachment and hatred prevent one from seeing the Divine. Prayer and Spiritual discipline are the means by which these clouds are dispersed. Spiritual discipline is the royal road to reach the Divine.

Baba, The Breath of Sai, p. 201

0128: We witness today humanity being racked by innumerable troubles and worries. No administration or authority can solve these problems. God alone can save mankind. Men have to develop faith in the Self. Thereby they should acquire the grace of the Divine. Humanity as a whole is in need of God's grace. To receive this, everyone has to fill his heart with love, render service to his fellowmen and thus redeem his life.   *Sanathana Sarathi, May 1996, p. 123*

EDUCATION

0129: Education does not consist in the accumulation of information and facts from a multitude of books. Reading of books can only enrich you in the information that you gather but can never give or promote good qualities. You will have to regard good education as a process by which your character is improved and by which you will be able to use your intelligence and sharpen your mind so as to distinguish right from wrong. Students must strive to attain strength connected with responsibility. They should also recognize the necessity for becoming aware of the defects in society and in mankind in general. Students must necessarily have three essential qualities: discipline, devotion and duty. It is only when the students have these three qualities that they will become useful to society.   *Summer Showers, 1973, p. 3*

0130: Education should be divorced from jobs. Its purpose should be the acquisition of the highest knowledge (Vijnaana). That is the concept upheld by Bharatiya Culture. Students will be ideal citizens of the nation only when they develop self-confidence and the feeling of spiritual oneness. Develop the spirit of sacrifice and become defenders of the nation's integrity and honor. You must strive to promote the welfare of society.

Sanathana Sarathi, February 1997, p. 32

0131: Education is the means of unfolding the moral and spiritual potentialities of man. Education reveals to man what is right and what is wrong.

Sanathana Sarathi, February 1997, p. 34

0132: Educational institutions should teach students to adhere to truth and to discharge their duties as a sacred obligation. Students should not allow success or failure to ruffle their minds unduly. Courage and self-confidence must be instilled in the students. Bend the twig and shape the tree, says the proverb. The molding of character must start with children at the earliest age. Begin developing human values from the primary school. Some are concerned about living in a "secular state". Secularism really means equal respect for all faiths and beliefs. There should be no hatred towards any faith. Other creeds and beliefs should be condemned or derided. I want each one of you to grow into a strong steady and straightforward person. Your eyes should not seek evil sights. Your tongue should not indulge in evil speech. Your hands should not do evil acts. Your mind should not seek evil thoughts. Be pure and full of love. Help those who are in a bad position and serve those who need your help.

Sanathana Sarathi, May 1997, p. 119

0133: Indifference, bad company, disrespect, arrogance and jealousy, there five tendencies reduce man to the level of the animal. No one with these vices can be called an educated person. To get rid of these vices, it is necessary to take note of some of the good qualities in animals and birds, Man can learn any number of good qualities in animals, birds, insects and worms.

One animal which is viewed with contempt is the donkey. The quality of patience to be found in a donkey is not to be found even in man. Whatever burdens may be heaped on its back, it bears them all with forbearance. It puts up with any amount of beatings. Even when it is starved of food and water, it presents a calm face. Man has thus to learn the quality of forbearance from the donkey.

The ant is one of the tiniest among insects. But there are many lessons to be learned from it. The ant has a capacity for foresight. With foreknowledge of the rainy season ahead, the ant starts storing food three months in advance.

Then there is the spider, from which lessons can be learned. Determination is one of its traits. However many times its web may be destroyed or broken, the spider will go on remaking it with relentless determination.

Then, there is the dog. The dog is treated with neglect and indifference. But the fidelity displayed by a dog is not found in any other creature. Getting a few morsels of food from man, the dog shows its gratitude to him by following him and wagging its tail out of affection. But such gratitude is lacking among students who have been nourished, educated and placed comfortably in life (by their parents). Many do not have even a fraction of the gratitude displayed by dogs. Has their education or intelligence any meaning?

Sanathana Sarathi, March, 1997, p. 59

0134: Humility is the hall-mark of education. Humility calls for actions free from egoism and self-importance.

The inherent goodness in man is covered by the ashes of attachment and hatred. Remove the ashes and the goodness will manifest itself.

Sanathana Sarathi, September, 1996, p. 246

0135: Education should promote discrimination and humility.
Gems of Wisdom, Education, p. 185

0136: Education confers beauty on man; it is his secret treasure. It confers pleasure, fame and happiness. It is the teacher of teachers; it is one's kinsman when abroad; it confers supreme vision. In a royal assembly it is learning alone, not wealth that counts. A man without learning is an animal.
Sanathana Sarathi, December 1993, p. 316

0137: Education today promotes greed instead of paralyzing it. The aim is to earn more monetary income. So the struggle is directed to the acquisition of degrees which bring higher salaries. The learned man is anxious to exploit society, to pilfer from society by means fair or foul. He is not eager to give to society, to benefit society. He is concerned with what he can get from society not with what he can give to it.
Gems of Wisdom, Education, p. 184

0138: The power of discrimination is definitely more valuable than bookish knowledge, wealth and physical strength. The coordination of thoughts, words and deeds is the first step in spiritual growth. Lack of correlation between ideas, utterances and actions leads to self-destruction, hypocrisy and spiritual bankruptcy. The proper study of mankind is man. The generation, expression and efflorescence of humanitarianism depends on the proper integration of thought, speech and action. In other words, the rapport between mental and physical activities is an essential ingredient of spiritual training.
Summer Showers, 1979, p. 15

0139: In the educational system today, the spiritual element has no place. This cannot be true education. Education must proceed primarily from the Spirit to Nature. It must show that mankind constitutes one Divine family. The divinity that is present in society can be experienced only through individuals. Education today, however, ends with the knowledge one has acquired to meet the challenges of life and to make all human beings happy as far as possible. Born in society, one has the duty to work for the welfare and progress of society.
Gems of Wisdom, Education, p. 189

0140: Today the heart of the educated man, has become the lair of wild desires and cruel habits. Educational institutions should be nurseries for tradition, loyalty to culture and the ideals of service to society. Education is to promote wisdom. Wisdom can grow, only where humility prevails. It thrives when man is afraid of vice and sin. The crisis of character, which is at the root of all the troubles everywhere, has come about as a result of neglect of this aspect in education.

As a first step in educational progress you must revere your parents. Students should consider that study is their first and only duty. Students should become strong physically, mentally and spiritually, imbibe as much as possible, the wisdom that has been gathered in the past; cultivate the skills by which you can serve society.

We now believe that the acquisition of knowledge is for the acquisition of wealth. But this is not right. Education should emphasize self-reliance and independent living. It should confer on the students the courage to stand up against injustice, immorality, and falsehood. Students should cultivate in their hearts the spirit of sacrifice and the virtues of charity.

Men crave for a prosperous future; for positions of authority, power, care-free lives; they never desire to possess pure, clear, loving intellects and a humble disposition.

Unless knowledge is transformed into Wisdom and Wisdom is expressed in Character, education is a wasteful process. The task of education is not over by merely providing with food, clothing and shelter. It should liberate man from greed, hatred, unrest, narrow loyalties and ego impulses. Earning money is not the end all of education. Greed to earn money, by any means, has led to the evils of today. Money breeds pride, pride fosters hatred.

Students have to also revere their deeds. Deeds elevate us or drag us down. Students should try to elevate themselves by doing good, speaking good, seeking good, and having the good of others in mind. The educated man must be ready to serve his parents and his country. Students are born in society, which has helped to guard, guide and foster the students, to educate them and fill them with dreams and ideals. Students should repay the society the debt they owe to it. It is the duty of every national being to assimilate and appreciate the historical and cultural heritage. The years of life allotted to man as a result of the enormous amount of merit earned and accumulated through many lives in the past, have to be utilized for the purpose of rising higher into divinity.

Animal instincts and impulses have persisted in human nature as vistages and proper education will help man to exercise control over them.

Gems of Wisdom, Education, p. 184

0141: If anyone blames, abuses or hurts you, do not return him with the same. Behave nobly and with patience. When a dog bites a man the man does not bite the dog in return. Education must lead you from darkness to light. It is only those who wander in darkness that fall into pits; can a man walking in the light fall into a pit? If he does, it means that he is still 'in the dark', Vid means light, and a vidyarthi must seek light and gain it. What is the use of an eye that does not reveal to you the pitfalls? Education must endow you with the type of eye which will reveal in time the pits that yawn in your path.

Sathya Sai Speaks, Volume X, p. 127

0142: Man needs today a mind free from attachment and hatred, speech that is untainted by falsehood, and a body that is totally free from violence. Of these, truthful speech is most essential. Unfortunately, man is not free from these taints. Hence, students should receive an education that produces purity of mind speech and body.   *Sanathana Sarathi, December 1993, p. 317*

0143: Wisdom flashes like lightening amidst the clouds of the inner sky; one has to foster the flash, and preserve the light. That is the true sign of the educated person. Do not believe that mastery of many tomes makes you wise. Wisdom can grow where humility prevails. It thrives when man is afraid of vice and sin and is attached to the Divine in himself and in all else.

Sathya Sai Speaks, Volume X, p. 3

0144: The end of education is character and the end of knowledge is Love. If we concentrate on book knowledge at the cost of its practical application, we will be spoiling the name of Education itself. Education should lead one to humility, which in turn equips him with all the eligibility. Eligibility provides him with necessary material wealth, which enables him to do some charitable deeds. Charity makes him happy both in this world and the higher one after this.

Sathya Sai Speaks, Volume X, p. 11

0145: Man's heart, which ought to be filled with compassion that is natural to it, is today full of cruelty and bitterness. Education, which should serve to refine man's nature and make him a hero, is failing in its purpose because in his conduct man is a "zero". An education which does not develop humanness is an utter waste. The educational system should ensure that along with knowledge, right conduct is also developed.

True education should produce a blossoming of human qualities. It should not be merely for earning a living, but should result in a ripening of the heart, filling it with love. "What happiness can one achieve if all his education makes him concerned only about filling his stomach and makes him forget the Supreme Lord?

Sanathana Sarathi, June 1994, p. 148

0146: Education can claim success only when it results in the student gaining awareness of the Divinity inherent in him and others. No academic degree can confer as much self-confidence and self-realization as that awareness. It has to be transmitted by teachers who have attained it through a sense of duty and in a spirit of love. It has to be accepted by students who have cultivated faith in the teacher and reverence for his role. The pot that pours and the pot that receives have to be steady and straight, eager to give and gain. If the teacher has the responsibility to inspire and illumine, the student has the responsibility to respond to the Love and Light, discarding all contrary thoughts. Thoughts that arise from the region of the pleasant cannot co-exist with those which arise from the tough challenges of higher life. The student must be equipped to prefer the latter to the former.

Gems of Wisdom, The Teacher and Tomorrow, p. 192

0147: It is often declared that knowledge is power. No, character is power. Nothing can be more powerful on Earth than Character. Riches, scholarships, status, authority are all frail and flimsy before it.

While earning a livelihood is important, what matters most is ideals for

which you live. The primary purpose of education is to enable one to manifest the Divinity within him. When students pursue education in this spirit, they will be able to promote the welfare of the nation, of society and their own good.
Gems of Wisdom, The Teacher and Tomorrow, p. 194

0148: Today neither students nor teachers are aware of the true meaning of education. Education should foster morality, righteousness and character. Man today has acquired prodigious knowledge in the fields of science and technology. But this serves only to promote a material civilization and teaches only knowledge of the external world to students. What man truly needs today is not this external knowledge. He needs refinement of the heart. This can be got only by internal culture.
Sanathana Sarathi, December 1993, p. 316

0149: The cultivation of a social consciousness is also very important. One must not learn to live like a drop of oil on a pond spreading all over the surface and resurging to merge with the water. One must join others in common tasks and contribute one's strength and skill to the common pool. A single thin string cannot bend even an ant, but hundreds of them twisted into a rope can hold back an elephant. This is the effect of united effort. It is a desirable trait to work for a common cause with others in co-operation; but today people unfortunately only believe in operation.
Sathya Sai Speaks, Volume X, p. 313

0150: You must forget the foolish idea that education is only acquiring a degree. Do not seek education for the sake of serving someone else. Have in your mind as the objectives of your education, the prosperity and good of yourself, your country and your society.
Summer Showers in Brindavan, 1973, p. 11

0151: You must realize that the Divine current that flows and functions in every living being is the One Universal Entity. When you desire to enter the mansion of God, you are confronted by two closed doors- the desire to praise yourself and the desire to defame others. The doors are bolted by envy, and there is also the huge lock of egoism preventing entry. So if you are earnest, you have to resort to the key of prema (Love) and open the lock; then remove the bolt and throw the doors wide open. The education must train you in this difficult operation.
Sanathana Sarathi, December 1995, p. 334

0152: The educational system today prepares students for pursuing worldly gains and comforts, but makes no attempt to cultivate in them the qualities of righteousness, love of peace and promotion of social welfare. Both students and educationists are mainly concerned about using education for getting jobs and earning large incomes. What kind of life do they lead in their earning career? After a so-called hard day's work, they spend their evenings in clubs, imagining that they get peace and rest there. If they wanted real peace they should have it in their homes. In the clubs they spend their time playing cards and having "bottles". Is this commendable? Does this befit persons calling themselves educated? Far from it. Not only do they ruin themselves this way, but also ruin their families. Instead of falling a prey to such pernicious habits, the educated should use their knowledge for the improvement of society and thereby redeem their lives.   *Sanathana Sarathi, August 1996, p. 205*

0153: Of what use is the acquisition of all kinds knowledge of one has not good qualities and has no moral values? What for is academic knowledge acquired? Is for deceiving others? Or is it for promoting one's selfish interests? Or for the selfish enjoyment of pleasures? Education today is being used largely for these purposes than to promote the well-being of society or the nation. An education that serves no useful purpose in daily life is utterly worthless.

Education today promotes largely intellectual cleverness. What is the good if the head is filled with bad thoughts, is the ears listen only to scandals, if the eyes look enviously and the mind is plotting misdeeds? All that is noble in human life is being destroyed. The students of today are divorced from all that is ennobling.   *Sanathana Sarathi, December 1996, p. 317*

THE EGO

0154: There is one disease with which all are afflicted to varying degrees. It is the disease of egoism. There is no basis at all for this conceit. There is no reason at all for anyone feeling proud about one's wealth or any other possession. The only thing about which one should feel proud is one's goodness. People should cultivate love and cherish the feeling of oneness with all beings.
                    Sanathana Sarathi, May 1997, p. 132

0155: Every human being should strive to destroy the ego. Unless the ego is eradicated, Divinity cannot be realized.   *Sanathana Sarathi, April, 1997, p. 90*

0156: Ego is enemy number one of the spiritual process.
                    Sathya Sai Speaks, Volume V, p. 93

0157: Egoism and divinity are incompatible. An egoist can never aspire for the life divine. Ego should be completely annihilated in order to progress along the path of spirituality. However, self-confidence, as different from ego, is of supreme importance in spiritual progress. A man who has no faith in himself cannot have faith in God. Self-confidence and faith in God are always found in juxtaposition. They complement each other.

Faith is a cardinal virtue and faith in God is a prop in life. Though God dwells in everybody, unless one has faith in God, he cannot become divine. Some people might say that they will believe only after they experience. But that is like putting the cart before the horse. In spirituality, faith always precedes experience.

Summer Showers, 1979, p. 142

0158: Only where there is no ego, or at least less ego, can peace, happiness, cooperation and love flourish. Man cannot claim to be a man until this ego which urges him to destroy others is overcome by the discipline (sadhana) of service (seva). By saturating the service with love, work is offered to God; it then gets sanctified into puja. This makes it free from ego. Only by reducing his wants and overcoming jealously and envy can man reduce his ego, since to overpower the ego is well-nigh impossible.

As a consequence of pride in one's own strength and power a person might injure thousands, but the pride will injure that person most, being like a devil that possesses man. Man cannot claim to be man until this ego, that prompts him to ruin others, and ride over others, is destroyed by sadhana (spiritual discipline). The Divine in him can manifest only when the dark forces of 'mine' and 'I' are rendered ineffective. To overpower the ego is a well-nigh impossible task. We have heard of the six internal foes that haunt man every moment on his life. But the sense of 'I' and 'mine' are far more deep-rooted. People have conquered the six foes- lust, anger, greed, attachment, pride and hatred. Indeed these are many who have achieved this victory. But rare indeed is the hero who has demolished his ego and escaped from its nefarious urges.

Saytha Sai Speaks, Volume X, p. 214

0159: The vision of the inner Atma will not be revealed to the spiritual aspirant as long as his ego continues to exist. It is only when egoism is given up that the inner significance of dharma (the code of right conduct) will be comprehended in its totality.

Summer Showers, 1979, p. 66

0160: Envy and greed also emanate from the ego and have to be carefully watched and controlled. Like a tadpole's tail, the ego will fall away when you grow in wisdom. Ego must fall away; if it is cut the poor tadpole will die. So, don't worry about the ego; develop wisdom.

Gems of Wisdom, Ego, p. 138

0161: Man is a pilgrim towards Dharmakshetra, the abode of dharma, which is the abode also of santi; but, on the way, he is led into the bylanes and alleys of objective pleasure by the senses to which he has become a slave. Man is eager to know about all kinds of trivialities, like the details of other lives and other places, but, he has no keenness to know about himself or the place from where he himself has come. Man is sunk in ignorance about himself, his source and substance, his goal and fate. He reduces himself to just one name and one form, and limits himself to just one individual; he, the inheritor of unlimited wealth and fortune, feels himself a pauper. Remove this ego boundary; then only can you recognize the vastness of yourself.   *Sathya Sai Speaks, Volume IV, p. 139*

0162: At birth, all are pure and innocent. But as they grow, they develop arrogance, pride and ostentation. But this is not proper. People should cultivate humility and discipline, which are the hall-mark of humanness.

Humanness means harmony in thought, word and deed. The absence of this harmony is degrading. Men should learn to respect one another. The Divine is present in everyone. Strive to make others happy as far as possible.

Everyone should manifest his divine essence as a spark of the Divine. It is a fruit of many lives to be born as a human being. Man must lean an exemplary life. Education and wealth are good in themselves, but when they are misused they become harmful. The fault lies in the conduct of the persons concerned. Humanness consists in leading a life free from egoism and acquisitiveness.
Sanathana Sarathi, December 1995, p. 331

0163: The worst enemy of man is his ego. Many have been able to overcome the six weaknesses: anger, pride, lust, greed, hatred and attachment, but rare indeed is the hero who has demolished his ego, which has jealousy as its companion trying to dominate the mind continuously. More than ordinary men, the scholars, sages, teachers and even devout spiritual aspirants are victims of ego. It is their ego which makes them declare that they are nearest to God and the most enlightened. The ego brings wave after wave of wants and wishes. When egoism enters man, envy follows fast. Sorrow is the shadow that haunts the ego.

How does the egoism get into our system? Where was the ego in the beginning? Is it a weed cultivated by us for our destruction? Where were we before we were born? Where will we be after death?

All our ideas and inferences are but products of the period between birth and death. When the girl you married was seriously ill as a child, you did not worry since she was not "yours". We ourselves grow this attachment. This is "mine" and "yours" attitude adopts colossal importance in our lives.

Egoism is a thorny bush, which when planted and fostered, makes us suffer. It makes enemies even of close friends and does not allow men to work together. Grief follows ego like a shadow.
Sanathana Sarathi, March 1996, p. 81

FAITH

0164: Faith is the basis of every act. You have faith in the driver of your bus and the pilot of your plane. Faith is the power. Without faith living is impossible. We have faith in tomorrow; that is what makes us take up activities that extend beyond this day. People without faith cannot plan; they court misery only. Faith must lead to effort. Faith makes us an optimist. So too, believe in God who is your Creator.   *Sathya Sai Speaks, Volume X, p. 227*

0165: Faith is the basis for the experience of bliss; faith is like our life breath.
                              Gems of Wisdom, Self Confidence, p. 122

0166: For what is the root of that faith in yourself? Who are you that you should believe in yourself? You believe in yourself because your self is God and you have an unshakable faith in God, deep down in you. Faith in yourself and faith in God are identical. You tap the strength of the God within when you face an enemy without.   *Sathya Sai Speaks, Volume II, p. 229*

0167: Spiritual progress in NOT merely intellectual exercise; it is right living, good conduct, moral behavior. These characteristics are automatic consequences of belief in a good, just, compassionate God who is watching and witnessing every act. So faith in an omnipresent, omnipotent, omniscient God is the first prerequisite to a good life.   *Sathya Sai Speaks, Volume VI, page 108*

0168: Humanity cannot exist even for a moment without perseverance and faith. They are the two wheels of the chariot of a man's life which should proceed towards the unfathomable ocean of God's boundless Grace.

God is worshipped by four kinds of devotees; "aartha", "arthaarthi", "jijnasu" and "jnani". God loves all of them. He grants them boons appropriate to their thoughts and attributes.

An "aartha" prays to God in times of distress. He prays for relief from the difficulties, troubles, trials and tribulations of the world. God gives him mundane happiness by removing his sorrow and sickness. With the cessation of his sadness, the relation between the "aartha" and God also comes to an end.

An "arthaarthi", is a devotee who prays to God for power, pelf and prosperity. He becomes an egoist as soon as his wishes are fulfilled. If his ambitions are not fulfilled, he blames God for his indifference to the welfare of mankind. When an arthaarthi's prayers are not answered, he becomes an angry agnostic.

A "jijansu" wants to understand the enigma of God and to solve the riddle of the universe. He is an inquirer, and explorer and an investigator. His aim is to unravel the mystery of existence with the aid of his limited intellect. This is a painful intellectual endeavor foredoomed to failure. When all his efforts fail he also becomes a disinterested man filled with indifference and apathy. But, if a "jijnasu" remains undaunted by failures and persists in his inquires with single-track mind, he will also win God's Boundless Grace.

A "jnani" is the only individual who has reached the summit of spirituality. He has attained the acme of wisdom. He alone can reach and know God. It does not, however, mean that the others cannot know God. They, too, can realize God if they dedicate all their actions to God in a spirit of self-abnegation. Killing of the lower self is more important than memorization all the scriptures.

This is the easiest path to God-realization. Every act should be treated as a sacrament. Meditation, yoga and rites and rituals are no longer essential to the "jnani". His life and his actions are dedicated to God in complete self-surrender. He remains unattached to the fruits of his actions.

Summer Showers, 1979, p. 66

0169: When faith dawns, fence it around with discipline and self-control so that the tender shoot might be guarded against goats and cattle, the moth-crowd of cynics and unbelievers. When your faith grows into a big tree, those very cattle can lie down in the shade that it will spread.

Sathya Sai Speaks, Volume I, page 68

0170: Faith is very essential for the pilgrim on the spiritual (adhyatmic) path. Man is now caught up in temporary and trivial preoccupations in the too short interval between birth and death, and he deceives himself by placing faith in these rather than on truer and more lasting realities and experiences. He does not hold onto discrimination and deeper realities and is carried away by every gust of doubt or disappointment.   *Sathya Sai Speaks, Volume X, page 225*

0171: No devotee should allow his faith in God to weaken in any circumstances. You will achieve victory by facing any adverse circumstances with faith in God.

Embodiments of love! Foster intensely faith in God. All other beliefs are of no avail.   *Sanathana Sarathi; October, 1997, p. 264*

0172: Whatever studies you may pursue, do not give up your faith in God. To give up God is to give up life itself. Life is God, Truth is God. All that you do as an offering to God will be an expression of human values.

Gems of Wisdom, Practice and Precept, p. 239

0173: There can be no creation without the Creator. But you are now attempting to possess the creation with no faith in the Creator.

Gems of Wisdom, Spiritual Quality is Essential, p. 277

0174: I will not accept if you say that you are an atheist with no faith in God. For what is the root of that faith in yourself which makes you say so? You believe yourself because your self is God and you have an unshakable faith in God, deep down in you. Faith in yourself and faith in God are identical since you tap the strength of God in you when you defy an enemy without. That is why there is a persistent whisper within, to sure that strength in the path of mercy, charity, helpfulness.   *Gems of Wisdom, Bhakthi (Devotion), p. 299*

0175: It is excessive attachment that is the cause of man's troubles. Do everything as an act of offering to the Divine. Without faith in God man ceases to be human.   *Sanathana Sarathi, May 1995, p. 120*

0176: We should understand that when there is no God; there will be no courage. All the human bodies will simply be reduced to mere leather bags, in which there is no life at all, if there is no contact with the Divine.

You have faith in the senses and the knowledge they garner; you believe in the fancies and fantasies of your mind; you have faith in the syllogisms of your reason, but alas, you have no faith in God. So you fear, you grieve, you doubt.

Have faith in Him and be free from fear, anxiety and agitation. Surrender to God. His Grace can save you, His wisdom can enlighten you. His power can overcome all your obstacles. Faith and surrender are the manifestations of devotion.

In all effort, if you trust in a higher power which is ready to come to your help, work is made easy. This comes out of worship, reliance on God, the Source of all Power.

Only those who have faith in themselves shall have faith in God.

Prayer is the very breath of religion, for it brings man and God together and with every sigh, nearer and nearer.

The stamp of devotion is what makes the prayer reach the destination, God; not the festoons, the fan fare, the heap of flowers on the festive nature of the feast-offerings. The simple, sincere heart is the stamp that makes the prayer travel fast.

Have the firm faith that Divinity is present in the human form. Perform right actions befitting the human form. Eschew selfishness, the attachments and hatred arising from it. The way to get rid of selfishness is adoration of God.
                    Gems of Wisdom, Bhakthi (Devotion), p. 308

0177: Self confidence is the basis of faith in God also. People who do not know who they are and who have no confidence in themselves assert that there is no God. But how can they declare that the God in whom you believe and who exists for you does not exist?   *Sathya Sai Speaks; Volume VIII, p. 88*

0178: When you are afraid of someone or something outside you, remind yourself that the fear is born, fed and fertilized in your own mind and that you can overcome it by denying it. How can fear counter the path of a spiritual aspirant? It can hide in no shadow, it can pester no devotee who has God in his heart. Faith in the Almighty God is the impregnable armor that the devotee can wear, and peoples of all lands are devotees, whether they know it or not. Be steady, do not waver; keep straight on. Hold fast to the ideal without despair. Pray until God relents; do not turn away sadly if God does not shower grace when you expect it.

Gems of Wisdom, Quality of a Devotee, p. 392

GOAL OF LIFE

0179: The main aim of a student should be to mold himself in such a way that he leads a purposeful and useful life in society. Unfortunately in the educational system today, there is no strength of purpose, no unity and no love. Whether one learns anything or not, whether one leads a meaningful life or otherwise, one's span of life melts away like a block of ice. Students should recognize this truth.

Students today are not aware of what is the primary goal of life. They do not seem even to be worried about this.
One in a million seems to be concerned about knowing the primary purpose of life. This concern is the first step in the ascent towards the goal.

Sanathana Sarathi, June 1996, p. 149

0180: As long as you disregard Truth, you cannot have even a trace of Bliss. Time is fleeting. You have to start inquiring into the purpose of this human life now itself. It is not for leading an animal existence. The goal of human life is progress from the human to the Divine.

Sanathana Sarathi, October 1994, p. 275

0181: It is doubtless essential to acquire skills of various kinds. But the purpose for which they are to be used should also be understood. They have to be used for the realization of the four main goals of human life, described compendiously as the "Purushaarthas" (The four goals are: Righteousness, Wealth, desire, and liberation).

Sanathana Sarathi, April 1994, p. 96

0182: What is the happiest day in your life? All are happy days to a person of true knowledge. Happiness is an internal conscious experience which comes as an effect of the extinction of mental or physical desire. The less the desire, the greater is the happiness, so that perfect happiness consists in the destruction or satisfaction of all desires in the Absolute being. Life is an experience meant to train the individual for a higher, deeper and more expanded state of existence through the experience of the results of action. The aim of everybody's life is the attainment of complete perfection in the spiritual Absolute.

Sanathana Sarathi, April 1994, back cover

0183: The span of life allotted to man is very short; the world on which he lives is very wide; time extends far behind and far beyond. What little man has to do here has to be done quickly, at the place that is assigned to him and within the time that is allotted to him. And, man has such a formidable task before him; it is to fulfill it that he has come as man, exchanging for this habitat all the merit he has acquired during many past lives. The task is no less than the manifestation of the Divinity latent in man.   *Sanathana Sarathi, January 1995, back cover*

0184: You are born as a human being for doing your duty (Karma). Had the goal for man being mere living or even happy living, the Atma could have been encased in the form of birds or beasts. Why it has taken this human form, with the power of reasoning through the intellect, is to achieve the goal of realization of the unity of self with God.   *Sanathana Sarathi, April 1996, p. 102*

0185: If one is able to control his senses, even if he is a blind person, he will reach the destination of moksha and attain liberation. On the other hand, if one's senses are not controlled, even if he is the best of men, he will not be able to reach the divine destination.   *Summer Showers in Brindavan, 1973, p. 103*

0186: Keep the memory of the Lord and His Glory always with you; that will quicken your steps and you will arrive soon at the Goal. The mother, coming from the well with a pot of water on her head, another on the hip and a third in her hand, hurries home, since she is always conscious of the infant in the cradle. If she forgets the infant, her gait slows down and she wanders around, chatting with all her friends. Similarly, if God, the Goal, is not cherished in the memory, one has to wander through many births and arrive home late.

Sathya Sai Speaks, Volume IV, p. 42

GOD

0187: Some people want to have uninterrupted happiness. When you eat at 10.00 AM you do not go on eating every hour thereafter without a break. You have to give a break for the food to be digested. So also when you experience pleasure it has to be digested before you meet with another bout of such experience. Just as you have to so some exercise for helping the food to digest, you have to go through the exercise of confrontation of pain after experiencing pleasure. Therefore, you must take whatever is given by God as good for you.
Sanathana Sarathi, February, 1994, p. 51

0188: Man is haunted by fear wherever he goes or stays. The only way out of this situation is for people to take refuge in God. The protective grace of the Divine will free men from fear. Where devotion and love exist together, there will be no room for fear. It is their absence that is the cause of fear everywhere.
Sanathana Sarathi, February 1997, p. 32

0189: God is the indweller in the human heart (spiritual heart). There is no meaning in going elsewhere in search of God. Realizing this, men should lead a life of kindness to all beings. A man without kindness is an animal.
Sanathana Sarathi, May 1997, p. 131

0190: God is omnipresent. Just as there can be no light rays without the sun, this cosmos cannot exist without God.   *Sanathana Sarathi, May 1997, p. 126*

0191: Do not think that God dwells in some temple, shrine or place of pilgrimage. He is omnipresent and His abode in man is the human heart.
Sanathana Sarathi, April, 1997, p. 94

0192: Cows are of many colors, but their milk is white. Living beings are numerous, but the indwelling spirit is one and the same.
Sanathana Sarathi, March, 1997, p. 57

0193: Man has but the right to perform action; to ask for the fruits thereof he has none. God alone can dispense the fruits of man's actions.
Summer Showers, 1979, p. 70

0194: There are two ways of God-realization. One is the path of devotion where the devotee considers himself a servant of God. By repeatedly declaring, "Daasoham" ("I am your servant") he goes reducing his ego till the bondage of worldly attachment falls off. The other means is the path of knowledge

(Jnaanamarga). By constantly developing the sense of oneness with the Divine ("Sivoham- I am the Divine") his consciousness expands to the point where it becomes one with the universal consciousness and all worldly bonds are snapped.

Give no room for the ego. If any one examines his position in this vast cosmos, he will realize his infinitesimal smallness. Egoism arises out of ignorance. Expel the ego and develop love. With love, develop the spirit of sacrifice. Sacrifice alone can confer immortality, says the Upanishad. Sacrifice can confer bliss and health. Experience the joy of sharing. Renunciation is the key to sound health.

Do not indulge in criticism of others. Count your own faults and rectify them. See the Divine in one and all. Elevate the quality of human life by living in amity with all. Chanting the name of God is the sure means of cultivation of this universal love. *Sanathana Sarathi, May 1997, p. 129*

0195: God is your best, unfailing friend at all times. All others are mere time-servers. People waste their lives believing in such petty fair-weather friends. Your best friend is residing in your heart as the Indweller.
Sanathana Sarathi, March, 1997, p. 60

0196: God will not reside in a heart filled with fraud and falsehood.
Gems of Wisdom, Characteristics, p. 83

0197: By letting himself be enslaved by his senses, man is degrading himself. The royal road to perfection consists of controlling one's senses, praying to the Almighty, and finally merging in Him.   *Summer Showers, 1979, p. 44*

0198: When the magnet does not attract the needle, the fault lies in the dirt that covers up the needle. When the Lord does not approach the devotee the fault lies in the heart of the devotee; it is not pure enough.
Sanathana Sarathi, June, 1997, p. 164

0199: It is essential to realize the basic truth that God is present in the form of human beings.   *Gems of Wisdom, Beliefs, p. 222*

0200: You may ask: Why, then, is God not visible? Why are some near to God and others remote? God is not to blame. People are immersed in worldly concerns.   *Sanathana Sarathi, September, 1996, p. 248*

0201: God is inscrutable. He cannot be realized in the outer objective world; He is in every heart of every being. Gemstones have to be sought deep underground;

they do not float in mid-air. Seek God in the depths of your self, not in tantalizing, kaleidoscopic nature, and the body is granted to you for this high purpose, but you are now misusing it like the person who cooked his daily food in the gem-studded gold vase that came into his hands as an heirloom.

Gems of wisdom, Preface

0202: The body is the temple of God. In everybody, God is installed, whether the owner of the body recognizes it or not. It is God that inspires you to good acts and warns you against the bad. Listen to that voice. Obey that voice and you will not come to any harm.   *Sathya Sai Speaks, Volume II, p. 26*

0203: God is bliss; you can feel Him but not see Him. Two plus two equals four; it is a fact, whether you accept or not.   *Gems of Wisdom, Faith, p. 114*

0204: Some ask, where is God to be found? God can be realized only after a long process of cleansing and at the end of systematic disciplined preparation. Without learning the alphabet, how can anyone dare condemn the classic?

Gems of Wisdom, Where is God? p. 337

0205: There is in everyone a spark of truth, no one can live without that spark. There is in every one a flame of love, life becomes a dark veil without it. That spark, that flame, is God, for he is the source of all truth and all love. Man seeks truth. He seeks to know the reality because his very nature is derived from God, who is truth. He seeks love to give it for his nature is that of God and God is love.

Sathya Sai Speaks, Volume I, p. 78

0206: All the living and non-living entities God projects are led towards acquisition of the very ecstasy whose overflow they are. God is the paramount principle of Bliss for the material world of Time and Matter. His bliss pervades all creation. That is the way His leela (Divine play) works.

Gems of Wisdom, Why is God not seen? p. 345

0207: Many say, we will believe in God when we see him. Then we can reply that we will believe in pain when we see it! God is a bliss you can feel (but) not see.

Sathya Sai Speaks; Volume VI, p. 110

0208: We should not be under the impression that God exists somewhere, having a special form and vested with special powers and so on. What is contained in man's heart as a clean thought and a supreme consciousness is itself God. All limbs in our body are nourished by the same blood, motivated by the same Will, the Will of God. This is called "viswarupa", the cosmic vision, which will create

faith in yourself and God and bestow everlasting peace.
Gems of Wisdom, Why is God not seen? p. 344

0209: It should be realized, that there is no greater friend than God. He is beyond the reach of praise and censure. He does not give up man on the ground of latter's failure to come up to His expectations. That is why God has been given the appellation, Suhrid (a good friend), who confers benefits on devotees without expecting any return. Never the less, man does not readily accept such a friend. Only the man who accepts God as such a friend and is guided by His advice can understand the full meaning of Divine friendship.
Gems of Wisdom, Where is God?, p. 339

0210: God is impartial. He is like a thermometer which cannot exaggerate or falsify.   *Gems of Wisdom, Why is God not seen? p. 349*

0211: God is but a witness to man's actions; He is above hate and anger. Man gets punished by his own actions and not by God.
Gems of Wisdom, Why is God not seen? p. 349

0212: The Lord is the unseen foundation on which your life is built. He is the source, sustenance, and strength. Without His will, no leaf can turn, no blade of grass can quiver.

Just as the same blood stream circulates in all the limbs of the one individual, the One Divine Principle activates the entire Universe. Do not get too involved in the turmoil of living and ignore the kinship of God. Ignore the beads; contemplate upon the unifying, eternal, ever-present thread. God is to be recognized in all that exists, all that is charming or suffering, blooming or drooping. He is the intelligence in the insect, faithfulness in the dog, latent energy in the rock! A gentleman may wear morning dress, evening dress, dinner jacket or luncheon slacks - he is the same inside all these dresses, isn't he?
Gems of Wisdom, Namasmarana, p. 378

0213: One of the first principles of straight living is the practice of silence. For the voice of God can be heard in the region of your heart only when the tongue is stilled and the inner storm is subdued and the waves are calm.
Sathya Sai Speaks; Volume IV, p. 274

0214: There is no greater form of meditation than constant remembrance of God at all places and on all occasions. God is the indweller in the heart. When you experience this you will lack nothing and will fear none. Your conscience will be your guide. Love all.

You can see God only through the eye of wisdom (Jnaana-chakshu). Realizing that God dwells within you, you must treat God as the universal Guru, as the preceptor for mankind, irrespective of differences in names.
Sanathana Sarathi, August 1997, p. 202

0215: God is omnipresent, but you are unable to see Him. You see his external form and not the Divine in him. But without the power of the Divine how can he exist? You cannot deny the existence of the air all around you, though you cannot see it or grasp it. Likewise God is everywhere but is subtle and invisible. You will experience Him in your heart, when you make it absolutely pure.
Sanathana Sarathi, September 1997, p. 229

0216: God is adored as mother, father, kith and kin, friend, wealth and everything else in the world. God is immanent in every atom of the universe. All that you see, the mountains, trees, insects, birds and beasts, the food you eat, the air you breathe are all manifestations of the Divine.
Sanathana Sarathi, August 1997, p. 198

0217: God is omnipotent. Nature is a reflection of that omnipotence. All the powers present in Nature are present in every human being. Hence it should be recognized that God, Nature, and the individual are all equally divine.
Sanathana Sarathi, August 1997, p. 198

0218: God is not somewhere outside. He is the indweller in the body. Sin is the result of one's own actions. Hence it is folly to seek God elsewhere. Man wants to know all about the world and ventures to explore outer space. But he is unable to know his own nature. How is he to know his self? The self is called conscience. The spiritual quest means making use of the vibrations from the conscience to understand the Truth. Today man follows only the body and the mind and becomes a prey to all kinds of troubles.
Sanathana Sarathi, December 1995, p. 282

0219: God is your friend closer than even your own mother and father. He exists in you in the form of self. What I am conveying to you is the simple truth. What greater truth can I convey?   *Baba, The Breath of Sai, p. 223*

0220: God is no stony hearted despot. He is Compassion. He is Grace, personified. Once you have cleansed yourself by tears, He draws you near and grants you consolation and courage. Without a cleansed heart, realization is impossible. Wisdom can enter only a purified mind. Spiritual discipline, slow and steady, can succeed in purifying it. The Spiritual discipline for each Age has been prescribed by the Scriptures; for the Kritha or first Age, it is Meditation; for the

Thretha, the second, it is Righteousness; for the Dwapara, the third, it is Ritual Worship and for the present Age, the Kali, it is the Repetition of the Name of God.

The repetition of the Name of God, the Scriptures say, in this age of materialism is the one hope for man. Have the Repetition of God's Name on your tongue, the Form in your eye, the Glory in your heart, the thunderbolts will pass you quietly by. When you recite the Name of God, remembering the while His Majesty, His Compassion, His Glory, His Splendor, His Presence, Love will grow within you. Its roots will go deeper and deeper, its branches will spread wider and wider, giving cool shade to friend and foe, to fellow national and foreigner.

Baba, The Breath of Sai, p. 308

0221: Where there is confidence, there is love. Where there is love, there is peace. Where there is peace, there is truth. Where there is truth, there is bliss. Where there is bliss, there is God.   *Sanathana Sarathi, April 1994, p. 90*

0222: If the heart is polluted of filled with pride, God cannot be experienced even if one tries for endless years.   *Sanathana Sarathi, August 1996, p. 204*

0223: As butter is inherent in milk, God is immanent in the Universe. When it is churned, the butter separated itself and becomes cognisable. So too, by means of Love and the discipline of the recitation of the Name, God can be concretized.

Baba, The Breath of Sai, p. 234

0224: God showers His grace according to one's deserts. He is the embodiment of Love. One's bad qualities prevent one from realizing the grace of God. The fault lies with the individuals and not with God.

Sanathana Sarathi, September 1994, p. 229

0225: It is not open to all to understand the ways of the Lord. To know about God one has to develop godly feelings.   *Sanathana Sarathi, January 1997, p. 2*

0226: Scientists employ all kinds of instruments and declare that they have not found God anywhere. But the saints, seeing God with the inner vision, see Him everywhere. They use the power of Mantra to see God, they see God through the lens of Love. When some people ask you, "Can you show God?" you should reply: "You are God; that is why you are able to talk and act." There is nothing in the world other than God! To know divinity you should know the sacredness within you. Keeping salt in your mouth, you can't taste anything that is sweet. Only when you cast off the salt and wash your mouth you can experience the taste of the sweet. Worldly desires are like salt. Discard them. Then you can realize Divinity. You must shed the evil qualities of jealousy, hatred and anger and divest yourself of the ego. If you rectify your defects and cleanse your heart, you can realize Sathya and Dharma as the basis of your life. This is the Life Principle and with these you can lead a purposeful life. Making use of your intelligence as whip and the mind as the yoke, you can drive the chariot of life, with the senses as horses, to the right destination.   *Sanathana Sarathi, April 1994, p. 99*

0227: The idols that are worshipped are the answers to those who go about asking, "Where is God?" The truth is God is present is every atom. Every atom represents the power of the Divine. Every atom deserves to be worshipped. All objects in Creation have to be respected. Men have to cultivate this feeling of reverence for all things.   *Sanathana Sarathi, March 1995, p. 59*

0228: People imagine that God is an entity far beyond human conception and grasp. That is not true. Divinity is nearer than anything else in the world. If you consider It remote, It will appear distant, but if you regard It as near, It will be near. As long as man is conscious of the body, he cannot comprehend a formless Divinity. Hence, he must adore the Divine in human form. If, for instance, a buffalo or a fish thinks of God they can conceive of God only as a huge buffalo or a gigantic fish. Man also conceives the form of God only in terms of his own human form and attributes. As long as man is attached to the body, he cannot realize God.Only when he sheds his attachment, he can experience the Divine.   *Sanathana Sarathi, March 1994, p. 59*

0229: We use old newspapers generally to wrap different types of articles purchased in a shop. If jasmine is wrapped in the paper, the paper smells sweet like jasmine. Another person may wrap some edible like pakoda and the paper gives that smell. If dry fish is wrapped, the paper emits the smell of fish. Though the paper has nosmell of its own, it takes on the smell of the thing with which it is associated. In the same way our mind, too, gets polluted because of the illusion of body consciousness and attachment. When you think of a material object, it gets object-oriented, but if you turn the mind towards the Life P rinciple it makes the life sacred. If you turn it towards the world, it is binding you to the world. If you turn it towards Awareness, which is Brahman, you become Brahman.   *Sanathana Sarathi, May, 1993, p. 114*

0230: Cores of people all over the world are in quest of God. But where are they searching for Him? In my view, the very idea of a quest for God is mistaken. There is no need for you to search for God. God is omnipresent. He is everywhere. Devotees imagine they are searching for God. This is not true. It is God who is in search of devotees. Where is the devotee to be found who is pure in thought, word and deed? God is searching for such a devotee.

You need not search for God. God is nearer to you than your mother and father. You yourself are divine. How can you go in search of yourself? This is the mistake you commit. When everything is permeated by the Divine, who is the searcher of the Divine? It is because the world has lacked men who could

proclaim this Vedantic truth with authentic experience that it has sunk to such
degrading levels.   *Sanathana Sarathi, February 1995, p. 32*

0231: Man should remember that the same Divine Awareness (Prajna) is present
in all human beings. This truth is accepted by all faiths. It may be asked why God
is not visible if He is all-pervading. The answer is that though God is omnipresent,
He can be experienced only by those who have a pure heart. Just as a cow's milk
can be got only from the udder and not from any other part of the cow, God's
image can be visualized only by those with a heart full of love and which is pure
and free from selfishness. God cannot be perceived by those with impure minds
and polluted hearts. The sun cannot be seen when he is covered by a cloud. But
when the wind sweeps the cloud away, the effulgent sun becomes visible.
Likewise, man has to drive away the cloud of ignorance enveloping his mind be
meditating on God. In this Kali Age, there is no greater or easier means of
realizing God than chanting His name.
                    Sanathana Sarathi, January 1995, p. 24

0232: If you want to get near to God and to experience God, you have to
transform the heart. As you sow, so shall you reap. Sow the seeds of love and
reap the fruit of love. Sow the seed of immortality and reap the fruit of immortality.
Today you want sweet fruit, but you sow poisonous seeds. This is thoughtless
action.   *Sanathana Sarathi, May 1995, p. 120*

0233: Man is the embodiment of the Divine. All human bodies are animated by
the same Spirit, like the current that makes all bulbs shed light. The Divine
subsumes everything though invisible.
                    Sanathana Sarathi, December 1995, p. 317

0234: You see this magnificent hall, but you do not see its foundations. Likewise,
God is the basis, nature is the superstructure. The spirit is the basis, the body is
the superstructure. The body is like a rose in which the spirit is present as
invisible fragrance.   *Sanathana Sarathi, December 1995, p. 314*

0235: Truth is God. The Upanishads declare: "Raso vai Saha" (God is all
sweetness). This means that God is present in subtle form everywhere, like sugar
in sugarcane and butter in milk. Although it is difficult to have a direct perception
of God, His presents can be experienced in many ways. The sweetness in sugar,
the sourness in lime fruit, the bitterness of the margosa leaf, all testify to the
presence of the Divine. When you see a mountain or a waterfall or a forest you
feel happy. All these proclaim the presence of the Divine. Light shines, the stars
twinkle, the sun blazes, the planets revolve in their orbits. All these phenomena
are manifestations of the Divine. By understanding the nature of a flame you can
understand the nature of fire. By examining a drop of water you can know the

nature of the Ganges. Likewise by understanding the true nature of humanness, you can understand Divinity.

Despite all the activities in which man is engaged from dawn to dusk, he has no understanding of his true nature. He identifies himself with the body, the senses and the mind, forgetting that his true self is beyond all these. They are only instruments. Vedanta calls man to know himself. The insigniaby which a man is identified in ordinary life are not the indicators of one's true self. There are two entities in a man: the body and the indwelling Spirit. To know the Spirit is to know one's true self. *Sanathana Sarathi, December 1995, p. 281*

0236: If you do not feel the call at the sight of human distress, disease or deviation from the right, how can you muster the determination and dedication necessary to serve the unseen, inscrutable, mysterious God? When you do not love man, your heart will not love God. Despising brother-man, you cannot, at the same time, worship God; if you do, God will not accept that hypocrisy. God is resident in every heart; so, if you serve anyone, that service reaches the God within him: it brings to you the Grace of God.
Sanathana Sarathi, December 1997, back cover

0237: Embodiments of love! Take note of the fact that the rapid passage of time is consuming man's life-span at a rapid pace like the melting of an iceberg. The end comes even before man realizes his role in life. It would be a shame if human life is wasted in this manner.

Man suffers from numerous ills because he has not understood the purpose of life. The first thing he has to realize is that God is one, by whatever name and in whatever form the Divine is worshipped. The One chose to become the many. "God is one. The wise hail Him by many names." It is the imagination of the observers which accounts for the apparent multiplicity of the one Divine. The sun is only one, but his reflections appear in a myriad vessels. Likewise God is present in the hearts of different beings in varied forms and natures.
Sanathana Sarathi; October, 1997, p. 262

0238: God's ways are astonishing, inscrutable, and mysterious. God has made ample provision for all man's needs. He has also given to man much more in the form of luxuries. In addition, He has conferred on man the power to control all these things.

God has told man: "You are free to use as you like all the things given to you, subject one condition. You will have to face the consequences of your actions." This means that you cannot abuse the freedom given to you to misuse the things that are provided for you.

When you misuse anything, you have to bear the resulting misery. When you make good use of anything, you will enjoy the benefits therefrom. You have to take note of the purpose for which you use your sense or the objects given to you. Any misuse of them will bring misery in its wake.

You came with nothing into the world and leave it with nothing. What happens to your wealth or to yourself? Of what use is all other wealth unless a man realizes the bliss of oneness with the Divine? Scientists who are exploring the moon are not trying to understand their own minds. Without understanding one's own true self, all other knowledge is meaningless.

Sanathana Sarathi, December 1995, p. 321

0239: The great teaching of the Gita is: "Put your trust in God, carry on your duties, be helpful to everyone and sanctify your lives". Dedicate all actions to God. That is the way to experience oneness with God. God is in you. You are in God. This oneness is the basic truth. Chant the name of the Lord and render social service in a spirit of selflessness and devotion to God.

Sanathana Sarathi, September 1995, p. 232

0240: The truth is that sweetness is common to all, though the names and forms may vary. Similarly, in the world the different nations and countries have diverse forms and names. But the Divine in all of them is one and the same. The Indwelling Spirit is the same in all beings. The Divine energy is common to all, like the current which activates all bulbs, fans etc.. God is present equally in everyone. The differences among human beings are the result of the differences in their capacities. When one is immersed in thoughts of God, his capacity will grow.

Sanathana Sarathi, July 1996, p. 172

0241: Giving up narrow ideas and feelings, people should show compassion towards their fellow beings. Compassion is the hallmark of devotion. No one can hope to please God without showing compassion towards his fellow-men. A loving heart is the temple of God. God cannot dwell in a heart without compassion.

Sanathana Sarathi, April 1996, p. 88

0242: All beings experience the presence of the Divine through the five elements, the five senses, and the five life breaths. Some may ask, "When the Divine is omnipresent and is in all beings, why is He not visible to us?" If investigation is made on right lines, God can be perceived. Some human effort is essential to get this perception. Just as the reflection of the sun can be seen in all its purity only in clear and still water, though reflections may be noticed in ponds, wells and oceans, God can be perceived only when the heart is pure and unselfish. How can God be expected to appear before a person whose mind is wavering and whose outlook is self centered? The wavering mind will experience only a hazy figure. In a strong mind, God will present a clear image.

Sanathana Sarathi, January 1996, p. 3

0243: Love is Divine. Have love for all. Impart your love even to those who lack love. Love is like a mariner's compass. Wherever you may keep it, it points the way to God. In every action in daily life, manifest your love. Divinity will emerge from that love. This is the easiest path to God realization. But why are not people taking to it? This is because they are obsessed with misconceptions relating to the means of experiencing God. They regard God as some remote entity attainable only by arduous spiritual practices. God is everywhere. There is no need to search for God. All that you see is a manifestation of the Divine. All the human beings you see are forms of the Divine. Correct your defective vision and you will experience God in all things.   *Sanathana Sarathi, August 1996, p. 212*

0244: All of you are embodiments of the Divine. Recognize this fact and strengthen this feeling within you. The idea that God is different from you should be given up. You have to develop the feeling that God is not different from you.
Sanathana Sarathi, April 1996, p. 93

0245: The man of faith need not worry about who will take care of him of he devotes all his time to thoughts of the Divine. The Lord who is the universal provider will take care of his devotees.
Sanathana Sarathi, October 1996, p. 264

0246: How is God to be experienced? God is present in everyone like butter in milk. Your heart is the container. Love is the milk present in the heart. When this love is offered to the Lord, it acts as the churning process for getting butter. There is then the direct experience of the Divine.
Sanathana Sarathi, July 1996, p. 170

0247: All the pains and pleasures man experiences are the results of his own actions and not due to any act of the Divine. God is only a witness. God is like a postman. He delivers to you whatever letter is addressed to you. The grief or joy you derive from the contents of the letter are your own. Likewise, the suffering or happiness one experiences are the results of one's own bad or good deeds, and are not derived from God. However, there is the operation of special grace on certain occasions. When you pray to God with a pure heart, without a trace of selfishness and with sacred feelings, God confers special favor. Moreover, when a person has done some unique act of sacrifice in a previous life or at any time in the past, the Divine confers an appropriate reward for it at the proper time.
Sanathana Sarathi, August 1996, p. 218

0248: Reawakening of man is at hand. Reawakening to the knowledge that man himself is God. The human body is not you, it simply houses the soul or the spark of Divinity within, for God dwells in the heart of every man and that dwelling spark of the divine is you- yourself. All else is illusion.
Sathya Sai Speaks, Volume IV, p. 76

0249: We should understand that where there is no God, there is no courage. All the human bodies will simply be reduced to mere leather bags in which there is no life at all if there is no contact with the divine.

Summer Showers in Brindavan, 1973, p. 110

HEALTH

0250: All the diseases which afflict man are the result of agitations in the mind. The enormous growth of disease in the world today is due to the loss of peace of mind. To get rid of illness and to lead a calm, healthy life, man has to cultivate mental peace.

Gems of Wisdom, Mind, p. 41

0251: Evil thoughts cause ill health. Anxiety, fear, and tension also contribute their share. All these results from greed, which in turn results in sorrow and despair. Contentment can come only from a spiritual outlook.

Gems of Wisdom, Health, p. 177

0252: Fear is the biggest cause of illness.

What are the main causes of ill health? Millions of living beings grouped as species, sustain themselves by the food provided by Nature. But man, in order to satisfy the craving of his tongue, changes the composition and characteristics of things provided by Nature and prepares food through the process of boiling, frying and mixing concoctions, which have hardly and nourishing value in them. Thus, vitamins and proteins that are valuable nourishment are destroyed. The billions of cells in the body are so interdependent that when one is weakened or damaged, all of them suffer.

Gems of Wisdom, Health, p. 176

0253: It is death that teaches us to love life. Diseases which torment man are many in number, of these, hatred, envy and egoism are the worst. Even the doctors cannot cure them, for most of them suffer from these!

Gems of Wisdom, Health, p. 179

0254: Anger is another enemy of health. It injects poison into the bloodstream.

Gems of Wisdom, Health, p. 179

0255: Man should try earnestly to live long, without falling into the hands of doctors. Moreover, the drugs they recommend are mostly spurious, since the manufacturers want to amass wealth by hook or crook. Most illnesses can be cured by simple living, simple mental and physical exercises and by not succumbing to the taste for the tongue.   *Gems of Wisdom, Health, p. 179*

0256: The means to prolong or shorten one's life lie in one's own hands. Your life span is prolonged when you are full of joy, when you are calm and filled with pure thoughts. When you are filled with envy, anger, hatred and conceit your lifespan gets shortened. The envious man gets no sleep at all. Sleeplessness ruins the health even more than lack of food. Envy torments a man all the time. These troubles lead to shortening one's life. As for hatred, the man filled with it cannot even bear the sight of his enemy. He suffers from hallucinations which consume his body and spirit. Anger is the cause of destroying the divine potencies in man. Hatred ruins a man's circulatory system. Envy drives the man crazy by depriving him of his sleep. In that condition he cannot relish his food. Thus, these three evil qualities, hatred, envy and anger are wasting diseases. When you consider yourselves as devotees of God you should get rid of these three evil qualities. Lead peaceful and pure lives. To call yourselves devotees but to look with envy at others is totally unbecoming. Exude joy always. That joy will manifest itself when you experience your oneness with the Divine within you. If you are unhappy, it is because you have not experienced the Divine.

Sanathana Sarathi, August 1993, p. 203

0257: By eating flesh one develops violent tendencies and animal diseases.

Gems of Wisdom, Health, p. 180

0258: Excessive eating does violence to the body. Moderation in food is conductive to happiness.   *Sanathana Sarathi, March 1996, p. 69*

0259: Food and recreational habits are the two main causes for ill-health. Great care has to be bestowed to ensure that injurious tendencies do not affect these two. At present, though drugs have multiplied and more hospitals exist, ill health is also widespread. This situation is attributable to the spread of deleterious food habits and pastimes.   *Sathya Sai Speaks, Volume X, p. 54*

0260: Life sustained by food is short; life sustained by Atma is eternal. Do not lay claim to lone life; but to Divine life. Do not pine for more years on earth, but for more virtues in the heart. The Buddha know and made known to the World the Truth. Everything is grief. Everything is empty. Everything is brief. Everything is polluted. So the wise man has to do the duties cast upon him with discrimination, diligence and detachment. Play the roll but keep your identity unaffected.

Gems of Wisdom, Food, p. 183

0261: Strong will is the best tonic. The will becomes strong when you know that you are a child of Immortality or a person who earned the Grace of the Lord. Medicine and hospitalization are for these who doubt and hesitate and argue about this doctor being more efficient than the other and this drug being more powerful than the rest. For these who rely on the Supreme Doctor, His Name is the drug that cures.   *Gems of Wisdom, Degradation, p. 148*

0262: By making an offering of all that you eat to God before taking it, the food gets purified and sanctified.   *Sanathana Sarathi, October 1996, p. 257*

0263: Mere medication will not cure a sick man. He must also control his diet for quick recovery from illness. There is no single panacea for the great world-sorrow. Each individual has his own specific type of suffering. Nevertheless, meditation on God is an unfailing remedy for human suffering if it is supplemented with the practice of dharma (code of right conduct) and the strict observance of moral restraints. We are all interdependent. We must learn to share the joys and sorrows of other people. A practitioner of meditation must pray for the welfare of others as sincerely as he prays for his own welfare.
                    Summer Showers, 1979, p. 92

0264: A person who is sick will always want to take several medicines. Certain birds will always be wanting to look at cool moonshine. Good people will always want to help the bad people and to see that the badness in them is removed and they bare cleansed. It is only one who has a disease and is sick, that wants a doctor. A healthy man does not want a doctor. Similarly, people who are suffering from the disease of disbelief can be cured by good people.
                    Summer Showers in Brindivan, 1977, p. 219

0265: For leading a good life, good health is a prerequisite. It is better not to fall sick rather than search for remedies later. The quantity of food taken by the rich is far too much. Overeating has become a fashion. Shortage of good grains are mainly due to wasteful eating habits. Man will remain healthier by eating the minimum than the maximum.   *Gems of Wisdom, Behavior (Conduct), p. 399*

0266: Illness is caused more by malnutrition of the mind than of the body. Doctors often speak of vitamin deficiency; I will call it the deficiency of vitamin "G", and I will recommend the repetition of the name of God. That is vitamin "G"! That is the medicine; regulated life and habits are two-thirds of the treatment, while the medicine is just one-third only. Fear is the biggest cause of illness.
                    Sanathana Sarathi, March 1996, p. 75

0267: We can say that there are three types of hearts. The first one is the physical, which causes problems of diseases that are mainly due to overeating and sedentary habits. By regulating the diet and by proper exercises, the heart disease can be prevented. It is necessary to keep the body in a fit condition to do service. In China, people follow certain type of yoga called "Taichi". They get up early in the morning and do this; exercise. We can see thousands on citizens practicing this in the open. India has a rich tradition of yoga which relates to breathing, sitting and walking. A massive educative campaign is needed, especially in the rural areas, to prevent heart diseases, by propagating such Yogic exercises.

The second heart is that of the Chakra, which is the seat of emotions, radiating love; compassion and hatred too. This accounts for the psychological aspect of diseases of the heart patient. That is why they administer holistic medicine nowadays.

The third one is the spiritual heart. The "Purusha" or Supreme Power resides in the innermost recess of this spiritual heart. This is referred to as the many-splendoured effulgent Joythi. The three-dimensioned (Physical, Emotional and Spiritual) heart is the secret of human consciousness, which is the direct like with the Divine. This is what the great sages of the Upanishads proclaimed when they had a vision of the Divine. They experienced the Supreme Purusha as the effulgent one shining with the brilliance of a thousand suns.

Sanathana Sarathi, January 1996, p. 16

0268: There is no worse disease than desire. Contemporary man is afflicted by endless desires. These desires are the cause of innumerable diseases. There must be a limit to desires. Today desires grow limitlessly. Consequently, diseases also increase limitlessly. Owing to endless desires, man is affected mentally and this gives rise to many bodily ailments. Hence everyone should try as far as possible to keep a check on desires.

Sanathana Sarathi, September 1995, p. 225

0269: Young people should realize that the root cause of all their bad thoughts and bad actions is the food they consume. The nature of the food determines the state of the mind. Food does not mean merely what is eaten, but includes all that is received through the senses and stored in the mind. The mind, as Dr. Subba Rao said, has the power of attraction. It attracts impressions of all kinds from the external world.

What do we find in every home today? There is a television set. T.V. sets are installed in every room in the houses of the rich. From the moment television made its appearance, the mind of man has been polluted. Before the advent of T.V., men's minds were not so much polluted. Acts of violence were not so rampant previously. Today T.V. is installed in every hut. People watch the T.V. even while taking food. The result is that all the foul things seen on the T.V. are being "consumed" by the viewer. Concentration on the T.V. affects one's view of the world. The scenes, thoughts and actions displayed on the T.V. set fill the minds of the viewers. Unknowingly, agitation's and ill-feelings enter their minds. In due course they take root and grow in the minds.

Hence, while taking food, you should not discuss dreadful incidents. No room should be given to subjects which excite the mind. Silence should prevail during eating. Even sound waves enter into us and affect our minds. Hence people should avoid seeing T.V. while taking food.

There is now what is called "Star TV. It is doing great harm to human life. The temporary satisfaction given by it is followed by lasting damage. It is like a sword coated with honey. As you lick the honey, the sword will cut your tongue.

Not Bharat alone, but the whole world is suffering from the consequences of TV. The world is racked by disorder, discord and frustration.

Sanathana Sarathi, February 1996, p. 45

THE INTELLECT

0270: Knowledge of Brahman is denied unto them who discard the intellect and are enamored of ephemeral knowledge. To the man who stands on the shores of the sea and observes the stultifying external manifestations, the waves alone appear. Only the daring, expert diver who can search the sea-bed finds the precious pearls lying there. The Bhagavad Geeta declares that knowledge of Brahman is attained only by the person who seeks the Atma in the innermost recesses of his subtle being.   *Summer Showers, 1979, p. 155*

0271: To exercise the power of discrimination, man is endowed with Buddhi (the intellect). The intellect has to be unwavering and steady. Man fails to use this discrimination power properly and fully because of his qualities of attachment and aversion (Raaga and dwesha), his obliviousness to his inherent divinity and his preoccupation with mundane desires. If these tendencies are removed, the intellect will come into its own as an instrument of discrimination.

The intellect is the highest among man's endowments starting with the body. Above the body are the senses. Subtler than the senses is the mind. The intellect is subtler than the mind. Above the intellect and much more subtle is the Self (Atma). Because of its proximity to the Atma, the Buddhi is very subtle.

Sanathana Sarathi, November 1997, p. 295

0272: Buddhi (intellect) is the most superior faculty of man, and its preeminence, is due to its proximity to the Atma. Below intellect is the mind; below the sensory organs is the body. In actual fact, intellect should always exercise control over the mind, and the mind over the senses. But today mostly the reverse is occurring and hence all the chaos.

Birth as a human being is a unique chance, for man in endowed with a discriminating intelligence. Intelligence must be the Lord and Master.

It is not enough if one has human form or the basic human equipment, physical, mental and emotional. With the help of discriminating intellect, one must bring it to perfection, as a sculptor does after the stone is brought to a definite shape.   *Gems of Wisdom, Intellect (Buddhi), p. 48*

0273: Man is blinded by the objective world and he believes that world to be real, meaningful and worthy of pursuit. The cataract grows in the eye and robs it of its efficiency. The cataract is the enemy of the eye. Ignorance, the cataract of the inner eye, blinds the intellect and robs it of its efficiency. So, it cannot see the Divinity that is your real nature. It misleads you into the impression that you are a man, whereas you are really God.   *Sathya Sai Speaks, Volume IV, p. 3*

0274: The mind is subject to unsteadiness because of desires. Desires are rousedby the impressions received by the senses from outside. The only way to avoid these external impressions is to turn the senses inwards. To effect this change in the use of the senses, the power of discrimination derived from the intellect should be employed. The intellect should be used to determine what impressions should be kept out and which should be let in. The intellect should determine what kind of company we should keep, what kind of food we should eat and what are desirable practices and what are undesirable. It is by the right use of their intellectual judgment that the ancient sages achieved spiritual eminence.   *Sanathana Sarathi, November 1997, p. 296*

0275: Man, although he is inherently the embodiment of Sath-Chith-Ananda (Being-Awareness and Bliss), unaware of this truth, seeks this bliss in the phenomenal world as the ultimate reality and forgets his own true Divine nature. This is a mark of his ignorance. When one's vision is turned Godward, this ignorance disappears.

Many persons yearn for God, worship God or contemplate on God. God cannot be realized by any of these means. All these activities are based on separating themselves from God. What is needed is a sense of oneness. How is this to be obtained? When you cultivate the feeling: "I and you are one". This oneness is beyond the grasp of the mind and the senses. It is only the Buddhi (Intellect) that can experience what is beyond the senses.
          Sanathana Sarathi, October 1996, p. 263

0276: The body is intended for rendering help to others and not for self-enjoyment. Unfortunately because of the perversions of the mind, man loses himself in worldly pleasures. He is a slave to the vagaries of the mind and ignores the counsel of the intellect (Buddhi).   *Sanathana Sarathi, January 1995, p. 24*

KARMA

0277: When you are born, you are not born with garlands and necklaces. You have no pearls or diamonds. You have no golden ornaments. But, around your neck hangs the garland of your past karma and acquired "samskaras" (tendencies). And when you die you do not take anything with you except the consequences of your good and evil actions. You are always decked with the invisible garland of your inexorable karma, which pursues and burdens you. This burden of karma can be lightened by God's grace and your own realization of the oneness of your soul with the universal soul. Karma can be destroyed by karma alone.

Summer Showers, 1979, p. 56

0278: Creation has no predetermined limits. It is an eternal process whose beginning or end cannot be known. In the process of birth, growth and dissolution, besides the Will of the Lord, the role of human effort can also be recognized to a certain extent. Man's destiny is determined by the nature on his actions, thoughts and desires.

The sacred Scriptures of this land loudly proclaim that the individual is the architect of his own fate: high or low status in society, luxury or poverty, liberty or bondage. Whatever form the person craves for now while alive in this world, that form he attains after death. Therefore, it is clear that karma decides birth and that the luxury or poverty, the character and attitude, the level of intelligence, the joys and griefs of this life are the earnings gathered during the previous life. The inference, therefore, is inevitable that the next life of the individual will be inconsonance with the activities prompted by the level of Karma in this life.

God is not involved in either reward or punishment. He only reflects, resounds and reacts. He is the eternal unaffected Witness. You decide your own fate. Do good, be good, you get good in return; be bad, do bad deeds, you receive bad results. Do not thank or blame God. He does not even will that creation, protection and destruction shall take place. They follow the same law, the innate law of the maya-ridden universe.

Gems of Wisdom, Fate, p. 87

0279: You are born as a human being for doing your duty (karma). Life is given to you only to recognize Divinity, and the body is the instrument for achieving this purpose.

Gems of Wisdom, Karma, p. 89

0280: Karma is the life sustaining force and is the cause of birth. The body is the instrument of the vital force. Every action done by man is termed as karma. Man performs actions for the fruits thereof. He takes birth again to experience the results of his actions. Hence it is considered that man's life in this world is bound by karma. Man cannot get away from action. Man's condition in life is dependent by his actions, and his habits are then governed by the actions. Habits determine conduct, and conduct determines his future. Hence, it is very important how we act. Good and evil in life are determined by the nature of our actions.

Gems of Wisdom, Karma, p. 89

0281: The distinction between karma and karma yoga should be clearly understood. Actions performed selfishly with egoism and desire for reward are karmas that bind. Actions performed unselfishly without ego and any expectation of reward become karma yoga.   *Gems of Wisdom, Karma, p. 90*

0282: Karma or action means life force. Man is the instrument of this life force. The human body is made up of action. Hence, the Scriptures described man as "karmajaa", i.e., born as a result of action. All actions performed by man with his limbs and organs are rendered possible by the Divine. Hence man must regard all actions as sacred.   *Gems of Wisdom, Karma, p. 90*

0283: On your land, you can grow food as you like, or you can be idle and let it lie fallow. You owe yourself the cause of ruin or progress. The tools are in your hands; you can learn the skills and break the shackles and escape, but if you decide to spend life is slavery and bondage, who can save you? Do not blame fate. The status in the present life is decided on your actions in the previous life.
Sanathana Sarathi, December 1995, back cover

0284: Karma is the supreme maker of one's destiny.
Gems of Wisdom, Karma, p. 90

0285: Actions of man determine his destiny. Through righteous actions, the mind is purified which results in awakening of wisdom. Man should pray each morning to the deity of karma, "let me do today only pure, purposeful and helpful actions".
Gems of Wisdom, Karma, p. 90

0286: The circumstances of one's birth are the result of past actions.
Summer Showers. 1974, p. 243

0287: It is not possible for any one to abstain from action. Action is the basis for our existence. This body has been given to us for the sake of action. It is the need of Man's life that he must sanctify it through action and purify his time by right action. This stream of action flows through Jnana (wisdom) also and ultimately leads us to the highest stages of realization.
Summer Showers, 1972, p. 275

0288: The art of engaging in karma without getting involved in karma is the thing that has to be learned. Karma has to be done because it is part of one's nature, not out of any external compulsion.   *Sathya Sai Speaks, Volume III, p. 96*

0289: It is only when you recognize your own faults that you begin to understand the ways of the Lord. Today the tendency is to ignore one's own fault and blame God for one's suffering. Nothing can happen without a cause. Good actions will earn good returns and bad actions will result in bad consequences.

Gems of Wisdom, Law of Karma, p. 98

0290: Every activity of man has a goal, an end in view. Proceeding to the market, going to school, each has a purpose. When such short duration activities are motivated by goals, how can man pass 60 or 70 years of life on earth with no purpose guiding him and leading him on?

Gems of Wisdom, Law of Karma, p. 102

0291: Whoever it may be, whether he is a devotee or a believer, an aspirant or an unbeliever, his actions will determine what rewards or punishments he gets in life. Your good behavior shall be your shield of protection.

Gems of Wisdom, Law of Karma, p. 100

0292: Whoever is dependent on objects for happiness or pursues sensory pleasures, whoever is motivated by impulses and desires is bound by karma. But those free from these cannot be affected by the temptations of sound, touch, form, taste, smell and other attractions of the senses.

Gems of Wisdom, Law of Karma, p. 108

0293: As per inescapable law of Karma, the results of good or bad actions are not like the milk that you get immediately as you draw it from the udder of a milk cow, but are like fruits that you get from a tree, long after the seed is planted. Therefore, do not feel elated just because your bad actions have not given you the bad results immediately; you are sure to experience them in due course.

Gems of Wisdom, Law of Karma, p. 98

0294: Our condition in life is determined by our actions. Our habits are governed by our actions. Habits determine conduct; and conduct determines our future.

Gems of Wisdom, Law of Karma, p. 103

0295: An idle man is the devil's workshop. When one is busy with some work there shall be no room for any thoughts. A peaceful mind is the abode of love, which is inherent in every man, even a thief, but it has to be nourished by dedicated service.   *Gems of Wisdom, Law of Karma, p. 101*

0296: Appreciation the importance of actions, you must see that everything you do is pure and holy. Action is not limited to what you do with your hands. What

you hear, what you see, what you speak and what you think - ALL OF THEM
CONSTITUTE ACTION. This means that the things you see, the words you hear,
the thoughts you think and the speech you make, should all be pure.
Gems of Wisdom, Law of Karma, p. 103

0297: Devote yourself in worshipful acts, do everything for the Glory of God; that
is more fruitful than the "meditation" which you are relying on. Just as a
thermometer indicates the temperature, your talk, conduct and behavior indicate
your mental equipment and attitudes and show how high is the fever of
worldliness that afflicts you.   *Gems of Wisdom, Law of Karma, p. 103*

0298: Actions of man should be done in a spirit of detachment to the world, not by
cutting himself off, but by being in it as an instrument in God's hands; by subduing
all tendencies toward egoism, by concentration on Dharma (code of right
conduct). Food and drinks; housing and clothing must be subsidiary to the needs
of spirit. Man's age, youth, strength, wealth and status should not make him feel
very proud, since these are but transitory.

Carry on your legitimate duties, discharge your obligations, but do not
allow attachments to grow.

A wise man has to do the duties cast upon him with discrimination,
diligence and detachment. Play the role, but keep your identity unaffected. Have
your head in the forest (ashram), unaffected by the aimlessly rushing world. But, it
is your duty which you cannot escape, to fully engage yourself in your work,
unconcerned with loss or gain, failure or success, slander or praise.

God is but a Witness to man's actions; He is above hate and anger. Man
gets punished by his own actions and not by God.

A man is judged by the nature of his actions; if they are good, then he,
too, is a good man, and if they are bad, than he too, is considered a bad or
wicked man. Man's qualities and actions are interdependent.
Gems of Wisdom, Law of Karma, p. 103

0299: When the strength of your body, the strength of your mind, and the strength
of your intelligence are good and powerful, if you cannot use your life for helping
others, what is the use of your life? It will be a waste. You cannot lead your life
like the oil drop on the surface of water, without touching the water. Your birth,
your life, your mode of conduct are all connected intimately with the community
around you. If that community around you is not remembered by you and if all the
time you think of your selfish interest, you are not going to be any good at all to
any one.   *Summer Showers in Brindivan, 1977, p. 89*

0300: One meaning of Karma, which is mostly accepted, is that it is one's destiny
of fate, the inescapable writing on the brow, which has to work itself out, and
there is no escaping it. But people forget that it is written by one's own hand and
not by someone else, and hence the hand which wrote it can also wipe it off. The

husk with which paddy (rice) is born can be removed with effort; similarly, the maya which persuaded you to write that destiny can also be conquered by doing good deeds.   *Gems of Wisdom, Law of Karma, p. 107*

0301: You are born as human beings for doing your duty (Karma). Had the goal for man been mere living or even happy living, the Atma could have been encased in the form of birds or beasts. Why it has taken this human form, with the power of reasoning through the intellect, is to achieve the goal of realization of the unity of self with God.   *Gems of Wisdom, Duty, p. 109*

0302: Man's present situation and status are determined by his acts and thoughts in the past.   *Gems of Wisdom, Education, p. 190*

0303: You came alone into the world and you go out alone. When you are born, you are not born with garlands and necklaces. You have no pearls or diamonds. You have no golden ornaments. But, around your neck hangs the garland of your past action and acquired "purification's". And when you die you do not take anything with you except the consequences of your good or evil actions. You are always decked with the invisible garland of your inexorable action of which pursues you and burdens you. This burden of action can be lightened by God's Grace and your own realization of the oneness of your soul with the Universal Soul.   *Baba, The Breath of Sai, p. 136*

0304: The causes are many and complex as to why all this has happened. It is even more difficult to predict as to where all this is leading the world to. But there is no doubt that the law of cause and effect (karma thatwa) operates with the same ubiquity as the law of gravity. Nothing can escape it. Thus the wheel of cause and effect is forever revolving. The results of today are the fruits of the causes of tomorrow. Action begets reaction begets action- and so on endlessly. Only the Lord Himself can amend it. It is indeed impossible to analyze all the various causes of the past which are resulting in the happenings of today, and for the same reason to predict the happenings of tomorrow.

However, we can see that the basic tendency today of man is a search for attainment of joy and peace.

The variety of knowledge has smothered the searching endeavor of the intellect and this is hindering the conquest of man's internal foes. It is a dangerous pride, as it captivates man's most useful servant "the intellect" which, instead of being a tool in the hand of man, has become the master.   *Gems of Wisdom, Weaknesses of Mankind, p. 136*

0305: Whatever the level of intelligence may be, you must keep on doing work, with your thoughts on the Lord. The result of all good work will only be good. Whatever work you have done in the past, Brahma will put all that, the good and the bad together, as a garland round your neck when you are born. You will be born with this garland of good and bad round your neck and you have to suffer all the consequences thereof.   *Summer Showers in Brindivan, 1977, p. 26*

0306: I have often declared that God does not come down as avatar to relieve individuals of their troubles and sorrows and to confer joy and happiness on them. Difficulties, troubles and worries come in the natural course as a consequence of past actions. The Gita says: Human beings are bound by Karma in the world. As human birth is the result of Karma there can be no escape from the consequences of Karma. As is your action, so is the reaction to it.
Gems of Wisdom, Avatar, p. 287

0307: The sacred Scriptures of this land proclaim that the individual is the architect of his own fate; high or low status in society, luxury or poverty, liberty or bondage. Whatever form the person craves for now while alive in this world, that form he attains after death. Therefore, it is clear that karma decides birth and that the luxury or poverty, the character and attitude, the level of intelligence, the joys and griefs of this life are the earnings gathered during the previous life. The inference, therefore, is inevitable that the next life of the individual will be in consonance with the activities prompted by the level of Karma in this life.
Sanathana Sarathi, September 1997, back cover

0308: By planting the seeds of a lemon tree, you cannot expect to grow mangoes and by sowing the seeds of a mango tree, you cannot expect to get lemons. In a similar manner, by doing a bad act, you cannot expect to get a good result and if you do a good deed, you cannot get a bad reaction from it. The kind of seeds you sow will determine the nature of the crop they will yield.
Summer Showers in Brindivan, 1977, p. 26

0309: Actions determine the course of the Intellect. In the actions performed by a person, there are two types: the proper and the improper. Man's intellectual tendencies depend on the nature of his actions, good or bad. Bad actions pollute the intellect. Good deeds purify the intellect. Hence, the condition of the intellect is determined by one's actions.   *Sanathana Sarathi, April, 1997, p. 92*

0310: When a man is born he does not have round his neck any necklace of pearls or gems or any possessions. But he is endowed by Brahma with the garland of the effects of his past actions, good or bad, which hangs invisibly around his neck. If you do good you will enjoy good results and if you are bad you will not escape suffering the consequences thereof.
Sanathana Sarathi, October 1994, p. 266

0311: God has provided everything for man's good in the world. But there is one condition that has to be observed. The results of your actions will be according to their nature, whether they are good or bad. Men today want to reap the fruits of good deeds without performing good deeds. This is impossible. Nor can they escape the consequences of their evil actions. God is only a witness.

Sanathana Sarathi, March 1995, p. 64

0312: You might say that the Karma of the previous birth has to be consumed in this birth and that no amount of grace can save man form that. Evidently, some one has taught you to believe so. But I assure you, you need not suffer from Karma like that. When a severe pain torments you, the doctor gives you a morphine injection and you do not feel the pain, though it is there in the body. Grace is like the morphine, the pain is not felt, though you go through it! Grace takes away the malignity of the Karma which you have to undergo.

Sathya Sai Speaks, Volume IV, p. 225

KNOWLEDGE

0313: Everyone goes about trying to see what he can get from society. Today, thanks to the influence of the Kali age, two kinds of diseases have grown: One is the insatiable thirst for wealth. In every city there is a mad rush for making money. No doubt money is necessary, but only up to a limit to meet one's needs. Owing to excessive desire, people lose all sense of proportion. Men turn into demons in the pursuit of wealth.

It may be asked whether at least they make good use of their immense wealth. No. Ultimately, the money may fall in the hands of robbers or others. What you get from society, give it back to society. That is the primary value to be cherished by every one.

The second malady is the thirst for power. The thirst for power and position is unquenchable. Afflicted with these two maladies, man is converting the whole world into a madhouse.

The desire for wealth and power is not wrong as such. But wealth and power should be used for right ends. Whatever position you occupy, see that it is used worthily. A cobbler stitching shoes is pursuing as worthy an occupation as a Prime Minister governing the country. Therefore everyone has to do his duty properly. There is no high or low in these matters. To each person, his occupation is a matter of pride. Hence, do your duty sincerely. Everyone should be filled with this feeling. He should see that he does his job well without any lapse or defect. When everyone does his duty in this spirit the well-being of the whole world will be automatically ensured.

People proclaim that they desire the well-being of one and all in the world, but they do nothing to promote it. They are concerned only about their own well-being.

Sanathana Sarathi, May 1997, p. 122

0314: Bodies and temperaments may differ from individual to individual, but the Divine is one and the same in all.   *Sanathana Sarathi, February 1997, p. 41*

0315: We do not go from falsehood to truth, or from unreality to reality. Truth cannot be derived or deducted from falsehood. Spirituality is a hierarchy of reality. We have to ascend from a lower level of reality to a higher level of reality. Absolute truth is the highest level of spiritual reality.
Summer Showers, 1979, p. 64

0316: Some people ask "How are we to believe in God when we have no notion of His form?" This is sheer folly. Here is a flower. It has a form, but the fragrance emanating from it has no form. Can you deny the reality of the fragrance because it has no form? Fragrance has a form, but that form is manifested in the flower.

Take, for instance, PREMA (love). What is the form of love? Is it your fault if you do not recognize its form. Love has a form derived from the persons who exhibit love. Without someone expressing love, love cannot exist, just as fragrance cannot exist without a flower. So, in these examples we can see the inextricable relationship between what appears to be formless and the source of its form.

To take another example: here is a person whose form can be described in terms of various physical features. But does this description in terms of height and weight reveal anything about his internal qualities like forbearance, peacefulness, compassion, love and sacrifice? Are not these qualities very real and significant? He is prized mainly for these qualities, not for his physical features. To judge him only in physical terms is meaningless. His formless virtues are more important. When one is judged in respect of his qualities, the form is irrelevant.

Those who judge anything on the basis of the external form are utterly foolish. No purpose is served by trying to explain to a blind person the nature of something he cannot see. Likewise, how can anyone speak about God to a person who has no intimacy with the Divine or yearning for God?
Sanathana Sarathi, April 1997, p. 88

0317: A guru is a spiritual preceptor. He transmits wisdom to his disciple. His duty ends here. It is the disciple's duty to receive and respond to his master's spiritual wisdom. He must put into practice what he has learned. A guru is like a "guide-post" in the highway. He shows the path to the disciple. A sign-post indicates the road to be followed, but does not indicate anything about to ups and downs and the pitfalls on the road. It is the traveler's duty to beware of all pitfalls and obstacles on the road.   *Summer Showers, 1979, p. 67*

0318: Secular knowledge is no doubt necessary for getting on in life. The bliss of spirituality cannot be achieved without the minimal necessities of life. But, secular knowledge is not the be-all and end-all of human existence. Spiritual knowledge is, as a matter of fact, more important than material knowledge. All branches of human knowledge are like rivers and spirituality is like the unfathomable and uncharted ocean. Just as the rivers flow into the sea and merge in it, all secular knowledge fulfills itself in spiritual knowledge.   *Summer Showers, 1979, p. 120*

0319: Everyday from morning till night you spend your life in merely earning the means of your livelihood. What great happiness have you attained by employing your skill and education in only filling your stomach forgetting the lotus-eyed lord? O, man! Ponder over this with deep regard.   *Summer Showers, 1979, p. 70*

0320: Man is on a long pilgrimage towards God. He moves from one life to another. On the way he has to take shelter in many caravan sarais (rest houses), but he cannot strike root and has to remind himself of the journeys end.
Sathya Sai Speaks: volume VI, p. 123

0321: Knowledge obtained directly from sastras and scriptures is like sea water. By exercising the faculty of discrimination and by entering the meditative state of mind, the pure water of wisdom can be distilled from the saline sea water of scriptural knowledge. This knowledge is humanized by experience and divinised by selfless love.   *Summer Showers, 1979, p. 95*

0322: Bookish knowledge divorced from experience leads to fanaticism and intellectual arrogance. Knowledge by acquaintance is always superior to knowledge by description. Practice is better than precept. We must live the scriptural injunctions rather than merely talk about them. Self-imposed discipline is more effective than discipline enforced by some external authority.
Summer Showers, 1979, p. 96

0323: To realize the Supreme, the path of devotion is the only royal road. It is the panacea for all worldly aliments and for the most effective means for awakening the spiritual urge.   *Sanathana Sarathi, September, 1996, p. 235*

0324: "Why should you study and stuff your mind with all sorts of useless knowledge and then die in ignorance to be born again and again? Acquire that knowledge which will make you immortal", said Venana. You may be well-versed in worldly knowledge, but without knowledge of the Self you will remain an ignoramus. Man searches in the world outside but fails to find his true self therein, just as a person who looks for some article in a room is unable to see himself. Seek within, realize the Self which resides there, and then experience the bliss of God.   *Summer Showers, 1979, p. 167*

0325: Man must engage himself in constant process of self-correction instead of finding faults in others   .*Gems of Wisdom, Gunas, p. 53*

0326: During youth, when a person is physically strong and mentally alert, he should conquer the six vices of: kaama (desire), krodha (anger), lobha (avarice), moha (attachment), mada (pride) and matsarya (envy). Above all, a young person should acquire self-confidence. Faith creates love. Love creates tolerance and compassion, and God reveals Himself to those with tolerance and compassion. Thus faith in yourself is of primary importance. *Summer Showers, 1979, p. 173*

0327: When qualities like greed and anger enter the heart, the brightness disappears and darkness dominates the vision, and man becomes the target of countless griefs and losses.   *Gems of Wisdom, Heart and Love, p. 77*

0328: Man's primary aim should be to recognize the unity that underlies the diversity in the phenomenal world. To break up what is one into many pieces is easy. But it is difficult to bring them together into a meaningful unit. It is in the unifying process that the utility of things can be understood. The role of both diversity and unity in life has to be properly understood.
Sanathana Sarathi, September, 1996, p. 237

0329: What is it that people need today? There are three things: A heart pure and white like the moon, speech soft and sweet like butter, a face that is loving and kind. These are lacking in the world today. The entire atmosphere is frightening. There is harshness in speech. There is no softness in the heart. The heart should be pure and soft like butter. Today, on the contrary, people are hard-hearted. Fill your hearts with compassion. Let your speech be sweet and truthful. You will then be truly human.   *Sanathana Sarathi, June, 1997, p. 148*

0330: Knowledge does not mean worldly knowledge. Only the person who has recognized the oneness of the individual spirit and the universal Spirit is a real Jnaani (One who possesses the supreme wisdom). True wisdom consists in the awareness of the unity of the individual and the whole.
Sanathana Sarathi, June, 1997, p. 145

0331: The six demons, kama (lust), kroda (anger), lobha (greed), moha (attachment), mada (pride) and matsara (hate) pursue you and turn you into wrong paths and make you servile, stupid and sad. Fight against them resolutely. That is the life-long war you have to wage. It is not a seven years war or a thirty years war; it may be a hundred years war, if you live a hundred years. The struggle knows no respite. This is a civil war, where vigilance alone can bring dividends.

You have six fires raging inside you, but you also have four effective fire extinguishers- righteousness, truth, peace, and divine love (dharma, sathya, shanthi and prema). All of them can help you to overcome these flames. It is the duty of man to ensure the four wheels of the chariot (body), i.e., dharma, sathya, shanthi and prema move along the road to the goal of liberation (moksha). The chariot will move easily only if it has less luggage (less worries, desires and fears). Faith is the air in the wheels and it must be periodically checked for even balance. Man must realize that he is the owner of the body and not the body itself. Mind, intellect and senses are his to manipulate as he wishes and not the other way around.   *Gems of Wisdom, Weaknesses of Mankind, p. 133*

0332: Man is enslaved by money. He lives a superficial, hollow, artificial life. This is indeed a great pity. Man should seek to possess only as much money as is most essential for his living. The quantity of riches must be compared to the shoes one wears; if too small, they cause pain; if too big, they are a hindrance to physical and mental comfort. When we have more, it breeds pride, sloth and contempt for others. In pursuit of money, man descends to the level of the beast. Money is of the nature of manure. Piled up in one place, it pollutes the air. Spread it wide; scatter it over fields; it rewards you with a bumper harvest. So too, when money is spent in all the four quarters for promoting good works, it yields contentment and happiness in plenty.

Sanathana Sarathi, June, 1997, back cove

0333: All actions in the world and their consequences originate in the head, and these relate to the external path, and those which arise from the heart relate to the inward path in feeling like peace, kindness, compassion, forbearance and love.   *Gems of Wisdom, Heart and Love, p. 76*

0334: If man wished to be happy, the first exercise he must do is to remove from his mind every bad thought, feeling and habit.

Sathya Sai Speaks, Volume XI, p. 183

0335: Truth is more fundamental than the atom. Every atom and every star manifests the truth to those who have an eye of wisdom. What is the special nature of man? If he too lives and dies as any animal, how can his supremacy be justified? His supremacy lies in his capacity to become aware of his truth.

Sathya Sai Speaks, Volume X, p. 126

0336: Men may have superabundance of food, clothing and housing; but their hearts may be dry and their spirits gloomy. Sense-control, self-confidence, contentment, absence of hatred and greed are far more precious as possessions than land, money or houses.   *Gems of Wisdom, Degradation, p. 147*

0337: Society, indeed, is the school where man will learn that God is ever with you everywhere.

Man in his ignorance, finds contentment is separating himself from the rest for the search of his own happiness, forgetting that he cannot be happy unless all are happy. He pollutes himself through the cultivation of pride. He uses time for degrading himself to the bestial level.

Gems of Wisdom, Society and Company, p. 201

0338: Man is shaped by the company he keeps; so, be ever vigilant of the air you breathe; it is fouled by foul thoughts of the men among whom you move.

Gems of Wisdom, Society and Company, p. 201

0339: Teach children not to receive anything for nothing. Let them earn by hard work the things they seek.   *Sathya Sai Speaks, Volume V, Children, p. 212*

0340: Inner purity is even more important than outer purity. By practicing patience and forbearance we will be able to acquire all the other important spiritual qualities, such as Mind Control, Faith, Renunciation, Endurance and Concentration. This will bring a state of inner purity. God is ever present both inside and out. Therefore, both must be purified and sanctified. Then the indwelling God will protect you wherever you go.

Gems of Wisdom, Purity of Body, p. 271

0341: Today parents are worried about the conduct of their children. They do not realize that they are themselves to be blamed. If the parents had brought up the children on the right lines and by good personal example, would they go astray? Pampering children in various ways, they are allowed to go about like street dogs! How can such children be reformed? It is impossible. When wealth grows, arrogance increases and morality declines. The father must encourage the son by example more than precept.

Why blame the boys and girls that they do not respect elders or obey their parents or believe in God or adhere to high principals of character? The elders are not providing them examples to show those traits on character are useful or valuable or essential.   *Gems of Wisdom, Children, p. 213*

0342: You are living now in the dark, in ignorance. The knowledge that you are the divine spark, encased in the sheaths of bliss, intelligence, feelings, sensations and organic substances, this knowledge is the light. You must light your own lamp. You cannot walk in the light of another's lamp. Knowing is not enough; you must experience it. A well has water, but that is not enough. It must be brought up in a bucket and used to bathe and quench thirst.

Gems of Wisdom, Truth, p. 250

0343: You must realize that the Divine current that flows and functions in every living being is the One Universal Entity. When you desire to enter the Mansion of God, you are confronted by two closed doors- the desire to praise yourself and the desire to defame others. The doors are bolted by envy, and there is also the huge lock of egoism preventing entry. So if you are earnest, you have to resort to the key of prema (Love) and open the lock; then remove the bolt and throw the doors wide open. The education must train you in this difficult operation.

Sathya Sai Speaks; Volume X, p. 85

0344: An empty iron box gets valued when it contains jewels; the body is honored when it contains the jewel of consciousness and values known as virtues.

Life has to be lived through for the sake of the chance to unfold the virtues. Otherwise, man is a burden upon the Earth, merely a consumer of food.

A virtuous character is the lamp which illuminates the path to peace and joy.

Some consider themselves great because they have vast territory, some because they have a lot of wealth, some because they have a large population; but the greatness is virtue which earns the Grace of God.

Gems of Wisdom, Virtue, p. 229

0345: Avoid factions, quarreling, hating, scorning, fault-finding; they recoil on you. You find fault in others because you have faults in you. Remember, every one is a pilgrim towards the same goal; some travel by one road, some by another.

Sathya Sai Speaks, Volume X, p. 70

0346: The complete harmony between thought, word and deed is the mark of a high souled being. Without unity of thought, word and deed there can be no fulfillment in life. The consummation, of all sadhana (spiritual practices) is purity of the heart.   *Gems of Wisdom, Practice and Precept, p. 239*

0347: Man does not realize the value of the precious gift of the number of days of life he has received from the Lord. He fritters them away for temporary yearnings. That is the tragedy of man everywhere.

Gems of Wisdom, Spiritual Level, p. 263

0348: Man today has forgotten his true nature and looks upon the world entirely through the senses and the mind.   *Gems of Wisdom, Spiritual Level, p. 260*

0349: The genuine outer signs of devotion are: faith, humility, and apprehension.

Qualities like forbearance, sympathy, truth, love and compassion are the spiritual qualities of mankind and are essential for people anywhere in the world at all times.   *Gems of Wisdom, What is Realization? p. 270*

0350: You cannot hide truth for a long time. However much you may try to hide, the truth will always come out. In fact, the Divine strength in man's heart will always be pushing him to proclaim truth.   *Gems of Wisdom, Truth, p. 250*

0351: Change and evolution are natural to mind. But the presence of the unchanging Divinity should be experienced within the changing body.
Gems of Wisdom, Beyond the Senses, p. 256

0352: Science can offer only temporary worldly comforts; spirituality alone can give you enduring bliss.   *Gems of Wisdom, Spiritual Level, p. 260*

0353: God and the devil, good and bad are denizens of one's own heart. Where God is, there the devil cannot be.   *Gems of Wisdom, Spiritual Level, p. 262*

0354: No one is competent to determine the length of anyone's life. Why, then, is there mention of a hundred years span for man in the scriptures?
This is not mere fancy of the authors of the scriptures. It is the truth. Every man should live for a hundred years. What is the reason for premature death?
The wicked tendencies in man, such as arrogance, envy, bad thoughts and misdeeds, go on shearing the life of man into pieces. His bad qualities shorten the life of man. When a man's life is filled with good thoughts and good actions, he can live for a hundred years. The secret of the longevity enjoyed by the ancient sages is precisely this. Man today wastes his life in bad thoughts and bad actions and ends his life in a bad way.
Gems of Wisdom, Spiritual Level, p. 263

0355: Man's attitude towards God should not be based on the fulfillment or nonfulfillment of petty desires. You must feel that whatever happens to you is for your own good.   *Gems of Wisdom, What is Realization? p. 270*

0356: There are four kinds of tendencies in man: the animal, the demonic, the human and the divine.
When man ignores the mind and the Atma and identifies himself with the body, he manifests only his animal qualities. When the body and the Atma are forgotten and only the mind alone is predominant, one becomes demonic.
When the body and the mind are forgotten and one is immersed in the Atmic consciousness, one becomes Divine.
Gems of Wisdom, Characteristics of Man, p. 283

0357: The proof of rain is the witness of the ground. Likewise, the proof of true devotion is in the peace of mind; that the aspirant has been able to attain, the peace that protects him against the onslaught of failures, the peace in which he is unruffled by loss and dishonor.   *Sathya Sai Speaks; Volume V, p. 308*

0358: Raising the standard of living must also mean raising ethical, moral, and spiritual standards.   *Gems of Wisdom, Spiritual Quality is Essential, p. 277*

0359: It is the identification with the body and the slavery to the senses that it breeds which cause all the cruelty, injustice and violence that stalk the world.
Gems of Wisdom, Avatar, p. 294

0360: Marvelous are the beauties presented by Nature. They are sacred as well as wondrous. What Nature promotes or destroys, what it bestows or takes away are equally amazing. It is not easy to understand these marvels.

Man is born in this world but does not realize the purpose of his birth Forgetting this purpose, he regards himself as the master of Nature and in his insane conceit forgets his own divinity. He is unable to recognize that it is Nature that provides or takes away, that blesses or punishes, that Nature's sway is extensive. Nature presides over every aspect of life. In his deep involvement with mundane concerns man tends to forget his divinity and what he owes to Nature. All things in creation are equal in the eyes of God. God is immanent in all of them. Hence God and Nature should not be regarded as distinct entities. They are inseparably interrelated like the object and its image. Man, however, looking at Nature externally, considers it as purely physical and intended to provide the amenities he seeks.

Nature is the best teacher for man. Every object, every individual, is offering lessons of various kinds to man every moment.
Sathya Sai Speaks; Volume X, p. 229

0361: Not all living beings can recognize that in all living beings the Divine exists as the indwelling spirit. Only a human being has the capacity to recognize this. Man alone has the ability to discriminate between the transient and the permanent. The other unique faculty with which man is endowed is VIJNAANA (the ability to acquire the highest knowledge).
Gems of Wisdom, How is Man?, p. 283

0362: The body is the ball filled with air of Divinity; it is kicked in play by six players on one side (the six FOES: Lust, Anger, Attachment, Pride and Hate) and six on the other side (the six FRIENDS: Truth, Righteousness, Peace, Love, Compassion and Fortitude). The goal-posts are on each side and if the ball is kicked so that it passes through them, the Dharmavidya (Moral Attainment) and Brahmavidya (Spiritual Attainment), those who kick it so, can claim victory.
Gems of Wisdom, Characteristics of Man, p. 283

0363: There are four kinds of worship. The first kind of worship is undertaken whenever one is in trouble or distress, then God is forgotten after relief is obtained. The second kind of worship is carried on by the worshipper seeking the good things of life from the deity he worships without depending on others. The third type of worshipper offers worship for the sake of others, praying for the welfare of all. The fourth kind, which is the highest form of worship, is worship done in a spirit of complete surrender to the Divine and dedicating all actions to the service of the Divine. Man's attitude towards God should not be based on the fulfillment or nonfulfillment of petty desires. You must feel that whatever happens to you is for your own good.   *Gems of Wisdom, Bhakthi (Devotion), p. 300*

0364: Prayers for worldly ends do not reach God. They will reach only those deities, who deal with such restricted spheres. But all prayers arising from pure love, unselfish eagerness to render service, and from hearts that are all-inclusive will reach God.   *Sathya Sai Speaks; Volume II, p. 68*

0365: Prayer has to be united with practice. You should not pray for one thing and practice another. Such prayer is only a means of deception. The words you utter, the deeds you do, the prayers you make must all be directed along the same path.   *Prashanthi Vahini, p. 34*

0366: Between Concentration and Meditation, there is border-area which covers both and that is the area of Contemplation. To be in that area of Contemplation is to free yourself of worldly attachments. If you break away all the worldly attachments- all the routine attachments in the world- then you enter the region of Contemplation. When you have completely broken away all your attachments, you break through this area of Contemplation and you get into the area of Meditation.   *Gems of Wisdom, Dhyana (Meditation), p. 320*

0367: There is no need to establish a new society. It is our duty to recognize what good already exists in us.   *Summer Showers in Brindivan, 1977, p. 246*

0368: The distinctive feature which renders man different from animals is wisdom or intelligence. The animals do not have intelligence and if man does not use his intelligence properly, he is just like an animal, animals have no inner vision. They have only external or outward vision. They do not remember the past, nor plan for the future.   *Baba, The Breath of Sai, p. 252*

0369: Cause and effect are indistinguishably interwound; silver is the cause and a plate of silver is the effect; clay is the cause and the earthen pot is the effect. In the same way, Divinity is the cause and humanity is the effect.
                    Gems of Wisdom, Why is God not seen?, p. 349

0370: One only, not two. If it is not two, it could be three; so it is defined also as One only. It is the inner motivator of all, like the string running through all the beads. If it is inside all, why is it not visible in all? Picture a rosary if different types of beads - coral, pearl, tulsi, crystal, rudraaksha, conch, etc. the string passes through each and holds all the beads together no doubt; but it is only in the transparent beads that it is visible. So too, you have to make yourself transparent, free from wish and will that hide or befog; then only can the inner motivator be seen. You cannot say that since it is not visible, it is not there. To earn transparency, purity of intuition, impulse and instinct is essential. That can be achieved by systematic and sincere discipline.

Gems of Wisdom, Sins and Repentance, p. 356

0371: For a trouble-free journey, there is nothing as reliable as the remembrance of the Name of the Lord.   *Baba, The Breath of Sai, p. 317*

0372: I do not condemn worldly happiness. I feel glad when people are happy. I want that you should study all the arts and sciences for acquiring worldly happiness. But, please do not believe that this happiness is permanent.

Gems of Wisdom, Sai Baba's Directives, p. 454

0373: When divinity is immanent in everything, conscious and un-conscious, in every form of being, how can a thing be condemned as bad or commended as good?

Water quenches thirst and can also drown people. Fire gives light and warmth, but can also burn a thing to ash. Sound terrifies and also thrills. They are all three Divine. Divinity is not so easily understood. To recognize this Unity one needs training, though to be deluded by diversity one doesn't need any. For grass to grow quickly no effort on our part is needed, but if grain is to be harvested, the field must be ploughed, weeded, watered, manured and fenced. So also to get a harvest of virtue, intense sadhana is needed, though no such effort is necessary to contract vices. Man has to struggle hard in order to attain the higher stages of spiritual development. He has to overcome many hurdles and put up with many difficulties and disappointments.   *Sathya Sai Speaks, Volume X, p. 186*

0374: Man must realize the immensity of the play of the Divine will which manifests itself in such abundant variety. But what does science say of this Will? It only declares that we should not believe things that we do not see. The Divine Will is beyond our power to see, so it cannot be tested to be real! This attitude is not correct. Take this kerchief which I drop from my hands. It falls to the ground instead of going up in the air. We attribute this to the gravitational pull even though we do not see the pull.   *Sathya Sai Speaks, Volume X, p. 186*

0375: One must give a shape to one's life in such a way that one earns the grace of God. We should follow a sacred path. Having been born, we should do all that is necessary to see that we are not born again. When we meet our death, we should not meet it a second time. This is indeed the secret of man's life. But today, in man's life to the extent to which the knowledge of science has grown, to that extent the strength of man has become less. As science has progressed, the sense that is present in human beings has become less and less. What you call Science can give you material pleasure but it cannot give you any bliss of self. Spirituality leads you to the aspect of completeness. Every human being must realize this completeness of the total knowledge contained in spirituality.

Baba, The Breath of Sai, p. 227

0376: The intelligence that has been given to you so that you may understand who you are is being used to understand the rest of the world and not yourself.

If the intelligence that has been given to you for the purpose of introspection and search of your atma is used to procure food, there is no meaning to your life. Even the birds and the animals are searching and procuring food. It is a shame to be born as a human being just for the sake of getting food to eat. If a mirror that is given to you to look at your own face is used to see the faces of others, how are you going to know your own face?

God has gifted this intelligence to you so that you may be able to understand yourself and to realize your own true nature. Make an attempt in the first instance to find out who you are. It is this esquire that will automatically become the esquire of self and lead to questions like who am I? Am I this body? Am I this mind? Am I this intelligence? Etc.

When you examine each of these questions, you will realize that you are none of these. For example, you say, "It is my body" When you say that, you imply that you are separate, the body is separate and that you are not the body. This truth must be understood by you. If I take this as my kerchief, the kerchief can be thrown away at anytime and I can become quite separate from the kerchief When you say that this is my body, my mind, my intelligence and so on, it simply means that you are different from the body, the mind and the intelligence. You are in the body, you are in the mind, you are everywhere, but they are not in you. They belong to you but they are not the same as you.

Summer Showers in Brindivan, 1977, p. 33

0377: Heaven is not a supra-terrestrial region of perpetual spring; it is an inner experience, a state of supreme Bliss.   *Baba, The Breath of Sai, p. 259*

0378: There are some qualities which are always accompanying the jeeva (individual). His sorrows, his birth, his work, his hatred, his likes and dislikes, his lack of discriminating power and his ignorance are qualities which are always accompanying the jeeva. Ignorance gets mixed with lack of discriminating power. Lack of discriminating power gives rise to attachment. Attachment gives rise to anger. Anger gives rise to hatred. Hatred gives rise to birth and sorrow. All these qualities are related to each other in an inseparable manner.

For sorrow, birth is responsible and for birth, one's own karma is responsible. However, we may ask if sorrow is natural to man or is it coming half-way through one's life? Truly, if sorrow is natural to man's life, he cannot get rid of sorrow all through his life. There is no basis for us to think that sorrow is a natural quality for a human being. If that is so, it could not be got rid of by any method.

Summer Showers in Brindivan, 1977, p. 84

0379: Man has three things that animals do not have:
1. The power to reason out.
2. The power to renounce.
3. The power to decide on right and wrong; use the sacred body for the purpose of seeing truth.   *Baba, The Breath of Sai, p. 253*

0380: There is no basic conflict between man and nature. Man is entitled to enjoy the fruits of nature even as a child is entitled to the mothers' milk or a bee to suck the honey in a flower. The creation is greater than mankind. It is humanity's privilege to understand the secrets of creation. Man should also seek to know the relationship between creation and creator.

Sanathana Sarathi, November 1997, p. 281

0381: It may be possible to teach a person the posture, the pose, the position of legs, feet or hands, neck, head or back, the style of breathing or its speed. But the meditation is a function of the inner man; it motivates deep subjective quiet, the employing on the mind and filling oneself with the light that emerges from the divine spark within. This is a discipline that no text-book can teach and no class can communicate.   *Sathya Sai Speaks; Volume VII, p. 356*

0382: Human life is much more meaningful than that of birds and beasts. Man has in him a spark of the Divine; his body is the temple of God. So he must live in such a manner that the innate Divinity expresses itself through Love, through service of others, and through the recognition of the constant presence of God in him and all around him. When man dedicates his skills to the search for food, he estranges himself from the light that shines within him, the Self.

Baba, The Breath of Sai, p. 243

0383: Man is considered to be the crown of the animal kingdom; he is the summit of living beings. Of whatever is born from the womb of a mother, it is said, he is the highest. Why? Because he is the only animal that can investigate his own self and realize and reveal the Divinity which is his reality. Other animals have no thirst for the basic inquiry and no hunger for this satisfying wisdom. This thirst has let many posit that there is God, and others to deny the existence of God.

Baba, The Breath of Sai, p. 243

0384: Man consumes as food many living beings, plants, eggs, fish, cattle, sheep, etc.. These are born as human beings, on account of this act of consumption. But since they have not had the education; which can reveal the God within they vegetate or stay brutish, without appropriate ticket or passport for rising higher than the human status in which they have been hurriedly placed. Like most men, they roll along from womb to tomb, bond slaves to the senses and the ills that the bondage brings inevitably in its train. Do not be content with slavery; yearn to reach the sun of Splendor, the Source of Perfect Wisdom.

Baba, The Breath of Sai, p. 243

0385: When you scatter seeds on the surface of the soil, they do not germinate. You have to keep them inside the soil. So too, Bodha (knowledge), if it is scattered on the surface, it will not germinate, grow into the tree of knowledge and yield the fruit of wisdom. Plant it in the heart, water the plant with divine love, manure it with Faith and Courage, keep off pests with the insecticides of Bhajana (group singing of holy names) and Sathsanga (company of the holy), so that you can benefit in the end. You have not yet got started in Sadhana; still you demand Saanthi; you demand Grace. How is it ever possible? Start! Then, everything will be added unto you. *Sathya Sai Speaks, Volume IV, p. 101*

0386: There are three types of behavior among human beings. The Divine, the human and the animal. What we are witnessing is the growth of animality and decline of humanness. The reason for this trend is the limitless growth of desires and the steady disappearance of ideals. Selfishness is growing, selflessness is declining. Trickery is spreading, Integrity is vanishing, Attachment to the body is waxing; Love for the country is waning. The result is that the character of the people is getting degraded. *Sanathana Sarathi, November 1997, p. 283*

0387: Joy is a deceptive trap; grief is the real preceptor, teaching caution, circumspection, discrimination, detachment, awareness and vigilance. Death is not the merciless foe he is made out to be, he is the friend and companion, the teacher, the kindly kinsman who takes you into his fold and clothes you with the halo of remembrance. The heart of man has to be toughened, not hardened; it has to be made soft, not slithery, this can be achieved only by the blows of loss, grief and distress. It is God's way of shaping us, in the Divine mold. But man is blind to His mercy; he revolts at the first blow of the sculptor's hammer. Do not lose the great chance of association with the Divine, by identifying God with your trivial likes and dislikes, your tawdry aim and ambitions. Having come into this un-eternal un-happiness filled world, adore Me in order to save yourself."

Baba, The Breath of Sai, p. 290

0388: When you are able to control your desires, it will be possible for you to have the entire world in your palm. If you become subservient to your ambitions, then you will become subservient to everything around you. If you become a slave to your desires, then you become a slave to the entire world. But if you control and conquer your desires, you can conquer the whole world. If you want to keep them under control only apparently, the lasting results will not follow. If you go and beat on the surface on an ant-hill with a stick, will the snake inside the ant-hill die? Controlling desires only superficially will not be the right thing to do.

The bad ideas and thoughts that come within your body have to be controlled. Mind is like the ant-hill. Out of the ant-hill of your mind, several poisonous thoughts like poisonous snakes will be pouring out. By using sacred thoughts of God and by using quiet and calm ideas about God, you should be able to put the snakes to sleep. Yours is an age which is a sacred age. To waste such sacred age and not to get good results out of that age is deplorable. You should not desire to imitate or copy others in all your actions. If from today, you are able to get rid of such qualities and control your thoughts, in future you will be able to acquire strength by which you can go close to God.

Summer Showers in Brindivan, 1977, p. 37

0389: Charcoal is dark and signifies ignorance in the form of darkness. Fire throws light or brightness and signifies knowledge. So long as the fire and the charcoal are separated from each other, the charcoal can only look at the fire but cannot get any of its brightness. However, when the charcoal is put into the fire and brought into contact, it will become b right and will become a part of fire. Therefore, when one comes into contact with the divine form, the ignorance in the body will be removed. If we also do a little fanning, the charcoal will become fire faster. The spiritual discipline constitutes such a fanning. By spiritual discipline, even an ignorant person can become a wise person.

Baba, The Breath of Sai, p. 319

0390: No one need be afraid of what others say or think as long as one is doing the right thing according to his conscience. Courage should go along with good action. If your heart is good, no harm can come to you.

Sanathana Sarathi, November 1997, p. 285

0391: Generally, man seeks only happiness and joy; under no stress will he desire misery and grief! He treats happiness and joy as his closet well-wishers and misery and grief as his direct enemies. This is a great mistake. When one is happy, the risk of grief is great; fear of losing the happiness will haunt the man. Misery prompts inquiry, discrimination, self-examination and fear of worse things that might happen. It awakens you from sloth and conceit. Happiness makes one forget one's obligations to oneself as a human being. It drags man into egoism, and the sins that egoism leads one to commit. Grief renders man alert and watchful.

So misery is a real friend; happiness spends out the stock of merit and arouses the baser passions. So it is really an enemy. Really, misery is an eye-opener; it promotes thought and the task of self-improvement. It also endows one with new and valuable experiences. Happiness draws a veil over experiences that harden a person and make him tough. So, troubles and travails are to be treated as friends; at least, not as enemies. Only, it is best to regard both happiness and misery as gifts of God. That is the easiest path for one's own liberation.

Baba, The Breath of Sai, p. 291

0392: Through activity man attains purity of consciousness. In fact, man has to welcome activity with this end in view. And why strive for a pure consciousness? Imagine a well with polluted and muddy water so that the bottom of the well cannot be seen. Similarly within man's heart, deep down in his consciousness, we have the Atman. But it can be cognised only when the consciousness is clarified. Your imaginings, your inferences, your judgments and prejudices, your passions, emotions and egoistic desires, muddy the consciousness and make it opaque. How then can you become aware of the Atman that is at the very base? Through seva (service), rendered without any desire to placate one's ego and with only the well-being of others in view, is it possible to cleanse the consciousness and have the Atman revealed.

Sanathana Sarathi, November 1997, back cover

0393: Meditation is the inward journey, away from the objective world and the senses that run after it. The Upanishads declare, the Self cannot be attained by one devoid of strength. Strength means physical, vital moral intellectual and spiritual toughness. For all these are essential to establish mastery over the senses.

Baba, The Breath of Sai, p. 307

0394: The power of thought is immense. Thoughts survive unchanged the death of man. Therefore, everyone should foster noble thoughts.

Sanathana Sarathi, August 1994, p. 220

0395: There are no shortcuts in the spiritual field. As a matter of fact, devotion is even more difficult than wisdom, for to get the attitude of "Thou" not "I", one has to surrender completely to the Higher Power, personified as the Lord. The ego has to be fully curbed; the faith, that not even a blade of grass can shiver in the wind without His being aware of it and thus having caused it, has to be implanted in the mind. Devotion is not a leisure time job. Erase sensual desire; clear the heart of all blemish; then the Lord will be reflected therein as in a mirror.

Baba, The Breath of Sai, p. 328

0396: Renunciation is the real secret of happiness. Everyone should share with others to the extent of his capacity his income and possessions and contribute to the well-being of others. There are so many people who are destitute and suffering in various ways. It is the duty of those who are better off to go to the help of these unfortunates.

Sanathana Sarathi, November 1997, p. 284

0397: The heart has a precious treasure of Bliss, but man does not know the key to open the lock; that key is the repetition of the Name of the Lord with a pure heart. Purify the heart with the four instruments: Truth, Righteousness, Peace and Love.   *Baba, The Breath of Sai, p. 318*

0398: But why is this Bliss eluding man? Because he has not recognized the Divinity within him. Man is considering nature as entirely a creation of Providence for his enjoyment. This is a mistake. Nature exists for enjoyment by man according to certain limits.   *Sanathana Sarathi, November 1997, p. 281*

0399: It is essential to limit one's desires and keep the senses under control. This the only way to true happiness. The most important organ which has to be controlled is the tongue, which, unlike the other sense organs- the eyes, the ears and the nose, has a double function: speech and taste. The ancient sages practiced silence for a variety of reasons. Silence serves to conserve energy, improve the memory and experience the Divine. Restraint in speech and avoidance of gossip and slander are commendable virtues. Help ever, hurt never. This should be the motto of everyone.   *Sanathana Sarathi, May 1996, p. 127*

0400: India and the world are today suffering form disorder and violence because people have lost faith in the Self (Atma-viswaasa). They are fostering attachment to the body and ignoring the Spirit. Man should not follow the senses which are wayward, the body, which is perishable, or the mind, which is fickle. He must follow the conscience, which tells him what is right and wrong.
                              Sanathana Sarathi, August 1995, p. 221

0401: The second evil is the passion for power. From the villager to the top most man in a city, everybody is after power. Power carries with it limits and obligations. There are five kinds of power (or strength): the power of knowledge, intellectual power, the power of fame, the power of character, and the power of sacrifice. Only a person who has all these five attributes should aspire for a position of authority.   *Sanathana Sarathi, December 1994, p. 311*

0402: It is necessary that everyone should recognize the proper role of the sense organs and use them properly. In this context it may be noted that different animals are victims to different kinds of sensory experiences. Deer are a prey to sound - the roar of a lion or other wild animal. The elephant is afraid of the touch of the mahout's goad. Insects are attracted by light or a flame and lose their lives. Fish are lured by the taste of the worm attached to the angler's hook. It is a pity that man who possesses all the five senses of perception (sound, touch, sight, taste and smell) is a bond-slave to all of them. Thereby he forfeits his freedom.

How then, can man experience real happiness? Only by turning his senses towards God. Man has five senses of perception and five senses of action. The master for all these are like ten wives pulling the mind in different directions. It is difficult for the mind to control the senses.

Man should realize that all pleasures derived from submission to the senses are momentary and leave a trail of suffering behind. He should realize that the senses are to be utilized for sacred purposes and the practice of human values. Only then he will understand the true purpose of human existence. The senses are gifted by God for humans to lead ideal lives. See good, think good thoughts, speak sweet words and listen to what is good. Be good and do good.
Sanathana Sarathi, November 1997, p. 291

0403: Because of the differences in external forms, you are victims of the ignorance of your true selves. From a pauper to a millionaire, from an ignoramus to a great scholar, irrespective of whether one is a male or female, young or old, anyone, when describing one's self, uses the term "I". The principle of "I" is the Atmic Principle.   *Sanathana Sarathi, December 1997, p. 309*

0404: Pomp and pride have to be given up to experience the Divine. People talk about meditation, but how much of it is concentrated on God? Nor is formal meditation necessary when you realize that the Divine is within you. The purpose of meditation is to recognize one's unity with God. This realization can come only when one removes the three- layered cloak that covers the Atma in the form of the three Guna (influences): Thamas, Rajas and Sathva.
Sanathana Sarathi, December 1995, p. 321

0405: People should realize that there is nothing closer to them than the Divine. Even one's mother may occasionally be remote from the child, but the Divine is never far from anyone at any time. This means that everyone is Divine. But each one must strive to recognize this indwelling Divinity that is the eternal Reality. Most people waste their lives in the observance of external rituals and forms of worship. Together with external observances, people should also try to achieve internal purity. How long should one waste his life in external forms? All knowledge and skills are of superficial value and effect no internal change.
Sanathana Sarathi, April 1994, p. 87

0406: Every man should have a compassionate heart. Without compassion, all wealth or scholarship is of no use.   *Sanathana Sarathi, February 1995, p. 39*

0407: The divinity in you is changeless, blemishless, without beginning or end. Just as a dhoby removes the dirt in a cloth and restores its original whiteness by washing with soap and beating it on stone, man should try to regain his vision of the pure effulgent Atma by washing his heart in the water of love with the soap of earnestness on the stone of sacrifice. This is the way to realize one's Inner Reality.   *Sanathana Sarathi, May, 1993, p. 126*

0408: Thus in all religions and philosophies through the ages, these three have been declared as the forms of the Divine Atma. Truth is the form of the Divine. Love is the form of the Divine. Righteousness is the form of the Divine.
Sanathana Sarathi, February 1995, p. 35

0409: People may judge things as good or bad according to their own predilections. But for God, all things are the same. In this world, nothing will appear bad if one views it from the Divine point of view. Seen from the worldly point of view, there will be differences of good and bad.
Sanathana Sarathi, May 1995, p. 133

0410: He must realize that whatever he perceives is essentially Divine. All his actions should be dedicated to the Divine. Thereby work will be transformed into worship.
Sanathana Sarathi, January 1995, p. 12

0411: You should never divorce spirituality from worldly life. The cloth in my hand (a kerchief) is spirituality. It is made up of threads which represent worldly life. The cloth is there only because of the threads. If you segregate the threads there will be no cloth.
Sanathana Sarathi, May, 1993, p. 128

0412: All religions teach one basic discipline; the removal from the mind of the blemish of egoism, of running after little joys. Every religion teaches man to fill his being with the glory of God and evict the pettiness of conceit. Foster love, live in love; spread love; that is the spiritual exercise which will yield the maximum benefit. God has a million names; sages and saints have seen Him in a million forms, they have seen Him with eyes closed and eyes open.

The human body, so filled with skills, so capable of great adventures, is a gift from God to each of you. It has to be used as a raft on which you can cross this never calm sea of change that lies between birth and death, bondage and liberation. Pursue nobler ends; have grander ideals; sensory pleasures are trinkets, trivialities.

In homes and schools, training of the minds of the young on these lines has to be taken up earnestly by teachers and parents; of course, they must equip themselves for this work by steady practice of meditation and recitation of the name of God. Parents and children must join in singing the glory of God.
Sanathana Sarathi, January 1994, p. 25

0413: We say, God is father, mother, friend, relative, knowledge, wealth and all. God is the energy which drives us to action. We should not waste our energy on useless things.
Sanathana Sarathi, May, 1993, p. 129

0414: Truth, Righteousness and Peace are all in you. You are the embodiment of

Truth, Peace, Love and God. Recognize this fact.
Sanathana Sarathi, January 1996, p. 26

0415: Don't rely on the body. It is a water bubble. Don't rely on the mind, which is like a man monkey. Follow the conscience. When you follow the conscience with full self-confidence, you can accomplish anything.
Sanathana Sarathi, October 1993, p. 257

0416: Goodness is a synonym for God. Hence, it is only by contemplating on the qualities of God that human existence finds fulfillment. The body of a human being who does not think in this way is merely a lump of clay.
Sanathana Sarathi, May 1995, p. 113

0417: Love and service are like a bird's two wings for a man. He can soar to any heights with those two wings. To cultivate these two qualities one has to achieve the triple purity in thought, word and deed.
Sanathana Sarathi, May 1996, p. 114

0418: It is unfortunate that the vast majority of mankind lead mundane lives forgetting God. Make God the foundation of your life. Carry on your normal duties. Duty is God. Work is worship. Spiritualise all your actions and treat whatever happens as actions for your good. Learn to experience perennial bliss by seeking union with God. Never forget God. Do not go after the things of the world. Have no fear of death. When your life is rooted in these three maxims, you will realize the Atman.
Sanathana Sarathi, November 1997, p. 303

0419: If you develop the sense of spiritual oneness of all mankind the conflicts of today will vanish. Discord has become ubiquitous. At the root of all this is the loss of faith in God. Get rid of jealousy and egoism. Then you will experience the Divine.
Sanathana Sarathi, March 1996, p. 61

0420: Give up the bad qualities in you. Banish the ego and develop the spirit of surrender. You will then experience bliss.
Sanathana Sarathi, February 1996, p. 41

0421: New year days come and go. Of what use are they? "Samvatsara" (the year) is one of the names of the Lord. Every moment is new. Why wait for a whole year to make the change in yourselves? As long as you are caught up in worldly celebrations of New Year, Vaikunta Ekaadasi and the like, God will elude you. You can realize God only when you forget the phenomenal world and the body consciousness.
Sanathana Sarathi, February 1996, p. 40

0422: So many are engaged in formal spiritual practices of various kinds; but of what use are they to win the grace of the Divine? Are you searching for the path that will help you to earn God's love? When you earnestly search within, you will get the answer.   *Sanathana Sarathi, October 1996, p. 264*

0423: Man needs God's grace to experience real happiness. But by his own thoughts, words and actions, man forfeits the grace of God. See no evil; see what is good. But men today look at only other people's faults and do not think of their own failings. Examine your own faults and rectify them.
Sanathana Sarathi, May 1996, p. 126

0424: Awareness is total understanding. This total understanding is within the capacity of every human being. Everyone must strive to express this awareness.
Sanathana Sarathi, March 1996, p. 70

0425: The observance of non-violence has been described as the highest form of Dharma. All the violence in the world today is due to the fact that people do not lead righteous lives. People do penance and perform various kinds of rituals, but they have secured on peace. Why? Because they have not sought to find out who they really are.   *Sanathana Sarathi, June 1996, p. 154*

0426: Studies should not end with mastery of books. The hearts should be filled with right knowledge. The students should see that the darkness which envelops the mind is dispelled.   *Sanathana Sarathi, February 1996, p. 32*

0427: The easiest and most fruitful method of keeping yourself free from dust and rust is Sathsang (good company). The company of the good and the godly will slowly and surely chasten and cleanse the persons prone to straying away from the straight path towards Self -Realization.
Sanathana Sarathi, June 1996, p. 152

0428: The duty of everyone from today onwards is to cultivate true, unsullied love. With love of God you can secure anything. Without that love, you will only be steeped in misery.   *Sanathana Sarathi, December 1996, p. 313*

0429: It is by accumulating the benefit of many good deeds in many earlier lives of yours that you are now born as a human being. Because you are not aware of the great good treasures that you have thus accumulated as a result of which you have the reward of your present life, you are not assigning the necessary value to human life. If you are only aware of the extent of the goodness of your previous births that has brought to the stage of your present life, you will never waste this present life.   *Summer Showers in Brindavan, 1973, p. 47*

0430: Turn the love that arises in you towards God. Dedicate your body to the Divine. This is the true mark of devotion. There are three constituents in man: mind, the power of speech and the body. These three are called "Trikaranas"- the three active agencies in man. It is when all three are used for sacred purposes, man becomes sanctified.

Every human being needs to cultivate the spirit, irrespective of his beliefs. All need devotion. It is only spirituality that can purify the heart (and mind) of man. The second requirement is morality. Morality helps to purify speech (vaak). The third is "Dhaarmikam". All righteous deeds done by the body (or hands) sanctify a man. It is through spirituality, morality and righteousness that the three instruments get purified. Only the one who has achieved this triple purity can realize the Divine. If any of these instruments are impure, he cannot realize the Divine.   *Sanathana Sarathi, February 1996, p. 40*

0431: There are some spiritual teachers who advise you to keep a daily diary, where you note down every item of evil that you did; they ask you to read is as a spiritual exercise and resolve to correct yourself. Well, reading it, and writing it will only tend to impress it more effectively on the mind. It is better to substitute good thoughts for the bad and cleanse the Jmind of all evil by dwelling on righteous deeds and holy thoughts. Forget the things that you do not want to remember. Bring to memory only those things that are worth remembering. That is the sane way to achiever spiritual progress.   *Sathya Sai Speaks, Volume IV, p. 7*

0432: Today, your foremost duty is to enthrone sacrifice. Only when sacrifice reigns, love will come into its own. All your latent potentialities will then manifest themselves. You will succeed in all your legitimate undertakings. When love becomes the ruling principle, sorrow and disappointment will disappear. That was why the Vedas declared that sacrifice alone is the key to immortal bliss.
                    Sanathana Sarathi, December 1996, p. 312

0433: Discipline is vital to every living being. For man it is even more important like the spinal column. Without discipline mankind will be ruined.

Discipline means the observance of certain well-designed rules. Without such regulation it is not possible to maintain humanness. Such regulation contributes to the glory of human existence.

Discipline cannot be acquired from books. Nor can it be learned from teachers. It has to be a natural component of one's daily life in the discharge of one's duties. Discipline is essential from the moment of waking to the time of going to sleep.

Discipline is essential for every group, for every society and for every political institution. Without discipline there can be no society or Government. No

nation can exist without discipline. It is discipline that unites man to man, and one society to another. Hence discipline is one of the basic insignia of social life.
Sanathana Sarathi, July 1996, p. 174

0434: The preciousness of human birth is indicated by the declaration in the Gita that every human being is a spark of the Divine. Everyone should look Godward while attending to worldly duties. If you dedicate all actions to God there will be no obstacles. Good thoughts will lead to good actions which produce good results.

Students, you should seek to earn the love of God and His grace. All other acquisitions are worthless and impermanent.
Sanathana Sarathi, October 1996, p. 274

0435: It is a hard job to know about your own self. Why, take the case of the food that you eat with your own mouth. You feel it in your stomach and after that, you do not experience what happens to it at each stage. How then can you know, without acquiring the special means for it, the truth that lies behind the sheaths that encase and enclose you- - - the Annamaya, Praanamaya, Manomaya, Vijnaanamaya and Aanandamaya (sheaths of material, vital energy, mind, intelligence and bliss)? Clear your intellect or intellectual power of the cobwebs of the ego, the dust of desire, the soot of greed and envy, and it becomes a fit instrument for revealing the Swarupa- - - the Inner Truth. "Know yourself, know the Inner Motivator, the Antharuaaamin" - - - That is the exhortation of the scriptures of all faiths. For, unless you are armed with that knowledge, you are like a ship without a compass, sailing on a stormy sea.
Sathya Sai Speaks, Volume IV, p. 93

0436: Practice; that is the real thing in spiritual matters. Scholarship is a burden, it is very often a handicap. So long as God is believed to be far away, in temples and holy places, man will feel religion a burden and a hurdle. But, plant Him in your heart and you feel light, burdenless, and even strong. It is like the food basket; when carried on the shoulder, it feels heavy; you are too weak even to carry it. But, sit near a stream and eat it. Though the total weight has not decreased, you feel lighter and stronger. That is the consequence of taking the food in: do likewise, with the idea of God. Do not carry it on the shoulder, have it "in".
Sathya Sai Speaks, Volume IV, p. 41

0437: Do not respect men who are caught up in the tangle of the senses. Give respect according to the knowledge each possesses of himself, i.e., of the Immanent and the Transcendent.

How do you fix the price of cane? According to the sugar content, is it not? You evaluate oranges in proportion to the juice they contain, is it not? So too, a man is worthy of honor in proportion to the knowledge of the Self he has acquired. The knowledge alone can confer steadiness and strength. Without it, all profession of renunciation, all pretense of devotion, all performance of charity are but tongue-deep or skin-deep!
Sathya Sai Speaks, Volume IV, p. 48

LIFE

0438: People should realize that human birth has been given to them to lead ideal lives. Good qualities enable one to lead a good life. But even for the good life a price has to be paid. That price is good conduct. This means that you derive the happiness that results from a good life only when you discharge your duties. Pleasures are of two kinds: temporary and lasting. Permanent happiness can be got only by performing your duties. First do your duty and then enjoy the fruits.
Sanathana Sarathi, February 1997, p. 30

0439: Youth is the stage in life when the slightest turn towards wrong will spell disaster. Thoughts shape the career. You plan to earn much wealth, because you imagine that rich people are very happy. The rich have plenty to eat, but they have no appetite. The rich wield power over others but they are held down by disease. The rich can have many servants but they cannot live in peace. So, plan to be rich in virtue, in devotion and dedication to good causes. Be rich in sovereign character. What exactly is character? Steady adherence to truth, renunciation, genuine love, selfless service, these are the essential components of character. Follow the dictates of your conscience; you can never be wrong.
Sanathana Sarathi, May, 1997, back cover

0440: While one is alive one should engage himself in good deeds and lead a sacred and meaningful life. All relationships are confined to the living. God alone is the only unfailing kinsman throughout life and beyond it. He is the only constant companion wherever you may be. Realize that life is impermanent. Only your good deeds will protect you. Peace, truth and virtue have to be acquired only through your actions. Achieve proximity to God and then become one with God.
Sanathana Sarathi, May 1997, p. 124

0441: Human life is related to both material and spiritual wealth. The combination of material wealth for daily life and spiritual wealth for achieving supreme bliss constitutes the meaning and goal of human life.
Sanathana Sarathi, September, 1996, p. 227

0442: Man has passed through many animal lives before he has come to earth in human form. Strains of animal nature such as cruelty, anger, greed and hatred still persist in him. Man is many animals in one. He has the jackal, the buffalo, the tiger, the elephant all in him. He must cast off these traits from his composition. When he indulges in useless controversy on matters beyond his understanding, he is behaving like a sheep; when he jumps from one ideal to another, from one project to another, without fully involving himself in any, he is exhibiting the nature of the monkey.
Sathya Sai Speaks, Volume X, p. 134

0443: Man should be courageous. Lack of courage leads to doubts, despair, dejection and depression. A person with a faultless and blemishless character shall never behave like a frightened, trembling sheep. Therefore, developing intellectual integrity and strength of conviction, man should proceed ahead and conquer the evils and temptations of the world.   *Summer Showers, 1979, p. 153*

0444: The life span of man is melting away every moment like a block of ice. Youth is transient. The only permanent and changeless entity is the Divine. Forgetting this, man is going after fleeting, trivial pleasures.

What is it that is permanent in this world? What is the purpose of human life? When one puts these questions, he does not get the right answers. Men pursue studies, jobs, wife and children in the search for happiness. They find no peace in any of these. Why? Desires are the cause of peacelessness. Without purifying the heart, all desires can only lead to unrest. Moreover, impurity in the heart is the source of many diseases. When the heart is pure, man will be free from disease.

How, then, is the heart to be purified? There is no other way except cherishing godly thoughts. All other rituals are of no avail except to provide temporary mental satisfaction. But the mind does not get satisfied easily. It is continually wavering and is uncontrollable.

Sanathana Sarathi, May 1997, p. 126

0445: Human life is related to both material and spiritual wealth. The combination of material wealth for daily life and spiritual wealth for achieving supreme bliss constitutes the meaning and goal of human life.

Sanathana Sarathi, September, 1996, p. 227

0446: The seat of thoughts is the mind. The mind has been described as symbolizing the form of Vishnu. Vishnu means one who pervades everything. The mind has the power to reach out for anything in the universe. Hence the cosmos is rooted in the mind.

The thoughts emanating from the mind find expression in words or speech. Thus, the heart, the mind and speech together constitute humanness. Sanctifying these three has been described as "Trikaranasuddhi", purity in thought, word and deed. The worship of the Trinity really calls for purification of the mind (Vishnu, the heart (Easwara) and speech (Brahma). Men today are immersed in transient worldly activities. They should sanctify all actions by purifying their feelings.   *Sanathana Sarathi, May 1997, p. 121*

0447: Divinity is permanent while human life is impermanent. We see around us many creatures that are born, grow up, live for some time and perish. This way, we are aware of the sequence of birth, growth, decay and death. Nevertheless, we delude ourselves and live considering ourselves immortal beings. This is a sign of ignorance and spiritual bankruptcy.   *Summer Showers, 1979, p. 144*

0448: The various journeys by car, bus, train or airplane undertaken by man in daily life are regulated by considerations of time. But the journey of life has been going on ever since creation began and shall go on forever. Unlike other journeys, this journey can never be canceled or even postponed! It is inevitable for all men, be the prince or peasant, messiah or mendicant. Forgetting that this ultimate journey is unavoidable for all those who come into this world with a body, man is foolishly arrogating immortality unto himself. Engrossed in the transient matters of the world, he is becoming a victim of misery and suffering.

Childhood is spent with companions and playthings; youth is thrown away in romance and dance; middle age is wasted in the pursuit of wealth; and old age is a sad tale of repentance and relentless attachments. Unable to discard evil habits and seek the path of liberation, man wallows in the mire of worldliness and fritters away the precious gift of human life!   *Summer Showers, 1979, p. 135*

0449: Sometime or other what has come from the Divine has to merge in the Divine. This is the natural destiny of all living beings. Taking birth as a man, leading a godly life, one ultimately merges in the Divine.

Considering the Divine as formless, some scholars have raised controversies regarding this process. The truth is that there is no object in the world which is formless. Even the minutest sub-atomic particle has a form. Only the ignorant can think otherwise.

It was for this reason that the ancient sages adored the Divine in various forms. Holding that all forms are made up of atoms, they recognized the Divine in all forms.   *Sanathana Sarathi, April 1997, p. 86*

0450: It is by accumulation the benefit of many good deeds in many earlier lives of yours that you are now born as a human being. Because you are not aware of the great good treasures that you have thus accumulated as a result of which you have the reward of your present life, you are not assigning the necessary value to human life. If you are only aware of the extent of the goodness of your previous births that has brought to the stage of your present life, you will never waste this present life.   *Summer Showers, 1973, p. 47*

0451: The foremost goal modern youth should set before themselves is to sow the seeds of love, rear the plant of forbearance and distribute the fruits of peace to society through dedicated service.

The secret of peace is not in the external world but is within each individual. He should realize that the whole universe is permeated by the Divine. Today the world is filled with strife. It is not possible to make a distinction between a human being and a demon. Man, who evolved from the animal, instead of proceeding towards Divinity, is regressing to animality. Man's primary duty is to uphold the human values of Truth, Righteousness, Peace and Love.

Man today is enveloped in attachment and hatred. The moment he casts them off, he will realize his divinity.

Sanathana Sarathi, September, 1996, p. 231

0452: As a child, man seeks toys to have fun and joy. As a boy, he demands a cycle for the same purpose. When he becomes a young man, he demands a car to have fun and joy, a good position with a pretty girl as his wife. Then in middle age, he learns to shoulder more responsibility. The actions of his previous birth have by now molded his mind fully, his ideas have become set, whether it be for a good or evil. But, the desire for ananda (bliss) is as strong as ever.

Now his quest for happiness follows different paths depending on three gunas (influences) on his mind:
a) If it be truthfulness which is supreme, then the path will be straight and
b) narrow, that of rectitude where thought, wo rd and deed merge.
c) If it be worldly which is predominant, the path will lead towards ceaseless activity to amass riches, power and fame.
d) If greed has the upper hand, the path will lead downwards towards destruction, towards a life of shame and perversion.

Gems of Wisdom, Gunas, p. 54

0453: When we saturate the air with sounds full of reverence, humility, love, courage, self-confidence and tolerance, we, too, will benefit from them. Therefore, always do good, see good, remember good and be good. When you are engaged in finding faults and failings in others, you will be paving the way for developing those faults and failings in yourself. Dwell on the good in others. Ideas which are opposed to spiritual tendencies, that narrow the limits of love, that provoke another, or greed that cause disgust - these you have to shut out from your heart. A devotee (sadhaka) must sublimate such thoughts before they cause an impact on the mind and should concentrate on the very source of the thinking process. This can be achieved by practicing equanimity, unaffectedness and balance.   *Sathya Sai Speaks; Volume X, p. 71*

0454: Grief is caused, as joy is caused, by the attachment of the senses to objects, once you know that you are not the senses or the mind, but HE, who operates the senses and wield the mind, you cross the bounds of pleasure and pain.   *Gems of Wisdom, Suffering, p. 171*

0455: Just as there are four stages in man's life, boyhood, youth, middle age, old age, so too, there are four stages in his acquisition of wisdom:
1. To be trained by parents, teachers, elders, being led, guided, regulated, warned, reprimanded.
2. To be eager to establish happiness and justice in society; to know the world, its worth and values.
3. To pour out energies to reform, reconstruct the human community.
4. The realization that the world is beyond redemption by human effort, that one can at best save oneself.

Gems of Wisdom, The Teacher and Tomorrow, p. 195

0456: Your age, your youth, your strength, your wealth, your status should not make you feel very proud because with your advancing age all these will vanish. In this context, what is the point in your feeling proud of this leather bag of a body.

Man had discovered electricity and is proud to use it for giving light. But what poor glory is this! When the sun rises even the brightest bulb pales into insignificance. Man's handiwork of brick and mortar is laid in ruins, with roofs flying in the air due to a storm. On what basis can he erect his pride? The sun is but a star among billions in space. The earth is but a speck, rotating around the sun. The country to which he belongs is but a fraction of that speck; his place of residence is a microscopic dot in that fraction and he is but one among lakhs of people living therein. He struts about for a few winks of time, and prides himself most stupidly, as if he is the Lord and Master.

Gems of Wisdom, Attachment, p. 142

0457: Man is equipped with a return-ticket when he takes birth. Holding it in his grasp, he earns and spends, rises and falls, sings and dances, weeps and wails, forgetting the end of the journey. But, though he forgets the wagon of life moves towards the cemetery, which is its terminus. It brings no glory to man if he is tied helplessly to the wheel of birth and death. His glory and greatness consist in disentangling himself from that revolving wheel.

Gems of Wisdom, Degradation, p. 145

0458: Suffering and misery are the inescapable acts of the Cosmic drama. God does not decree these calamities, but man invites them by way of retribution for his evil deeds. This is the corrective punishment by nature, which induces man to give up the wrong path. All this is part of the grand synthesis in which the negatives serve to glorify the positives. Thus, death glorifies immortality; ignorance glorifies wisdom; misery glorifies bliss; night glorifies dawn.

Gems of Wisdom, Suffering, p. 170

0459: Everything that is born must die. But you can escape death by not being born again. When you realize that you are the limitless Atma, you are no longer subjected to the limitation of birth. That is the secret. How to know that? It is the result of a long process of sharpening and purifying the emotions and the impulses. You may do the most rigorous japa or submit yourself to the ordeal of austerities, but if you are not virtuous, all of it is sheer waste.

Gems of Wisdom, Virtue, p. 230

0460: Life is a mixture of good and bad, of ups and downs. Ignore the bad and enjoy what is good. In life you should forget the bad experiences and make use of the good ones. Instead man broods over the bad experiences and spoils even the good that comes his way. This is a sign of weakness in man.

Gems of Wisdom, Coconut Ritual, p. 382

0461: As a drop of water on a lotus leaf disappears in no time, even so, we should know that our life is transient and will disappear very much like that and in no time. The world is full of sorrow and the human body is full of disease. Our life of turbulent thoughts are like a dilapidated house. Under these circumstances, it is possible to live in a peaceful manner only by following the Divine path and getting over all our worldly attachments.

Gems of Wisdom, Spiritual Level, p. 265

0462: The earth is a caravan where man came and stay for the night and when dawn breaks, one by one, they tramp their different ways. Kith, Kin are the words, we use for the attachment to the travelers cultivated in the caravan during the short term of acquaintance. Husband and wife are like two pieces of wood drifting down a flooded river; they float near each other for some time and when current comes between, they are parted; each must move on to the sea at its own rate and in its own time. There is no need to grieve over their parting of the two, it is in the very nature of Nature that it should be so. *Gems of Wisdom, Family, p. 210*

0463: In this vast universe every creature lives according to the law of its being. Man alone, who has the gift of this extremely precious human birth, is failing to realize the purpose of his existence and ignores his duties.

Immersed in sensual mundane pleasures, man forgets his spiritual destiny. All scholarship is valueless without Self-realization. Ravana, Bhasmaasura and Kamsa were not lacking in scholarship or even religious practices. But all these were related to the externals and not to the cultivation of the Spirit inside. Hence their basic demonic qualities did not change.

It is only when impure and unholy thoughts are expelled from the mind that sacred feelings will enter it. To experience lasting bliss the heart has to be sanctified by filling it with love. Through that love has to be secured the highest wisdom.

Sanathana Sarathi, September, 1996, p. 231

0464: You have been given a human birth to enable you to understand your own nature. When you do not know the nature of yourself, how are you going to know the nature of the world? The aspect of divine creation is spread and present all through the world. The life force in this world and the life force that exists in you are inseparable aspects on one and the same divine aspect. Although air is present everywhere around you, yet we do not see it. So also, this life force, through present in the whole world, can be recognized only in some places and by some human being.

Summer Showers in Brindivan, 1977, p. 203

0465: Man today is like a horseman riding two horses at the same time. Man aspires for the Divine, but at the same time yearns for worldly pleasures. Man forgets that the Creator contains the Creation. Forgetting this truth, man runs after the phenomenal world. Man behaves like a fool, who cries for butter while having milk in his hand.   *Gems of Wisdom, What is Realization?, p. 269*

0466: To know is the function of the mind. To act is the duty of the body. To remain as the Eternal Witness is the function of the Atma. Mind, body and Atma together constitute humanness, The Divine is present in all three.
Sanathana Sarathi, March 1995, p. 64

0467: Do not think of the existence of two entities - this world and the next, here and hereafter. Realize the hereafter is here; this world is interwoven with the next.
Gems of Wisdom, What is Realization?, p. 269

0468: An empty iron box gets valued when it contains jewels; the body is honored when it contains the jewel of consciousness and the valuables called virtues. Life has to be lived through, for the sake of the chance to unfold the virtues. Otherwise, man is a burden upon the earth, a consumer of food.
Baba, The Breath of Sai, p. 262

0469: Life is a jungle, where there is a great deal of dry wood which harbors worms and insects. No one cleans the floor of the forest or cuts away the undergrowth of bush and bramble. To wade through the thorns and the leech-ridden floor of the jungle, one has to wear the boots of sense-regulation, if one has to pass through the jungle of life, without harming oneself.
Gems of Wisdom, Discipline, p. 411

0470: People do not conphrehend the preciousness of human life and all its potentialities. Men should learn to lead a moral life. When one's thoughts are pure, one's life becomes sacred and blissful. No room should be given for bad thoughts and bad actions.   *Sanathana Sarathi, December 1995, p. 287*

0471: Nowadays people are shy to pronounce the word "God". It is indeed difficult to understand why only an idler will complain of lack of time for meditating on God. Yearn, you will find a way; pray, you will receive grace. For a meal that takes only a few minutes, we spend hours to make it tasty. Then for a life of many decades should we not take the trouble to make it tasty?
Gems of Wisdom, Bhakthi (Devotion), p. 306

0472: A human being is like a seed. As a seed grows into a plant after sprouting, as the plant becomes a tree when it becomes bigger, so also a human being is born, then he grows and changes and transforms, acquires the fullness of human nature and ultimately through various stages will reach his destination.

Man has got two kinds of knowledge. One type of knowledge is that which relates to the day-to-day world. The second type of knowledge relates to the higher world, the world of spirit. The first has been described as that which helps you to carry on your daily life or earn your livelihood. The second one takes you to the ultimate destination, the objective of all life. By using the knowledge which relates to the world, you can carry on your daily life. By such a process, you generally enhance your reputation and your position in the society in which you live. You also use this knowledge in order to fulfill your responsibilities and your duties. It can also be described as the knowledge which enables you to live peacefully in the surrounding world. By this means, you can acquire ability and strength to live well.

The second type of knowledge which relates to the higher world, the world of spirit, enables you to answer questions like, who am I? Why have I come here? What is the basis of life? What is the secret of my birth? and so on. To enable you to answer such questions, we use the second type of knowledge. To answer these questions, you have to see the oneness in all creation. The worldly knowledge and spiritual knowledge are really one and the same are inextricably connected with each other. They are like two faces of the same coin. They are like two wings of the same bird. They are like the two wheels of a cart and you must understand that these two are not distinct or separate. We should coordinate these two branches of knowledge and see the connection between them and conduct our life accordingly.

Summer Showers in Brindivan, 1977, p. 239

0473: There are many unfortunate people who are not able to utilize the sacred opportunities that come their way. For one who cannot enjoy happiness and bliss, what does it matter what opportunity he gets? For a dog which can only lap out water, what is the use of a river with a large quantity of flowing water? We really get many sacred opportunities on occasions in our life. Without using those opportunities and discussing their values, we waste our time and our life.

Summer Showers in Brindivan, 1977, p. 242

0474: The hands of the clock keep on moving and we hear their ticking noise. This sound of the clock goes on continuously. Between one tick and another, there is an interval. Man's life is also like this interval. Through man's heart and through his blood vessels, his life stream is beating, this beat will come to an end at sometime. Truly birth is followed by death and death again by birth and so on.

We should try and understand the secret of this life. Like a man who is swimming and moving forward in a river, we should also forget the experiences through which we have gone in the past and swim forward. Only if the swimmer throws back the water which is ahead of him will he move forward. If he does not throw back the water that is ahead of him, he will stay where he is. As in this analogy, only if man attempts to throw back the experience which he has gone through, will he be able to move forward. If one follows such a path, one will find that in man's life there is no place for anger, no place for jealousy and his life will move on pleasantly.

Because man wants to go through the same experience which he has already experienced in the past, he enters the region of hatred, because he accumulates around him many attachments. If man really makes an attempt to understand his own nature and the comparison between the clock and his heart, it will be possible for him to experience truth. Even after experiencing so many things, if man does not understand his true nature, he will feel very unhappy. He wants always to be happy, but not ask the question whether one can get happiness in this world?

Man has great faith in collecting, acquiring and amassing wealth, but he has not got the same faith in giving up and sacrificing; but he can make an attempt to develop faith in the act of giving and sacrificing. When man can develop faith and recognizes the joy of giving away and of sharing things, he will enjoy his life. If man really wants peace and happiness, he must   be prepared to sacrifice. The Vedas have told us that what cannot be acquired through hard work, through learning, through any other means can only be acquired through sacrifice. We should also understand the inner meaning of sacrifice.

If the food that we eat is not excreted out and is not sacrificed, our health will be spoiled. If we do not exhale the air that we take in and send it out, our lungs will get spoiled. If the blood does not keep on moving but stays at one place, then there will be a boil at that place.

It is necessary for us to recognize the happiness that is contained in the spirit of sacrifice. But man always wants to have the same experience again and again everyday before he learns a lesson and because of such bad desires, man has become so unfortunate that he cannot even have a peaceful death not to talk of a peaceful life. If man wants to lead a peaceful life, he must realize the importance of sacrifice. The truth that is contained in the statement: that immorality can be obtained through sacrifice alone, should be understood well.
Summer Showers in Brindivan, 1977, p. 176

0475: There is a God who will answer all your prayers. Having obtained what is most difficult to obtain, namely the birth as a human being, your main objective now should be to find Him.   *Summer Showers in Brindivan, 1977, p. 205*

0476: The work that we do today will determine the consequences that we will enjoy in the future. You must do good work and get good out of it. Can we put the seeds on lemon and expect to get mangoes? Can we expect to put the seeds of mango and get lemons out of that tree? It is right conduct for a human being to recognize this and promote sacred ideas, sacred thoughts and do sacred work now so that he may reap the sacred fruit in future.
Summer Showers in Brindivan, 1977, p. 244

0477: You have been sent into the world in order that you may use the time and the opportunity to realize the truth that you are not man, but God. The wave dances with the wind, basks in the sun, frisks in the rain, imagining it is playing on the breast of the sea; it does not know that it is the sea itself. Until it realizes that truth, it will be tossed up and down; when it knows it, it can lie calm and collected at peace with itself.   *Baba, The Breath of Sai, p. 223*

0478: In every human being Divinity is present in a subtle form. But man is deluded by this unmanifested presence of the Divine into believing that God does not exist. The innumerable waves on the vast ocean contain the same water as the ocean regardless of their forms. Likewise, although human beings have myriad's of names and forms, each is a wave on the ocean of Sath-Chith-Ananda (Being-Awareness-Bliss).   *Sanathana Sarathi; October, 1997, p. 266*

0479: You have earned this human body by the accumulated merit on many lives as inferior beings and , it is indeed very foolish, to fritter away this precious opportunity in activities that are natural only to those inferior beings. Life moves so quick that people often wonder how they grew so old so soon. It appears only yesterday that they were in college or playing in the streets; but they have grandchildren playing about them! While life makes them force others to fall before them; humility does not induce them to fall before the Almighty!
Baba, The Breath of Sai, p. 165

0480: Man is not merely a creature thrown up by nature in the process on an evolutionary gamble. He has special meaning. a special mission, a unique role. He is Divinity encases in the human frame.   *Baba, The Breath of Sai, p. 258*

0481: Man is a combination of the body, the mind and the Spirit (Atma). He is thus the embodiment of these three. But, forgetting the mind and the Atma, when man identifies himself solely with the body, he reduces himself to an animal. When he forgets the Atma and the body and identifies himself with the mind alone, he becomes a demon. When one forgets the body and the mind and adheres only to the Atma, he gets divinised.
Sanathana Sarathi, November 1994, p. 282

0482: Everyone is proud about the body, the mind and the intellect, forgetting the indwelling Atma, which is the basis for all of them. The Atma has no birth or death. It is like the root of a tree, which sustains the branches, the leaves, flowers and fruits. It is the basis on which the superstructure of life rests.
Sanathana Sarathi, July 1994, p. 169

0483: Just as every drop of the ocean has the salty taste, the composition and the name of the ocean, so too every single being has the Divine taste and composition, and the name of the Lord.   *Sathya Sai Speaks, Volume IV, p. 22*

0484: Does real happiness lie in enjoying creature comforts? No. True happiness consists in manifesting all the potentialities in man. When you put into practice all the sacred thoughts that emanate from your mind you will realize true happiness. Most people do not practice the sacred impulses that arise in them with the result that they do not experience the bliss within them.

Sanathana Sarathi, August 1995, p. 200

0485: In ancient times, the sages and seers maintained purity in thought, truth in word and righteousness in deeds. But in this Kali Age today, people have forgotten human values and exhibit animal qualities such as lust, anger, greed and hatred. Purity of heart and selflessness are the hall-marks of the human life which one gets after passing through several births. Foolishness, pride, covetness and other such qualities are a hang-over from their previous lives as sheep, buffalo or cat. One who is in the habit of attacking and harming others out of hatred reveals the tendencies in his previous birth as a dog. One who lacks steadiness of mind and constantly jumps from one thing to another, reflects the quality of the monkey from which he has evolved. It is to get rid of such bad qualities that sacrifices are undertaken.

Sanathana Sarathi, January 1994, p. 12

0486: The Divine is omnipresent. The entire cosmos is permeated and sustained by this Divine Energy. Everyone should endeavor to experience the Divine. Man must make the effort and he is bound to realize the experience. The necessary sacrifice must be made. All the bad qualities have to be renounced the moment they invade the mind. True devotion means elimination of all the animal tendencies in man. Man should seek to realize the eternal Divine within him. That is the primary purpose of human life. All other accomplishments are valueless. Man should raise himself from the animal to the Divine. There is nothing great in earning a fortune. What one should seek is purity of the Self; that is the essence of humanness.   *Sanathana Sarathi, December 1995, p. 317*

0487: Duty is related to one's obligations to society. Freedom is related to expressing the will of the Divine. The phenomenal world (Prakriti) is a projection of the Divine. Hence, it should be regarded as holy. Duty means recognizing the sacredness of one's obligations to Prakriti. Each one must recognize that he (or she) is an image of the Divine and conduct himself on that basis. He alone is a real man who lives his life in this way.

Sanathana Sarathi, August 1995, p. 200

0488: The base traits which are found in man are the result of his food and other habits and do not arise from his Atma. Vices like lust, anger, envy and pride are the outcome of bad food and improper associations and are products of external factors. They do not arise from within. Qualities like love, compassion, consideration for others arise from within one's self. These are human values. Forgetting these values, following animal qualities, man are leading an animal existence. This is wrong. Men should lead lives based on their human estate.

Sanathana Sarathi, December 1993, p. 312

0489: Today men have invented many types of machinery by their experiments and researches. Science has been pursued with relentless energy. But, being unable to experience peace or happiness, they have become strangers to both. Despite his acquiring the sacred human birth, man is immersed in the pursuit of transient worldly pleasures, forgetting his Divine destiny. Concentrating on scientific investigations, inventing all kinds of mechanical gadgets, man is content to lead a proud but purposeless life.   *Sanathana Sarathi, March 1994, p. 57*

0490: Born as human beings, growing as human beings, men have forgotten the value of human existence. Developing religious differences, fostering demonic tendencies, they are destroying peace. What is the state of human life today? The foremost thing that should exist is respect for human values. However great an intellectual may be as a scholar or a man of learning, one has also to acquire humanness. Without humanness, scholarship and intellectual eminence are of no value.   *Sanathana Sarathi, March 1996, p. 68*

0491: Man has to rise above the animal nature. He has to express his divine potencies. For this, man has to acquire Atmic knowledge (knowledge of the Self). Atma is the all-pervading Universal Consciousness. It is immanent in everyone. Only as long as this consciousness is present in the human body it is called "Sivam". Once the consciousness leaves the body it becomes "Savam" a corpse.   *Sanathana Sarathi, August 1995, p. 220*

0492: The human birth is intended for the pursuit of Dharma. Dharma (Righteousness) implies harmony in thought, word and deed. When every person realizes his essential divine nature, the entire world will be transformed. The body and the mind are mere instruments. Man's reality is the Self (Atma). Man should use the instruments given to him to perform his duties well and realize his oneness with God.   *Sanathana Sarathi, March 1996, p. 66*

0493: In life, everything has to be governed by restraints. These restraints should be for the purpose of directing life in the ideal path. Men desire the fruits of good deeds without doing good deeds and want to avoid the consequences of bad actions while indulging in them.   *Sanathana Sarathi, December 1995, p. 317*

0494: As long as one is proud, men will not like him. Only when he suppresses his pride will he be liked by one and all. The man filled with anger will have no happiness. He will be immersed in misery. When he subdues his anger, he will be free from grief. When a man has insatiable desires he will never feel contented. When he controls his desires, he will be truly rich. A miserly person will never feel happy. When he gives up greed he will realize happiness.
          Sanathana Sarathi, March 1996, p. 63

0495: Man who should progress upwards from day to day, is going down the slope. This is not right learning. Every day you should make the ascent towards the Divine. "I am "God. God is not different from me". This is the conviction with which men should live. *Sanathana Sarathi, April 1996, p. 94*

0496: Obsessed with worldly desires and forgetting God, man is immersed in misery. Even devotion is tainted by selfishness. It does not stem wholly from the heart. It is only part time devotion and hypocrisy. All should realize that the Divine is the basis of everything in the universe. Having evolved from the animal, man should aim at realizing the Divine. Unfortunately, men today are descending to animality. As a result, peace and order are vanishing from every sphere of life. *Sanathana Sarathi, May 1996, p. 113*

0497: Man has immense capacities latent in him, waiting to be tapped and used. He has many talents which he has to bring to light. He feels the urge to love all beings, to share his joys and griefs with his kind, to know more and satisfy the curiosity of his intellect, to peep behind the awe and wonder that Nature arouses in him. He is able to gather information about all kinds of things from all the corners of the world, but he is unaware of what happens in the corners of his own mind. He knows who is who among all the rest, but, he does not know the answer to the simple question, "Who am I?

The fact is, he has to ask it himself and seek out the clue to the enigma himself. He has not felt that it is essential to know the answer; he is content to move about blindly in the world, groping his way in the dark. Without knowing who he is, he is rashly judging, labeling and even libeling other men. This is the fundamental reason for the hollowness of human life today, for the hate and fear that stalk the world. *Sathya Sai Speaks, Volume IV, p. 43*

0498: People should always remember that the ultimate end may come at anytime. One should reform one's life well before the end comes. Greatness consists not in wealth but in virtue. A true human being is one who recognizes the Divine within him. He should lead a godly life. Everyone should strive to recognize the Indwelling Spirit within, which is the master of the body and the senses. The highest education is Atma-Vidya. The spirit is invisible like the roots of a tree. But it is the basis of real bliss, just as the fruits of a tree are derived from the roots. The external pleasures you enjoy are based on the power of the Spirit within. The air you breathe, the light you see, the water you drink, are all derived from the Divine. *Sanathana Sarathi, June 1996, p. 146*

0499: Do not base your life on the body. It is impermanent. The spirit within is immortal. The body is "Karmakshetra", the field of action. The heart is "Dharmakshetra", the Abode of Righteousness. The human state is a combination of Karmakshetra and Dharmakshetra. *Sanathana Sarathi, April 1996, p. 96*

0500: Human life is precious, noble and virtuous. It is a pity human beings do not realize this. The whole purpose and goal of human life is to know one's true nature. Forgetting one's true nature, man is caught up in worldly concerns and plunged in misery. *Sanathana Sarathi, November 1996, p. 284*

0501: Man is the beneficiary of innumerable gifts of God: wind, rain, sunlight and so on. What gratitude is man showing to God for all these, while he is paying a big price for every small benefit he derives from civic services like water supply and electric power? God is the provider of all that is essential for life. What recompense is man making to God? On the contrary, he goes on praying for more benefits. This insatiable desire is the cause of all man's evil qualities. The truly human qualities are calmness, forbearance and compassion. Man should lead a contented life. *Sanathana Sarathi, August 1996, p. 205*

0502: Many of you have from immemorial times had links with the Atmic Self. This link is unbroken. It is eternal, infinite. Such sacred relationships should never be given up. All should return to the place wherefrom they came. That is the strident declaration in the Dhagavatham: "It is natural for every living creature to go back to the source from which it came". You have come from the Atma and you must merge in the Atma. Till the goal is reached, you must not treat lightly the sacred journey of life. *Sanathana Sarathi, November 1996, p. 288*

0503: At the time of death, one has to leave behind all that one owns. Wealth and status too do not accompany you. Your friends and relations may come to the burial ground to bury or cremate the body, and thereafter all will return home. Only the good and bad acts that you have performed in your life will accompany you. Your next birth will be carved out according to your deeds in this life. In order to remain good you must cultivate respect for truth which is permanent, whereas everything else including your body is subject to change, decay and death. So it is desirable to undertake various practices to win the grace of the Lord at this young age when you have the energy and ability to learn and concentrate.

It is quite probable that some of your friends may point out to you this is the age to make success of yourself in worldly affairs. They will advise you to earn money and enjoy life. According to their way of thinking, the pursuit of God can be kept in abeyance till the age of retirement from active life. But in actual fact, the young age being impressionable and formative is the right age to develop sacred ideas and practice spiritual sadhanas (disciplines). It is common knowledge that if throughout one's life one pursues maya, then at the time of death it will not be possible to divert ones thoughts towards God. Therefore now is the time for you to lay the foundation for a good future. *Summer Showers in Brindavan, 1973, p. 197*

0504: Life is a mirage; it comes from no visible rain; it falls into no recognizable sea. There was a man once who was pestered by a host of relatives when he was dying. Parents, wife, children, brothers, sisters . . . all surrounded his bed during his last moments and wailed. They asked him "What is to happen to us?" The dying man lifted his head a little from the pillow and asked in return, "What is to happen to me? I am now more interested in that problem, than being worried about what is to happen to you." Well, it is better every one asks that question even now and equips himself with the answer rather than wait until it is too late.

"What am I for?" "What ought I to do?" These questions you must pursue, and arrive at the answers.   *Sathya Sai Speaks, Volume IV, p. 78*

0505: The mind must become bhaktimaya (saturated with devotion); the intelligence must be transformed into jnaana-deepti (the splendor of universal wisdom), or jnaana (Divine knowledge). The body must be a willing and efficient instrument for saddharmacharana (the practice of righteousness). Such a life is indeed the crown and glory of humanity. The rest are contaminated, contained, caged lives!   *Sathya Sai Speaks, Volume IV, p. 129*

LOVE

0506: Embodiments of Love! Through love you can achieve anything. A man without love is as good as dead. Serve all with love, The Divine is both the lover and the beloved. He is the director of the play and He is also the actor.
Sanathana Sarathi, April, 1997, p. 89

0507: Divinity is embodied in all creatures and this fundamental truth should be exemplified in practice by man. He must extend the field of his love until it encompasses the entire creation. It is only then that he will deserve to be a worthy recipient of God's love.   *Summer Showers, 1979, p. 107*

0508: Expansion is the essence of love. When a lamp is lit from another, there are two where there was one. The first one did not stop emitting light. You can light a million lamps from one; yet; the first will not suffer at all! Love too is like this. Share it with a million, it will be as bright as when it was alone.
Gems of Wisdom, Heart and Love, p. 77

0509: Love all. Love is God's only property. It does not belong to man. It is not a purchasable commodity. It issues from the heart. It alone can be said to be Divine. Divine love is different from human attachments. It is timeless. It is omnipresent. Make it your sole ideal. It is inherent in you. Manifest it in the proper way. If there is sugar at the bottom of a tumbler filled with water, you can make the whole water sweet by stirring the sugar and dissolving it in the water. Likewise, your heart is a tumbler. At the bottom, there is Divinity. Take the spoon of Buddhi (intellect). Stir the heart by the process of sadhana (spiritual discipline). Then the Divinity in the heart will circulate through the entire body. Then, every action of yours will be sweet, your walking will be sweet, your looks will be sweet, your thoughts will be sweet, you will be sweet all over.

Realize that that sweetness is within you. Turn your intellect inwards and discover that sweetness by filling the intellect with love.

Sanathana Sarathi, April, 1997, p. 89

0510: Selfishness is like a balloon filled with air. If you puncture the balloon, the air inside will combine with the air outside. When the ego is deflated, altruistic love takes its place. Love all and cultivate universal compassion. Love of oneself should evolve into Divine love, which is the highest form of love. We should ascend from a lower state of love to a higher state of love, just as we ascend from a lower level of truth to a higher level of truth. It is only through altruism that you can achieve divinity.

The help rendered by us to others as well as the harm done to us by others should be completely forgotten. Do not brood over the injuries inflicted on you. At the same time, do not expect either recognition or reward for services rendered by you. If you expect good results for your actions, you will have to be prepared for bad results also.   *Summer Showers, 1979, p. 174*

0511: If a man cannot love a fellow human being who is visible before his eyes, how can he love what is not visible to him? This is not possible. Only a man who loves living beings around him can love the invisible Divine. Love must start with love for beings that have form. It must be extended to all beings.

Sanathana Sarathi, January 1993, p. 3

0512: There is no nobler quality in the world than love. It is wisdom. It is righteousness. It is wealth. It is Truth. Everything is permeated with love. Everything in the cosmos arises from love, grows by love and merges in love.

Sanathana Sarathi, June, 1997, p. 141

0513: Love is transformed into poison if hate contaminates it. Love some but never hate the rest, for that hate will foul the love and make it mortal. Love must flow not from the tongue or from the head only, but chiefly from the heart.

Gems of Wisdom, Characteristics, p. 83

0514: The true strength can be acquired only through love. All other efforts are of no avail. Thus we should ask from God only the strength of love.
Gems of Wisdom, Heart and Love, p. 77

0515: Embark on this path of love. You are liable to feel elated over trivial pleasures of depressed over petty losses. God's love is permanent and unvarying. Try to understand that love. How is it to be done? By cultivating the feeling that whatever happens to you, whether pleasant or unpleasant, is for your own good. When you have that firm conviction, the value of God's love for you goes up.
Sanathana Sarathi, February 1995, p. 34

0516: Realization, which is not possible through logic, which is not possible through offering sacrifice, and which is not possible through discussion and other disciplines, can be achieved only through love.   *Summer Showers, 1972, p. 249*

0517: When there is Love, there will be no hatred. Without hatred, there will be no threat to peace in society. To ensure peace, society has to promote Love. This means that the mind has to be filled with loving thoughts.
Sanathana Sarathi, August 1994, p. 199

0518: It is needless to search for God. Verily you are the Divine. Strive to realize this truth. There is a simple and easy way. Have the faith that every human being is an embodiment of the Divine. Love everyone. Serve all. The best way to love God is to love all.
Sanathana Sarathi, February 1995, p. 32

0519: The whole world and the objects therein are inter-related by the bond of love. It is love that binds the human race together. The world cannot exist without love. God is love and resides in the heart of every one as embodiment of love. Based on this Truth we pray, that all the people in the world should be happy.
Sanathana Sarathi, August 1997, p. 210

0520: The Lord is described as the indweller in the heart. Love and compassion are inherent in every person. Each has to share one's love with others. Failure to share this love is gross ingratitude to society, to which one owes everything. One should give one's love freely to others and receive love in return. This is the deep significance of human life.
Sanathana Sarathi, July 1994, p. 170

0521: Man, who should manifest his inherent loving nature, has become stony-hearted. To accomplish his desires man should cultivate forbearance, love and compassion and not resort to sinful means. Your desires will not be fulfilled by

causing harm to others. You cannot please God if you are full of envy, pride and ostentation. God will respond only to unsullied love and not wealth or position.
Sanathana Sarathi; October, 1997, p. 267

0522: The greatest quality in every man is love. When love is absent, evil qualities like hatred and jealousy rear their heads. Make love the breath of your life.
Sanathana Sarathi, January 1994, p. 6

0523: It is enough if Love is cultivated, the Love that knows no distinction between oneself and another, because all are but limbs of one corpus of God Almighty. Through Love alone can the embodiment of Love be gained. Here, no scholarship is needed; in fact, scholarship will be an impediment, for it caters to egoism and it breeds doubts and the desire for disputation and laurel of victory over others preening themselves as learned.
Sanathana Sarathi, March, 1994, back cover

0524: If one object has to combine with another, or one individual has to associate with another, love is the basis for the affinity. The entire world is filled with love. The world is Love and Love is the world.
In every human being love is present as an effulgence which shines in his feelings. Love is life and life is love. Even as the power to burn is natural for fire, and the power to cool is natural for water, love is a natural trait for man. Without it he ceases to be human. *Sanathana Sarathi, January 1994, p. 1*

0525: Love in action is Righteousness. Love in speech is Truth. Love in thought is Peace. Love in understanding is nonviolence.
Sanathana Sarathi, August 1995, p. 222

0526: The three great enemies of man are: lust or desire, anger and greed. These have to be eliminated. The greatest quality in man is love. Love is God. Live in love. *Sanathana Sarathi, March 1996, p. 66*

0527: Start the day with love, spend the day with love, fill the day with love and end the day with love. This is the way to God. The primary requisite for cultivating love is to get rid of doubts and disbelief and develop confidence.
Sanathana Sarathi, May 1994, p. 114

0528: Truth issues from love. In this world there is nothing greater than love. The more you love, the more blissful you become. Divinity is the embodiment of love. Love shines as the eternal truth in every one's heart. However, it will be dormant in the heart of the selfish. Love shines only in the heart of the person who is selfless. Love cannot co-exist with ego and pomp. Love is the royal path that can take you to the highest state of the Divine.

Sanathana Sarathi, June 1995, p. 162

0529: The nature of true love between the devotee and God cannot be understood by the unbelievers, the atheists. Only the loving devotee can experience the effulgence of the Divine. The man without love is lost in dialectical controversies, with the result that bitterness develops over arguments.

Sanathana Sarathi, September 1995, p. 229

0530: Live in love. Start the day with love. Fill the day with love. End the day with love. That is the way to God. This love should be considered Divine by people of every faith. Manifest your love regardless of how others behave.

Sanathana Sarathi, January 1996, p. 28

0531: Make love the basic impulse for all your actions. Share your love with others. Be unselfish. Self lives by getting and forgetting. Love lives be giving and forgiving. Develop confidence in yourself. Through self-confidence you can achieve self-realization.   *Sanathana Sarathi, January 1996, p. 25*

0532: Divine love is all-compassion and the whole cosmos is contained within it. Hence it is essential for man to comprehend the nature of this love. Today, the world is riddled with disorder, violence and unrest. Injustice, exploitation, corruption and immorality are ubiquitous. All these are the very antithesis of love. Only through the divine love can the world be transformed.

Sanathana Sarathi, August 1996, p. 215

0533: Men should lead selfless lives. This may seem difficult. But, in reality there is nothing easier. It is selfishness that creates all kinds of difficulties for mankind. Selfless love will give no room for any evil. Unselfish love may meet with opposition from one's kith and kin and from worldly persons. But one should not be deterred by such opposition. Love should be cherished as one's life breath.

Sanathana Sarathi, January 1996, p. 3

0534: The Divine is in every individual, but one's realization depends on one's own efforts. The Divine shines according to the degree of one's spiritual awareness. To manifest the full effulgence of the Divine, one has to adhere to the path of Love. Only through Love can the Supreme Divine be attained.

Sanathana Sarathi, September 1995, p. 231

0535: Love can conquer anything. Selfless, pure, unalloyed love leads man to

God. Selfish and constricted love binds one to the world. Unable to comprehend the pure and sacred love, man today is a prey to endless worries because of his attachment to worldly objects.

Man's primary duty is to understand the truth about the Love Principle. Once he understands the nature of love, he will not go astray. The various contexts in which the word love is used today have no relation to the true meaning of love. The affection between a mother and child or between a husband and wife is incidental to a certain temporary relationship and is not real love at all. True love has neither a beginning nor an end. It exists in all the three categories of time: past, presents and future. That alone is true love which can fill man with enduring bliss.   *Sanathana Sarathi, January 1996, p. 2*

0536: What is needed is total faith; in a simple word, Love. Abide by it and lead a worthy life. Love will confer every kind of strength you need to sustain you in life. If you recognize the Divine in all, you will be blessed with everything.
Sanathana Sarathi, August 1996, p. 210

0537: What is termed love in ordinary worldly love is not real love at all. It is only one or other form of attachment based on human relationships in the family or in society.   *Sanathana Sarathi, August 1996, p. 214*

0538: Realize that the path of divine love is the easiest, the sweetest and surest path to God.   *Sanathana Sarathi, August 1996, p. 213*

0539: Embodiments of love! Recognize the supreme significance of the Love Principle. Today, it is love of the Divine that should be fostered. This love transcends the mind. Various forms of meditation are purely mental exercises. But devotion which emanates from the heart transcends the mind. Communication with the Divine is true Yoga. All other yogic practices are merely physical exercises.   *Sanathana Sarathi, May 1996, p. 127*

0540: The heart is the film and the mind is the lens. Turn the lens towards the world, the worldly picture will fall on the heart; turn it towards God and it will transmit the picture of the Divine. How can God shine in a heart that is darkened by bad thoughts and intentions?

If there is righteousness in the heart, there will be beauty in character. If there is beauty in character, there will be harmony in the home. When there will be harmony in the home, there will be order in the nation. When there is order in the nations, there will be peace in the world.

The Lord is sweetness, you are sugar; He is fire, you are fuel. He has no heart; every heart where He is installed is His. Cleanse the heart by listening to spiritual discourses, seeking the company of the righteous, simple and sincere, and by cultivating goodness of character and sweetness of disposition.

Expansion is the essence of love. When a lamp is lit from another, there are two, where there was one. The first one did not stop emitting light. You can light a million lamps from one; yet the first will not suffer at all! Love too is like this. Share it with a million, it will still be as bright as when it was alone.

Work, Wisdom and Worship are the three paths to God, but because of desire (Kama), Karma is warped through Krodha (anger). Jnana is befogged and due to greed, "Bhakthi is ruined, but by developing Prema (Love), man can conquer all these weaknesses.

The true strength can be acquired only through Love. All other efforts are of no avail. Thus we should ask from God only the strength of Love.

Sanathana Sarathi, April 1996, p. 109

0541: The hall-mark of love is sacrifice. Love seeks nothing from anyone. It bears no ill-will towards anyone. It is utterly selfless and pure.

Failing to understand the true nature of love, man yearns for it in various ways. Love has to be cherished with feelings of selflessness and sacrifice. In what is deemed as love in the world, whether it be material love, brotherly love, or friendship, there is an element of selfishness. Only God's love is totally free from the taint of selfishness. Divine love reaches out even to the remotest being. It brings together those who are separate. It raises man from animality to divinity. It transforms gradually all forms of worldly love to Divine love. To experience this Divine love, men must be prepared to give up selfishness and self-interest. They must develop purity and steadfastness. With firm faith in the Divine, they must foster the love of God regardless of all obstacles and ordeals.

Sanathana Sarathi, July 1996, p. 177

0542: As a man grows from childhood to manhood, his attachments change from the mother to friends, to wife and children, and then to the acquisition of wealth. In the ups and downs involved in the pursuit of wealth, he begins to feel the need for God. This perpetual alternation of attachment and separation cannot be called real love which is spiritual and enduring.

The quality of true love is to give and not to receive. How many are to be found today in the world who love to give? Even a father hesitates to part with his property to his children. Only God can be the infinite giver. Hence love is a divine quality.

Although inherently love is present in every cell of the human being, it does not manifest itself because of the pollution of the heart. A man without love in his heart is as good as dead.   *Sanathana Sarathi, August 1996, p. 214*

0543: True culture consists in the recognition of the unity that underlies the diversity in mankind. The basis of that culture is one, which is essentially divine. Love is a much abused word today. What is called love is only attachment of different kinds based on relationships.   *Sanathana Sarathi, June 1996, p. 151*

0544: For achieving anything in life, two things are essential: firm faith and pure love. People should not think that pleasure and pain are caused by some external forces. It is not so. They are the result of one's own thoughts. There is no meaning in blaming others. If you develop love of God, that love will banish all sorrow and evil tendencies like attachment, anger and envy.

Sanathana Sarathi, July 1996, p. 178

THE MIND

0545: The transformation of man is based on transformation on the mind. When men are transformed, the nation is transformed. When nations change, the world is transformed, hence, if the world has to be changed, there has to be a mental transformation at the individual level. The human mind should be filled with love.

Sanathana Sarathi, March, 1997, p. 59

0546: The mind is a remarkable entity. When it is filled with wisdom, it makes a man a saint. When it is associated with ignorance, it turns into an agent of death. Hence it has been declared that the mind is the cause of human bondage or liberation. All change, in education or other spheres, has to begin with transformation of the mind.

Sanathana Sarathi, March, 1997, p. 59

0547: The mind has no independent identity of its own. It is a conglomeration of the desires that sprout from the impulses. A cloth is essentially a bundle of threads. Threads, in their turn, are basically cotton. Similarly, desires arise from basic impulses and the mind is constituted of these desires. Just as a piece of cloth disintegrates if threads in it are pulled apart, the mind too can be destroyed by the eradication of desires.

The heart can be compared to the sky; the mind, to the moon; and the intellect, to the sun. The thoughts that are generated in the mind are like the clouds that pass away. The cause for one's happiness and misery or pleasure and pain lies in his thoughts. However, these twin ideas of happiness and misery or pleasure or pain obtain relevance only in the world of duality. Just as the camera gives photographic impressions of the objects upon which it is focused, the mind absorbs the impressions of the objects it is directed at. The more it is directed towards the world of sensory pleasures, the farther it takes man away from God.

Summer Showers, 1979, p. 116

0548: Scientists are not examining in the correct way the relationship between matter and energy. Scientists hold the view that matter is convertible into energy and vice versa. But, in fact, the two are not separate. They are inseparably interlinked and are interdependent. The attempts to divide matter and energy have given rise to many doubts and confusions.

What is the new discovery which scientists have made today? All their discoveries are of what already existed. Take, for instance, gravity. Gravity has governing gravitation. Newton sought to find out the laws governing gravitation. He did not discover the phenomenon anew. He only found out what already existed. That the earth had gravitational attraction was known even before Newton investigated it.

Likewise, matter and energy have existed from the time of creation. Both are comprehended by the mind only. When the mind functions in relation to the Divine it acquires the form of energy. When the mind is turned towards Nature, the latter assumes the form of matter. Mind is the cause of experiencing joy or sorrow and for comprehending matter and energy. Recognizing this quality of the mind, the sages declared; "The mind is the cause of liberation or bondage for humanity".   *Gems of Wisdom, Matter and Energy, p. 254*

0549: The importance of the mind in the process of transformation should be properly understood because the mind is the cause of bondage or liberation. Your actions are the cause of your happiness or sorrow. Do not blame others for your condition. Every thought, every word and every action has its reflection, resound and reaction. It is a sign of weakness to blame others for your troubles. You have to bear with the consequences of your actions. It they are unbearable, pray to God for relief. God alone can give relief in such cases. He is all-powerful and therefore take refuge in Him.

Pray to God and draw from Him the magnet of His grace and offer to the world the power of His electrical energy.

This is the energy which man can mobilize for the good of all. It is all-powerful, because it is Divine. It is within you. What a pity that people should be unaware of this and feel themselves powerless! All energy and all bliss are within us. Because of ignorance people are resorting to all kinds of useless exercises. They are unnecessary. Have full faith in your spiritual power. Adhere to the truth of your faith, without criticizing others.

Whatever you do, have the name of the Lord on your lips and faith in God in your heart. Thereby work will be transformed into worship.
                              Sanathana Sarathi, April, 1997, p. 95

0550: It is only when the mind follows the Buddhi that inner vision is developed. Inner vision leads to the experience of the Bliss of the Atma. External vision, however, subjects man to untold suffering.   *Summer Showers, 1979, p. 76*

0551: Living under the impression that you are the body and you are destroyed with the death of the body is an illusion which is basically undesirable. Another illusion is, that happiness consists in accumulating money or knowledge, comforts or reputation. Trying to be happy through such accumulation is like getting into the Madras bus and hoping to reach Bangalore. What is happiness? It is the stateof mind which is, by fortune, good or bad. By systematic education, the mind can attain that state. If activity is done as worship, then the mind can attain that state. If activity is done as worship, then the mind will be steady and free from anxiety.   *Gems of Wisdom, Curbing the Mind, p. 47*

0552: The mind has no independent identity of its own. It is a conglomeration of the desires that sprout from the impulses. A cloth is essentially a bundle of threads. Threads in their truth are basically cotton. Similarly, desires arise from basic impulses, and the mind is constituted of these desires. Just as a piece of cloth disintegrates if threads in it are pulled apart, the mind too can be destroyed by the eradication of desires.   *Summer Showers, 1979, p. 116*

0553: The mind can act as a bridge leading from the tangible to the intangible, from the personal to the impersonal. Cleanse the mind and mold it into an instrument for loving thoughts and expansive ideas.
                    Gems of Wisdom, Shanthi, p. 128

0554: We need not search for Divinity in the external world. We have to realize it within our own selves. The divine effulgence of Sat-Chith-Ananda (being, consciousness and bliss) is concealed by the perverted nature of the human mind.   *Summer Showers, 1979, p. 13*

0555: An individual seeking to realize Divinity must possess the primary prerequisite of chittasuddi or purity of heart. Even as poisonous creatures like snakes and scorpions do not enter a clean and well-lit room, desire, anger, envy and hatred do not enter a mind which possesses purity and wisdom.
                    Summer Showers, 1979, p. 58

0556: When a well is dug, the earth that is removed from the pit forms a mound by the side. The mud in the mound is the same mud that was in the pit. Praise and calumny are like the mound and the pit, and are essentially of the same origin. Realizing this, the mind should be trained to develop equanimity in terms of man's relationship with and existence in society.
                    Summer Showers, 1979, p. 157

0557: To get close to God you have to go beyond the mind. To have control over the mind is the mark of wisdom (Jnana). To seek to achieve proximity to God you have to develop devotion. Millions of people all over the world are seeking God-realization; but all their efforts are at the mental level. They have to go beyond the mind to realize the Divine, who is the embodiment of Truth- Wisdom-Omnipotence.   *Sanathana Sarathi, November 1997, p. 294*

0558: Bliss or Ananda is a divine vibhuti. That is why it is said,"happiness is union with God". Your true nature is bliss. Know this and be cheerful always. The mind that is morose harbors nothing but malice and jealousy. Divinity cannot reside in such unholy minds. Cheerfulness is the first sign of spirituality. Therefore, strive to be happy always. Live in contentment and with cheer, and thereby qualify yourself for the experience of Divinity which is Bliss supreme.
Summer Showers, 1979, p. 167

0559: The mind will be a means of liberation when it is rid of the impurities residing in it. All spiritual exercises are designed only for cleaning the mind.
Do not condemn the mind as a monkey, etc. It is a fine instrument with which you can achieve either liberation or bondage; it depends as to how you manipulate it. It can lead you, if you so desire, right up to the door of realization or it will make you wander into blind alleys where every step will fall into dirt.
Gems of Wisdom, Intellect (Buddhi), p. 52

0560: Earning and spending, man fills his time with work. He has no peace. However, he is busy trying to earn happiness, but the success in not much. Man does not realize the panacea for all his ills, the effort that will result in total victory lies in the control of Mind.
Gems of Wisdom, Shanthi, p. 127

0561: Jnana (wisdom) cannot be had without a pure mind.
Gems of Wisdom, Shanthi, p. 127

0562: Mind can reflect the light of the Atma within. And the Atma can be known only through pure, deep love: all claims to the contrary are spurious and missing the mark.
Gems of Wisdom, Ganesa Worship, p. 383

0563: There is some small confusion of terms, for there is no mind as such. The mind is a web of desires. Peace of mind is no desires and in that state there is no mind. Mind is destroyed, so to speak. Peace of mind really means purity, complete purity of consciousness.
Gems of Wisdom, Shanthi, p. 129

0564: Just as we will not benefit much by merely looking at fruits instead of eating them, so also for cognizing the Divine, the mind needs to be used. It being the instrument that can bind or liberate.
Gems of Wisdom, Science and Spirituality, p. 253

0565: There is a certain joy in being master of the senses, rather than being their slave. Now, you are slave of coffee habit. Resolve not to cater to that attachment at least for 3 days, continuously. You become the master of the tongue your slave. If coffee is capable of conferring joy, all should get it equally from that beverage. But many prefer tea and some take it without sugar, while some others without milk. So, it is the mind that gives delight and not the coffee: it is not the object that caters to the senses.   *Gems of Wisdom, Happiness, p. 166*

0566: When air fills a balloon, it takes the form of the balloon- oval, sausage shaped, spherical or spheroid. Likewise, mind assumes the form of the objects with which it is attached. Hence, man should dwell on high thoughts, as the mind becomes petty if it gets fixed on small things.
Gems of Wisdom, Bhakthi (Devotion), p. 299

0567: When the mind is good, man can divinise himself. Only the one endowed with a mind can be called a man. Without the mind, one ceases to be a man. It is only when the subtle, invisible, inner base of the mind is in a proper condition that a being that has donned the human form can attain his true state.
Sanathana Sarathi, June 1994, p. 147

0568: Do you think I would confront you with pain were there not a reason for it? Open your heart to pain, as you do now to pleasure, for it is My will, wrought by me for your good. Welcome it as a challenge. Do not turn away from it, do not listen to your mind, for mind is but another word for "need". The mind engenders need, it manifested as the world, because it needed this. It is all My plan, to drive you by pangs of unfulfilled need to listen to My voice, which when heard, dissolves the ego and the mind with it.   *Santhana Sarathi, August 1974, p. 185*

0569: The mind will be a means of liberation when it is rid of the impurities residing in it. All spiritual exercises are designed only to cleanse the mind.
Gems of Wisdom, Beliefs, p. 223

0570: The mind attracts many objects that it sees. It promotes a variety of qualities, attitudes, attachments. Above all, it encourages the inflation of the Ego. Puffed by his Ego, man loses all powers of discrimination.
Gems of Wisdom, Spiritual Level, p. 259

0571: The person who is a slave to the mind will not find peace or happiness in life. The body is a mansion which has been built by the mind for its own joy and protection. The mind is the cause and the basis of everybody - every human being. Some persons are wasting their lives by expending all their energy in looking after the body, basing their existence entirely on food. Others increase their attachments through thoughtless repetition of spiritual practices, reducing them to mere physical exercises. The wise man controls the mind and purifies the heart by removing bad thoughts and replacing them with good thoughts. Do not underestimate the power of good thoughts. They are sacred and divine, having great impact on the individual entertaining them.

On that day when we free ourselves from the evil thoughts which have solidified within us, we will have a vision of God.

Gems of Wisdom, Why is God not seen? p. 350

0572: The constant recital of the name of God from amongst any of the million names by which he is identified by human imagination or intelligence is the best means of correcting and cleansing the mind of man.

Gems of Wisdom, Namasmarana, p. 373

0573: Separation from God is the cause of men's wallowing in sensuous pleasures. The mind is the cause of man's pleasure and pain. It should be directed towards God to secure freedom from pleasure and pain.

Sanathana Sarathi, February 1996, p. 32

0574: Take back this lesson from here, retain at least this much knowledge, that attachment causes pain and detachment results in joy. But, you cannot easily detach yourself from activity; the mind clings to something or other, make it cling to God.   *Sathya Sai Speaks; Volume V, p. 105*

0575: The ancient Indian Sages practiced self-control, entertained good thoughts and led a blissful life. When a man's inner self is filled with love, his life becomes full of bliss and he is always hale and hearty. Today man suffers from numerous aliments the root cause of which is a diseased mind.

Sanathana Sarathi, November 1997, p. 292

0576: The mind is the cause of both bondage and liberation. It is only by controlling the mind that man can achieve liberation.

Sanathana Sarathi, July 1994, p. 169

0577: The heart is like the lens of a camera. Our mind is like the plate in this camera. The thoughts that enter our mind will get imprinted on that plate. For this reason, we must not allow any bad thoughts to enter our mind.

Summer Showers in Brindivan, 1977, p. 252

0578: The mind is called an instrument. The senses are instruments, which are used to contact nature and gather information about objects. Mind is the over-all instrument, which controls and directs the senses. It is called the Inner instrument. Higher than the mind is the intellect which analyses and categorizes the impressions as gathered by the mind, through the individual. The mind has to be subordinate to the intellect but usually it serves the senses, which are but its servants. That is how the mind leads man into bondage.

But beyond the mind, and beyond reason and consciousness and the I-sense, is the Self, the Reality, the Cosmic I or God.

Baba, The Breath of Sai, p. 301

0579: There is no death for the mind, though when the body is facing death, the mind thinks it is dying. The mind, it has been said, is the cause of one's bondage or liberation. Bad thoughts beget bondage. Good thoughts lead to liberation. Hence, everyone should develop good thoughts and perform good deeds. Such good feelings can arise only out of love.

Today all man's actions are governed by mundane desires. To achieve liberation man has to go beyond the vagaries of the mind. He should follow the Inner Voice (Antahkarana). *Sanathana Sarathi, November 1997, p. 293*

0580: Today there are many incurable diseases, but these relate not to the body but the mind. In a sense, all diseases get into the body through the mind. Even ordinary ailments like a head ache or a stomach ache have their origin in the mind.

Whatever influences the mind affects also the body. But unaware of this profound truth, man attributes all ills to the body and not the mind. Most ailments are really mental and not physical. Because of this we witness a wide prevalence of psychic disorders. We find that mental illnesses are on the increase all over the world. The reason is that there is too much of mental tension and worry.

The mind is subject to varying moods- sorrow or joy, anger or fear, love or hate. For all the diseases arising from the mind, the basic causes are two: attachment and aversion. The mind is filled with these twofold feelings. Consequently, it tends to forget its basic human nature. The mind in this state considers the six basic enemies of man- lust, hatred, delusion, greed, envy and pride- as virtues. These six vices can poison a person's entire being. He then forgets his inherent divinity and ceases to be human. He is a victim of infamy. But a person filled with good feelings enjoys peace and happiness.

Sanathana Sarathi, November 1997, p. 292

0581: As the Gita declares, the devotee dear to the Lord is one who does not hate any being. You should not harbor hatred towards any one but keep away from bad company. You should not cultivate relationship with evil persons as this will spoil the purity of your mind. The mind is the cause of bondage or liberation. You turn it toward God and cultivate detachment. If you turn towards the world you develop attachment. Desire is an unnecessary burden in your life's journey. You must reduce your desires to a minimum, as it may not be possible to give up desire totally. *Sanathana Sarathi, May 1994, p. 116*

0582: Any happiness experienced through the mind is not spiritual bliss. It is transient physical pleasure. Not recognizing this truth many pursue so-called spiritual exercises with the mind. The mind should be ignored. It is concerned only with thoughts of one kind or another. The Atmic Principle cannot be understood by such thought processes. Divert your attention towards the Atma and dismiss all thoughts. If you cannot get rid of thoughts, then cultivate good thoughts. Turn your thoughts towards the Supreme Lord.

Sanathana Sarathi, November, p. 293

0583: For the development of the human personality, the development of the mind and the refinement of the heart are essential.

All actions of man originate in the mind. The mind functions through thoughts. Hence, thoughts are the root cause of man's actions. Humanness is the outcome of thoughts. When the thoughts are pure, the mind is also pure with a purified mind, man's conduct becomes pure. Thus, for the purity or impurity of one's actions, thoughts are primarily responsible.

Sanathana Sarathi, August 1994, p. 219

0584: Every man is endowed with a mind. The mind is a mysterious thing. It can appear totally stationary and yet move faster that the speed of light. Whatever births a person may undergo and whatever changes in name and form may occur, the mind remains unchanged. It follows one from birth to birth. It is the mind's peculiar behavior. In this context, how is one to manifest his humanness? Man must follow the example of the honey bee which sucks the sweet even from a bitter flower. Likewise, one must seek the good even in what is apparently bad. There is something good in what is bad.   *Sanathana Sarathi, April 1996, p. 92*

0585: It is easy for man to stand but it is difficult for him to run. But, in the case of the mind, staying still is difficult, but running is easy. This is the difference between man and his mind. The mind runs about swiftly. This is based on the power of the thoughts. When a stone is cast in a well, a series of ripples start from the point where the stone fell. From there, the ripples go up to the edge of the well and cover the entire well. In the same manner, when the stone of thought is cast on the lake of the mind, the ripples started by it fill all the senses and limbs in the body. When the thought is a pure and sacred one, the ripples emanating in the mind fill all the senses and limbs in the body, from head to toe, with pure reactions. This pure thought entering the eye, purifies the vision. The same thought, entering the ear, makes it listen to sacred sounds. Entering the mouth, this pure thought brings about purity in speech. Permeating the hands, the sacred thought induces them to engage themselves in sacred acts. The sacred ripples from the mind entering the feet, induce them to go on pilgrimages. It the thoughts are impure, they travel in ripples to the senses and induce them to indulge in unholy acts.   *Sanathana Sarathi, August 1994, p. 219*

0586: When a criminal is punished by a court after being found guilty, he is kept in prison. It is only the body that gets punished. But the real culprit is the mind. No one has got any right or ability to punish the mind which really causes the convict to commit the crime. The mind can travel anywhere even when a person is in prison. The Government or Policehave no contro l over the mind. It is only the supreme power of the Divine that can have control over the mind.

Sanathana Sarathi, July 1994, p. 176

0587: Just as the wind causes the leaves to move, the company one keeps influences a man's mind. You should flee from evil company, it gets polluted with such bad qualities as anger, jealousy and hatred. You should use your body, mind and intellect for the benefit of society at large and not for selfish purposes.

Sanathana Sarathi, May 1994, p. 114

0588: In the world today, various changes are taking place. There is no shortage of wealth and property, nor is there any dearth of amenities for comfortable living. There is no lack of facilities for entertainment or recreation. Nevertheless, modern man is oppressed by frustration, depression and disappointment. What is the reason? It is the failure to use the divine power of the mind properly that accounts for the frustration and the lack of peace of man today. The differences between man and man are growing continuously. These differences lead to disastrous conflicts. Hence, the first requisite is to strive for the proper use of the powers of the mind. The mind of man today is that of an intoxicated person because his mind is giving free rein to the senses.   *Sanathana Sarathi, June 1994, p. 147*

0589: Nature is a projection of the mind. The world is rooted in the mind. When the mind is turned towards the heart and the heart is filled with the Divine, the mind will cease to be a source of trouble. The mind is the master of the senses. When the senses are controlled, the mind is under control. Only the master of the mind can attain Madhava (the Divine).

Sanathana Sarathi, February 1996, p. 45

0590: Life is extremely precious. Time is highly valuable. The heart is tender. The mind is a great possession. Though endowed with all these valuable things, man conducts himself as a mean, ignorant and miserable being. He is unable to recognize what a rare, sweet and blissful thing is human life. The reason is, man, forgetting his divine nature, is immersing himself in worldly pleasures and in mundane desires.

Man should realize that he is subject to time and time has no respect for wealth or position. Man is devoting all his time to worldly pursuits and the demands of the body. Not realizing the significance of time, man leads an animal existence.

The heart, which is soft and compassionate by nature, has been hardened into stone by man. Humanness should manifest itself in a heart overflowing with compassion, but compassion has turned into hard-heartedness.

The mind is all powerful. It can see without eyes, hear without ears, speak without the tongue and move about without legs. Man tries to control the mind, but he is subordinate to it. As long as he is subject to the mind, man cannot understand the true nature of the mind.   *Sanathana Sarathi, May 1996, p. 116*

0591: For man's happiness and good appearance or for his misery and ugliness, the mind its behavior are responsible. What we see outwardly as a man and all the qualities he exhibits depend ultimately on what we do not see and that is the mind.   *Summer Showers in Brindavan, 1973, p. 144*

0592: Nature is a projection of the mind. The world is rooted in the mind. When the mind is turned towards the heart and the heart is filled with the Divine, the mind will cease to be a source of trouble. The mind is the master of the senses. When the senses are controlled, the mind is under control. Only the master of the mind can attain Madhava (the Divine).
Sanathana Sarathi, February 1996, p. 45

0593: Turn the key in the lock to the right, it opens; turn the same key to the left, it is locked. So too, turn your mind towards the objective world, it is locked, caught, entangled. Turn it to the right, away from the objects of the senses, the lock is loosened, you are free, deliverance is at hand. How to turn it right? Well, begin with remembering the Lord's holy name, as the first step. All journeys start with the first step. That will itself take you through the second and third, to the very goal.   *Sathya Sai Speaks, Volume IV, p. 19*

0594: When Tukaram was asked how man can keep this monkey-mind from running after sensuous pleasures, he replied to the inquirer, "Let the monkey run; you keep quiet where you are; do not let the body go along with the monkey-mind". Tell the mind, "I shall not give you the body as your servant". Then, the mind will desist and it can be defeated. Just as there is a method to be followed even in pulling down a house, there is a method even in pulling down the complex structure of the mind.

The mind can be pulled down by systematic efforts and you can become master of yourself. You might ask, can such a mighty force come down? Well, when we were nearing "Rishikesh on our way back from Badri, Governor Ramakrishna Rao also asked me the same question. I asked every one to come beyond a certain point on the road in a matter of minutes. Everyone was surprised that I was ordering them to get down from the cars and buses and scurry forward in hot haste. I told the Governor that the projecting rock on the mountain by the side of the road will slide very soon on the road and block it. He asked me, "Is it possible?" Within a few minutes, after everyone had come forward to a safe distance, the rocks fell and the road was blocked for a long time, until debris was cleared.   *Sathya Sai Speaks, Volume IV, p. 106*

0595: The mind must become the servant of the intellect and not the slave of the senses. *Gems of Wisdom, Spiritual Quality is Essential, p. 275*

MISCELLANEOUS

0596: I have often indicated the rule by which people should govern their lives. They have to follow the dictates of their conscience "Make conscience your master". You can then face any difficulties in life and overcome them. Never give away to despair in the face of difficulties.

Sanathana Sarathi, March, 1997, p. 61

0597: Control over sensory organs can be attained by constant, steady and systematic practice. It is the privilege of man alone to overcome his natural instincts and change his habits. The tiger in a circus can be taught many kinds of feats. However, it is by nature a carnivorous animal and can never be changed into a mild, herbivorous animal. The tiger wants meat when it is hungry. Can a tiger ever eat "purees" instead of meat? It is an instinct of the tiger to eat flesh. You cannot think of a vegetarian tiger. Instinct cannot be changed. You may feed a cat with milk and curds, but at the very sight of a rat, it will pounce on it and gobble it up. A cat's instinct is to eat rats.

Man has the ability to learn new things and to change himself. Unlike animals, he is endowed with infinite capacity for learning and can transform himself into a better person. He can sublimate and refine his instincts, and give up his vicious habits. He can achieve anything by his own effort.

Summer Showers, 1979, p. 130

0598: Chronic jealousy is the source of all mental and physical ailments in this world. In order to acquire mental equipoise and inner tranquillity, man should make his heart pure by purging his mind of this psychological mania called jealousy. Man must first humanize himself before attempting to divinize himself. To feel jealous of others even in trivial matters suppresses the humanitarian instincts of a person. Men, today, waste all their time and energy in blaming others without realizing that to search for and find faults in others is the most grievous and ghastly sin. *Summer Showers, 1979, p. 140*

0599: Some people imagine that God bestows excessive grace on a few, appears to be indifferent towards some others, and totally to ignore some others. All these are only the aberrations of the people having such thoughts. For God all are the same. You can see your true image only in a glass covered on the rear with the mercury of love. Everyone says he has not experienced God, it is not God's fault. The feeling that God favors some and not others is born of jealousy.   *Sanathana Sarathi, September, 1996, p. 241*

0600: Consider the example of earth's rotation about its own axis and its revolution around the sun. The sun, all of us know, is stationary and it is the earth that revolves round it. The so-called sunrise and sunset are effected by this revolution of the earth rather than by the movement of the sun. This is scientifically proved. Nevertheless, the scientists also do talk in the language of the layman in daily life and speak about sunrise and sunset concealing the truth which they know. Similarly, the language of words is gloriously inconsistent to express and explain the great truths of spirituality. The language of experience is the only means to comprehend spirituality.   *Summer Showers, 1979, p. 143*

0601: People are going about now advising that one should believe only things that one has "seen" and "experienced". Something happens somewhere and the news is published in the papers. It is believed without question. So, too, believe in the experience of seers and sages who had no other purpose than discovering the Truth and sharing It with others who were not aware of it. In India we have had millions who believed in God and in the seekers after God, and who have themselves realized the Truth of God. This has made their lives happy and contented.

Truth is born of love, which comes from the faith in God. I have often said: Where there is confidence, there is love; where there is love, there is peace; where there is peace, there is truth; where there is truth, there is bliss; where there is bliss, there is God.   *Gems of Wisdom, Faith, p. 114*

0602: Whatever you do, wherever you are placed, believe that God has put you there for that work.   *Sathya Sai Speaks, Volume IX, p. 20*

0603: Today we know that there is a material world in which there are all kind of material attractions. We think that because of the existence of those attractions, we are having pleasure and happiness. It is not so. So long as these material desires and material attractions do not reach your eyes, do not reach your ears and you do not participate in them, they cannot affect you in the least.   *Gems of Wisdom, Self Confidence, p. 121*

0604: When life flows merrily, people claim it is due to their own effort, and they forget God. When failure visits the "smooth flow", they start cursing and lose faith.   *Gems of Wisdom, Self Confidence, p. 122*

0605: Joy is the interval between two moments of pain, and pain is the interval between two moments of joy.

Do not count your tears of pain; do not pour over your griefs. Let them pass through your mind, as birds fly through the sky, leaving no trail behind.
Sathya Sai Speaks, Volume V, p. 330

0606: Through activity man attains purity of consciousness. Why strive for a pure consciousness? If a well has muddy water, then its bottom cannot be seen. Similarly, within man's heart, deep down in his consciousness, we have the Atman. But it can be cognized only when the consciousness is clarified. Your imagination, your inferences, your judgments and prejudices, your passions and emotions plus egoistic desires muddy the consciousness and make it opaque.
Gems of Wisdom, Service, p. 158

0607: There are two birds sitting on one tree, the Upanishad says, the Jivatma and the Paramatma, on the tree of this body, this world. One bird eats the fruits of that tree, while the other simply looks on, as a witness. But the wonder is, the two birds are really one, though they appear as two; they cannot be separated, since they are two aspects of the same entity. Steam in the air cannot be seen, but it is the same as ice-which is hard and heavy and cold. Niraahaara and Saakaara are just two ways in which the One manifests itself.
Sathya Sai Speaks; Volume III, p. 147

0608: A time honored proverb says: "real and lasting happiness cannot be won through physical happiness". Lasting happiness can come by the discipline of the mind and faith in the Lord which cannot be diminished by good fortune or bad.
Gems of Wisdom, Happiness, p. 161

0609: Happiness and peace do not follow when man is fed well, clothed well, housed well and educated up to a good standard and employed under comfortable conditions, with no injury to health or security. There are many who have all these in plenty but who are yet worried or in pain or discontented. They depend on the inner equipment of man, not on his outer skill or riches.
Gems of Wisdom, Happiness, p. 167

0610: Man has to cultivate the sense of equanimity in pleasure and suffering. Man today is racked by all kinds of troubles. Are these troubles designed to make man miserable or to elevate him to a higher level of existence? Every trouble is really a step in elevating man. If there are no troubles, man will have no proper lessons. Troubles constitute good lessons. Trouble and pleasure are inextricably mixed and cannot be separated from each other by anyone. Pleasure has no separate existence. It is the fruit of the pain. This basic truth is not recognized by man. When grief smites him he succumbs to it. He gloats over some happy experience. His entire life is bound up with these varying experiences of pleasure and pain.

Like the black bee which has the capacity to bore a hole through a strong bamboo, when it enters the lotus flower which folds itself and makes the bee get immersed in the enjoyment of honey and thus forget its own power. Man has forgotten the divine in him and is immersed in worldly concerns and is intoxicated with mundane pleasures. That alone is the cause of all his misery.

The sorrows of life cannot be ended through hatred and injustice; these will only breed more of the species. The sorrows will yield only to nobler and higher thoughts and experiences germinating from the pure heart, where the Lord resides. *Gems of Wisdom, Suffering, p. 169*

0611: The honor of a nation depends on the morality of that nation, a nation without morality will be doomed. *Gems of Wisdom, Virtue, p. 231*

0612: The nature of man is such that he experiences joy by mixing with other humans. Not to mix and to lead a secluded life is a sign of weakness and of fear, not of courage. Active compassion, sympathy, love, tolerance, equanimity and many other qualities help build man's character.
Gems of Wisdom, Happiness, p. 166

0613: No one can liberate you, for no one has bound you. You hold on to the nettle of worldly pleasure and you weep, like the kite is pursued by the crows so long as it carries the fish in its beak; once the kite drops the fish, immediately it is free. So you too should give up attachment to the senses; the sorrow and anxiety can harass you no more, and you can be happy.
Gems of Wisdom, Happiness, p. 161

0614: For the ocean, the waves are the ornament. For the sky, the moon is the ornament. For man's life, virtue is the ornament. Without good qualities, all other ornaments are worthless. *Gems of Wisdom, Character, p. 224*

0615: There is no object without fault or failing; there is no pleasure that is unmixed with pain; there is no act that is not tainted with egoism. So be pure and develop detachment, which will save you from grief.
Gems of Wisdom, Suffering, p. 170

0616: If you give joy to your parents, your children will be a source of joy to you in your declining years. *Gems of Wisdom, Women, p. 198*

0617: Moral and spiritual values have to be honored as much as, if not more than, economic and material values. Life must be a harmonious blend of these values with emphasis on moral strength.

Sathya Sai Speaks, Volume VIII, p. 179

0618: Only that person who has tasted the juice of cane sugar can describe the taste of the juice. To some extent, by experience one can describe the taste but one cannot describe its form. When we ask the question, how is sugar? We can say sugar is like white sand. But if someone asks you to describe the nature and the form of sweetness in the sugar, it is not possible to do so. In a similar manner only those people, who have immersed themselves in the experience of God, can even have the right to attempt to describe anything about God. Others cannot do this.

God is present everywhere in the form of atma. His effulgence is shining in every heart. If such effulgent atma is not present, man cannot live in this world even for a moment. It is present is all of them, and is at the same level in all the human beings. It is possible to establish and describe that kind of divinity only when we identify ourselves with divine features. Our names, our forms, our tastes, our likes and dislikes may differ from one person to another. These are simply differences which arise out of our desires.

Summer Showers in Brindivan, 1977, p. 129

0619: In our daily life, we follow so many different paths for the purpose of getting some happiness and pleasure. In this world, there are many rich people, there are many wealthy people, there are many strong people and there are educated people but we do not find any amongst them who enjoy peace of mind. The Kauravas has any amount of wealth, physical strength and weapons but still they never derived any benefit from all that. If man makes himself distant form God and from righteousness, in what manner can he get this peace of mind?

Summer Showers in Brindivan, 1977, p. 156

0620: Morality is the corollay dharma (spiritual duty). Morality does not merely mean the observance of certain rules in the workaday world. Morality means adherence to the straight and sacred path of right conduct. Morality is the blossoming of good conduct.　　*Sanathana Sarathi, January 1985, p. 2*

0621: Morality has to be grown in the heart by feeding it with love. Then only can we have justice, security, law and order. If love declines among the people, nations will weaken and mankind will perish.

Sathya Sai Speaks, Volume VIII, p. 80

0622: So long as man lives a life devoted to objective pleasures and objective victories, he cannot escape sorrow, fear and anxiety.

Gems of Wisdom, Suffering, p. 170

0623: People ask how we can manage to live in society without a dash of falsehood. This is a wrong approach. Truth speaking is natural to man; it is falsehood that is an artificial skill. Avoid even little misdeeds, for by repetition they warp character and develop into bad habits.   *Gems of Wisdom, Truth, p. 249*

0624: In all lands the true sense of values has to be restored, and faith in the divinity of man has to be implanted. This is the work for which I have come. The world has to be saved from the consequences of limited knowledge, and from the blinding pride that precedes a fall.

Love is the vital force. Love is the governing principle. It is only when the precious diamond of love is shining in one's heart that sacred and divine thoughts about God will arise in the mind.

Compassion and love are vanishing in today's world. Ostentatious living is the order of the day. The manifestation of true love is totally absent. Everyone may claim to love God. Hardly one in a million is a true lover of God. True love should remain unaffected by weal or woe. To deride God during times of adversity, and to praise Him during conditions of prosperity cannot be called true love. Divine love is that which does not flinch in times of difficulties, and does not gloat over prosperity, but remains equally serene in all circumstances.

Man should become the very embodiment of love. When he is filled with love the entire world will be transformed into a love-filled world. As long as he is filled with hate the world will appear as a hate-filled world.

It is only when love is developed that the dualism of good and evil can be transcended and the joy of oneness with the Divine experienced.

Sanathana Sarathi, May, 1993, p. 136

0625: Victory won through questionable means is as shameful as defeat; defeat while pursuing honest and compassionate means is to be welcomed as victory.

Gems of Wisdom, Practice and Precept, p. 243

0626: Spiritual discipline consists in recognizing the unity underlying the apparent diversity and realizing divinity.   *Gems of Wisdom, Truth, p. 248*

0627: The thought which prevails at the time of conception results in the kind of child that is born.   *Sanathana Sarathi, June 1993, p. 141*

0628: Human values are in everyone. What we need are persons who will provide the stimulus and the encouragement to bring them out. If the feeling that the divinity that is present in everyone is one and the same, is promoted among all, human values will sprout naturally in every person. To have this among all, human values will sprout naturally in every person. To have this sense of spiritual oneness is the prelude to experiencing the highest bliss.

Gems of Wisdom, Practice and Precept, p. 238

0629: This is a door and there is a lock on the door. To open the lock on the door, we put the key inside the lock. If we turn the key towards the right, the lock opens. If we turn the key towards the left, the lock gets locked. In the same manner, our heart can be compared to a lock. Our mind is the key. If we put the key of our mind in the lock of the heart and turn it towards Paramatma, we get detachment; if we turn it towards the world, we get attachment. We should, in that context, make an attempt to put the key of our mind in the lock of our heart and by using our intelligence turn the key towards Paramatma.

Summer Showers in Brindivan, 1977, p. 58

0630: Morality has to be grown in the heart by feeding it with love. Then only can we have justice, security, law and order. If love declines among the people, nations will weaken and mankind will perish.   *Gems of Wisdom, Virtue, p. 231*

0631: If you wish to safeguard your future you have to be grateful to those who have helped you in your difficult time and to enable you to obtain your personal needs.

I must also condemn the absence of gratitude which is rampant today. Ingratitude is the hallmark of wild beasts, not of man.

Even if you fail to be helpful to others, do not cause harm to others. All spiritual aspirants should cherish in their hearts with gratitude the good done to them by others and always remember whatever form in which help was rendered to them.   *Gems of Wisdom, Gratitude, p. 231*

0632: Truth is something people do not like. In affluent society people like to purchase intoxicating drinks but would not purchase health-giving things like buttermilk and curd, though they are cheaper. Man today is relying very much on his mental and physical strength, and he is not making any attempt to fall back on the Divine strength.   *Gems of Wisdom, Truth, p. 249*

0633: Some laugh at spiritual aspirants and call them idle visionaries who are seeking something that is not tangible, that cannot be weighed and valued! The unseen is the basis of the seen. You so not see your breath or weigh it, but breath is the very sustenance of life.   *Gems of Wisdom, Quality of a Devotee, p. 392*

0634: Man and God are like iron and magnet. God by His very nature attracts man near, for in man there is the Divine. Often we feel that God has surrendered us, but in actual fact the iron piece (man) is too thickly covered by rust and dust. Thus man (the iron) fails to realize his own defect and rushes to blame God (the magnet).   *Gems of Wisdom, Sins and Repentance, p. 356*

0635: The human being is a composite of man, beast and God, and in the inevitable struggle between the three for supremacy, you must ensure that God wins, suffering the merely human and the lowly beast.
Gems of Wisdom, Practice and Precept, p. 243

0636: The lesson is learned by man when he studies nature, analyzing it and trying to understand it..... Break the laws of nature and she boxes you in the ear, obey her commands and listen to her warnings and she will pass on to you your heritage if inner-ability.   *Sathya Sai Speaks; Volume II, p. 152*

0637: The driver of a car has to be alert not only on the smooth road but even more so on a rough road full of potholes. So too, you must know how to avoid the temptations of falsehood and how to sail along the smooth road of truth. When in difficulty, pray for guidance. Others can give advice as per their cleverness, but the Lord who illumines dullness into intelligence will reveal to you the way out of the dilemma.   *Gems of Wisdom, Truth, p. 250*

0638: Scientists can weigh, measure and analyze materials that already exist and convert them into different forms. But they cannot create anything new. That can happen only through the will of God.
Gems of Wisdom, Science and Spirituality, p. 253

0639: Truth is so all-embracing and integrating that it sees no distinction. Truth is the current and love is the bulb it has to illumine. Through truth you can experience love and through love you can visualize truth.
Gems of Wisdom, Truth, p. 247

0640: How much more sacred it would be if men thought about God even for a few moments out of the many hours they waste of thinking about worldly things? People should develop their faith in this truth. Whatever faith they have in themselves that faith they should have in God. That is the mark of greatness. One who has no faith in himself, how can he have faith in God? Turn your faith away from the temporal and the transient to the unchanging eternal reality.   *Sanathana Sarathi, September 1997, p. 240*

0641: It is to be noted that the spirit of inquiry was prevalent among the ancient Greeks centuries before Christ. Socrates was a great teacher who promoted the spirit of inquiry among the youth of Athens. Socrates was so mush wedded to the pursuit of truth that he preferred death in his home city, to making good his escape with the help of his disciples. He set no value on life, property or possessions.   *Gems of Wisdom, Sins and Repentance, p. 353*

0642: When you call out in all sincerity, the response will certainly come: Do not pray from the lips, as you do now. You worship the Lord with an eye on the dishes cooking in the oven. Your thoughts of God are vitiated by vishayavasana (the attachment to sensory objects). There is a vast gap between what you say and what you are capable of, what you accomplish.
Gems of Wisdom, Sins and Repentance, p. 354

0643: Man today is behaving with less gratitude than what birds, beasts and even trees display. He is ungrateful to his parents, teachers, society and even to God. He makes a parade of his adherence to truth, righteousness, peace, love and ahimsa but does not practice any of them. Why is this so? It is because of intense selfishness and pro-occupation with one's own concerns and interests. Only when man sheds his selfishness can he turn his mind towards God.

Animals live and die without change in their original nature. Man is different. By practice and discipline, man can change his nature from bad to good.
Gems of Wisdom, Serve ever, Hurt Never, p. 404

0644: Envy is a self-consuming malady. It is incurable. One who is always blissful will overcome all difficulties. The courageous man can face death without fear.
Sanathana Sarathi, February 1997, p. 31

0645: Humanness is a combination of the body and consciousness. Man has to embark on self-scrutiny as the first step in spirituality. Only then the reality can be comprehended.

No one undertakes self-examination, though everyone is ready to condemn others. Only the person who is prepared to examine and punish himself for his lapses is competent to judge others.
Sanathana Sarathi, September 1997, p. 241

0646: Give each problem the attention it deserves, but do not allow it to overpower you. Anxiety will not solve any difficulty; coolness comes from detachment. Above all, believe in God and the efficacy of prayer; the Lord has said that he who does good, thinks good, and speaks good will come to no harm.

Above all, do not be traitors to yourself. If you say one thing and do another, your conscience will itself condemn you as a cheat. You are your own witness.
Gems of Wisdom, Self Control, p. 414

0647: The cow transforms grass and gravel into sweet strength giving milk and gives it away in plenty to its master. Develop that quality and power to transform the food you consume into sweet thoughts, words and deeds of sympathy for all.
Sathya Sai Speaks; Volume VI, p. 150

0648: Everywhere we have a surfeit of preachers but a famine of practitioners. Heroes on platforms are zero on the ground.

Gems of Wisdom, Pilgrimage, p. 421

0649: To enable your prayers to reach God you have to affix the stamp of faith and address it with love. If you have faith and love, your prayers will reach God regardless of distance.   *Sanathana Sarathi, September 1997, p. 240*

0650: Ideas of suicide, let "ME" tell you, are born out of the most despicable form of cowardice. Do not allow them to affect you; be bold, so bold that you are determined to brave out any calamity that you may assail. When you have God installed in your heart, who can lead you to destruction?

Gems of Wisdom, Pilgrimage, p. 423

0651: Your attitude is the cause of your suffering or happiness. With whatever feeling you see and object, the same is reflected back. Vision determines your view of Creation. When you see the world through colored glasses, you will see everything in the color of the glasses you are wearing. Whatever happens, you should take it as a gift of God. Love is God. Live in Love. This is the proper way of worshipping God.   *Sanathana Sarathi, May 1994, p. 115*

0652: White ants appear little by little and they grow slowly. However, in good time, the whole piece of wood will be completely eaten away. Similarly bad qualities start in a small way. In good time, they will destroy the individual completely.   *Summer Showers in Brindivan, 1977, p. 160*

0653: There is only one common feature for all living things in this world and that is the eternal spirit. In all manifold forms of creation in unity and in diversity, we find only the spirit of atma and nothing else. It is the realization of this aspect that constitutes the essence of all learning.

Sanathana Sarathi, September 1997, p. 241

0654: Man has lost the ability to discriminate between the permanent and impermanent things. Because of the absence of such discriminating power, man simply gets excited and acts in a state of excitement. They are not even able to recognize that excitement is a weakness in them. It their desires and their ambitions are fulfilled, they are happy and contented. If their desires and their ambitions are not fulfilled, they get excited. They do not even try to find out the reason why their desires have not been fulfilled.

Summer Showers in Brindivan, 1977, p. 241

0655: Some people want to have uninterrupted happiness. When you eat at 10 A.M. you do not go on eating every hour thereafter without break. You have to give a break for the food to be digested. So also when you experience pleasure it has to be digested before you meet with another bout of such experience. Just as you have to do some exercise for helping the food to digest, you have to go through the exercise of confrontation of pain after experiencing pleasure. Therefore, you must take what ever is given by God as good for you.

Sanathana Sarathi, February 1994, p. 51

0656: The great scientist, Einstein, regretted in his last years that his scientific findings had led to the production of the atom bomb. Sir Isaac Newton ended his life in a hospital with a mental affliction. True knowledge must secure mental peace and enduring joy. For this, contemplation of God is essential.

Sanathana Sarathi, March 1994, p. 60

0657: So, you have to do good deeds of you want to experience good results. Doing bad deeds man wants to enjoy good and beneficial results. It is folly to expect good results form bad deeds. Nature is like a mirror, which reflects only the object before it. In every human being, good and bad are co-existing. One should strive only to do good deeds which alone will lead one to liberation. Liberation is not an object that can be acquired form outside. It is a way of life itself. When you follow your inherent nature and cultivate good feelings, you can attain liberation from worldly bondage.   *Sanathana Sarathi, May 1994, p. 114*

0658: Restrain your desires. Experience the bliss of the Divine at all times. That is true humanness, which manifests itself when you think of God. Happiness is union with God. How much bliss can you experience if you see God in yourself and in everybody! Let all differences cease. Recognizing the divinity that is present in all, you should foster the principle of love and develop compassion in the heart. Love is God. It transcends all human relationships based on attachment. Develop divine and selfless love which is enduring and infinite. A true lover of God will experience no sorrow. On this auspicious day, ponder over the sacred teachings and develop the spirit of oneness.

Sanathana Sarathi, April 1996, p. 97

0659: I would advise all, and especially the overseas devotees who have come here from far off countries, to subject themselves to a process of self-inquiry. Is it right to call yourself a man? It is only a half-truth. You should be able to assert: "I am a man. I am not an animal". You will have to get rid of the animal qualities of ego, jealousy and hatred and develop human qualities of love, truth, sacrifice and happiness. Consider pain and pleasure as passing clouds, Happiness can be attained only by union with God. Worldly pleasure is transient.

Sanathana Sarathi, May 1994, p. 116

0660: Those who are after sensuous pleasures do not readily listen to the words of those who advise them to give up their evil ways. On the contrary, they try to drag others down to their level.   *Sanathana Sarathi, April 1995, p. 98*

0661: Excessive talking must also be avoided as it is waste of energy. When one gets weak due to wastage of energy, he is prone to get angry and develop hatred. You must, therefore, use the God-given energy for good purposes. Energy is a divine gift. By curtailing unnecessary talk and keeping silent, you can conserve energy. "Talk less and work more" is the golden rule to be adopted.
Sanathana Sarathi, May 1994, p. 118

0662: Anything done with expectation of reward gets tarnished by the desire for fruits and cannot be deemed real devotion. Devotion has been defined as desireless love for the Lord. Any prayer to God for fulfillment of a desire cannot be called devotion. God should be loved for His own sake. Love should be fostered for its own sake.

True devotion is a combination of selfless service and love.
Sanathana Sarathi, May 1995, p. 131

0663: The tainted life of man has to be purified by expelling the pollutants within man. What is pure and sacred has to be taken in. This duty has been forgotten. If you want to fill the stomach with wholesome and delicious food, you have to empty it of what is impure. One cannot relish good food when the stomach is full of bad stuff. This is borne out of everyone's daily experience. Hence every one should get rid of all the bad thoughts, evil intentions and bad feelings in him and fill the mind with good thoughts and noble feelings.
Sanathana Sarathi, December 1995, p. 316

0664: Over the ages, by identifying the "I" with the body, its true nature has been grossly underrated because of ignorance, perversion and false attachments. The truth is this "I" is subtle and incomparable. It is beyond change. This is the characteristic of divinity. Men have to recognize their inherent divinity.
Sanathana Sarathi, April 1995, p. 97

0665: God judges the devotee's love by the intensity of the feeling and not by the number of ways in which worship is offered.
Sanathana Sarathi, January 1996, p. 4

0666: Man today is dominated by selfishness and self-interest. Every action is based on selfish interests. Man has become a plaything in the hands of selfishness. Consequently he has forfeited peace of mind.
Sanathana Sarathi, December 1995, p. 317

0667: One may claim to surrender all his wealth, kith and kin and power and position to God. But this is not real surrender. One must realize: "I am in You, You are in me". God is one. The sense of separation between God and the individual should go.   *Sanathana Sarathi, September 1995, p. 231*

0668: Man has progressed a great deal in the physical and scientific fields; but with regard to morality and spirituality man has declined considerably. The reason is the deep-rooted growth of selfishness over the centuries. The entire human life is permeated with selfishness. This selfishness should be brought under restraint. Only then human life can be meaningful. Man should look at the world from the Divine point of view. Life is full of ups and downs. All these are transient. Man should use what is temporary (the body) as the base for realizing what is eternal, the Atma. These are inter-related.   *Sanathana Sarathi, May 1995, p. 132*

0669: Man cannot develop a yearning for liberation without passing through the initial stage of desire for worldly objects.   *Summer Showers, 1979, p. 134*

0670: Thoughts lead to action. There can be no action without thoughts. Hence, it is essential to entertain sacred thoughts. Everyone should realize that all the sorrows and miseries of modern man are due to his bad thoughts. Every man thinks that someone else is responsible for his troubles. This is not so. You alone are responsible for the good and evil that befalls you. You blame others because of your weakness.   *Sanathana Sarathi, September 1995, p. 227*

0671: Man today should reflect on his true nature. The Lord declares in the Gita, "The individual on earth is a fragment of my Eternal self." The import of this declaration is: "Oh foolish man, don't think you are only a composite of the five elements. You are a fragment of Myself."
        Sanathana Sarathi, September 1995, p. 227

0672: Every moment is auspicious if you dedicate your actions to God. If your mind is pure, other things do not matter.   *Sanathana Sarathi, May 1995, p. 134*

0673: Trust everything as God's work, what ever your vocation or profession. By dedicating all actions to God, you sanctify every act in daily life.
        Sanathana Sarathi, December 1995, p. 322

0674: All the forms in which God is worshipped are products of the human imagination. The proper way to experience God is to feel with all your inner being that you are the Divine self. That experience will make you feel the presence of the Divine in all beings and in all things. With that experience there will be no

room for hatred towards anyone. Such a one will not do evil deeds.
Sanathana Sarathi, December 1997, p. 312

0675: When praying to God, you should have a feeling of total surrender. If you are really keen about realizing God, if you are hungering and thirsting for God, then you should cultivate this all absorbing love. Mere expression of desire is not enough. You should endeavor to experience union with the Divine. If your heart is full of selfishness, how can you experience the Divine merely by a wish?
Sanathana Sarathi, December 1996, p. 310

0676: Every human being is potentially a messenger of God. But, today, men have become messengers of the Lord of Death.
They are traitors to their true human state. Humanness demands that everyone should manifest the Divinity within him. Everyone should be a real messenger of God and strive to promote peace and security in the world. There is no other path to be followed. God's message is sacred and totally free from self-interest.
Sanathana Sarathi, January 1996, p. 2

0677: Love of God does not mean giving up your normal duties. In the performance of these duties, every action should be done as an offering to God. Look upon the body as a moving temple, wherein God resides. Recognize that God is always with you and around you.
Sanathana Sarathi, January 1996, p. 4

0678: The quest for Truth really means discovering one's own inner reality. This eternal Divine Principle is in one and all. To experience this Divine, one has to develop certain sacred qualities.		*Sanathana Sarathi, January 1996, p. 24*

0679: All that I want you to do is to carry on your duties, place your faith in God and realize that there is one fundamental Reality underlying all things. When you get this realization, detachment will develop in you of its own accord. Detachment in not acquired by compulsion. As love of God grows, indifference to worldly things develops naturally.		*Sanathana Sarathi, November 1996, p. 294*

0680: The process of change is going on everywhere. A seed grows into a tree, an egg becomes a chicken. But man is failing to grow into the Divine. Instead he is falling into the demonic state.		*Sanathana Sarathi, March 1996, p. 62*

0681: The year is not responsible for the unrest in the world. Human actions alone are responsible. Every one should strive to work well and achieve good results. Every one has twenty four hours at his disposal. If out of this, six hours are used up in sleep, six hours for one's own private concerns and six hours for one's job, still six hours remain. How does one spend them? One should utilize them for rendering social service. One must embark on divine activity. In the present state of the world, if people do not take to divine activity, the conditions will get worse.   *Sanathana Sarathi, April 1996, p. 87*

0682: Spirituality means getting rid of attachment and hatred and looking upon the whole humanity as one. Every one should understand this inner meaning of spirituality.   *Sanathana Sarathi, March 1996, p. 65*

0683: By not getting excited over the angry words of a critic, one becomes superior to the critic. Otherwise, one descends to the same level as the critic. Bear no ill-will towards anyone.   *Sanathana Sarathi, June 1996, p. 156*

0684: In human life, righteous living and a good reputation are the two that are everlasting.   *Sanathana Sarathi, January 1997, p. 1*

0685: When a person believes whole heartedly in God, he will not come to grief. With their interests primarily in worldly benefits and material gains, men pray to God with their lips not their hearts. Rather than pray with lips, it is better to serve with the hands.   *Sanathana Sarathi, June 1996, p. 168*

0686: Men are engaged in the pursuit of wealth and position, but not in the quest of the Divine. They forget that lasting happiness and peace cannot be got by wealth, scholarship or position. Only good qualities can confer happiness because a good man finds a place in the Lord's heart.
                    Sanathana Sarathi, June 1996, p. 168

0687: The hard working farmer has no fear of starvation. The one who chants the name of God has no fear of worldly worries. The man of few words will be free from enmity. Though excessive talk man falls prey to quarrels. Everyone should cultivate moderation in speech. Restraint in speech is conductive to friendly feelings. The one who is careful in his behavior, doing all actions after due deliberation, will have no fear of danger.
                    Sanathana Sarathi, February 1996, p. 29

0688: With faith in the omnipresence of the Divine, man should engage himself in good deeds, cherish good thoughts and dedicate his life to good practices. His words should be words of truth. The ornaments he should cherish are truthfulness in speech, charity for the hands and listening to sacred lore for the ears.

Develop faith in your divinity. Then you will redeem your life. Follow your conscience. Make your heart pure.   *Sanathana Sarathi, February 1996, p. 40*

0689: You young people have to learn many things. First and foremost, get rid of arrogance. Earn a good name as a scholar, a man of character, endowed with a spirit of sacrifice. Realize that if you please God, you can please the whole world.
Sanathana Sarathi, February 1996, p. 33

0690: Pain is a gap between two moments of happiness. Happiness is an interval between two moments of pain.   *Sathya Sai Speaks, Volume IV, p. 29*

0691: When all are sliding down the easy path of flippancy, those who advise against it and warn the victims about the inevitable disaster are ignored and laughed at. Sunk in the search of pleasures and cheap recreation, people become deaf to the councils of the past and calls of the sublime.
Sathya Sai Speaks, Volume IV, p. 84

0692: Man cannot secure enduring bliss through physical pleasures. He has to discover that the source of this bliss is within himself.
Sanathana Sarathi, February 1996, p. 44

0693: If there is righteousness in the heart, there is beauty in character. If there is beauty in character, there is harmony in the home. If there is harmony in the home, there is order in the nation. If there is order in the nation, there is peace in the world.   *Sathya Sai Speaks, Volume IV, p. 42*

0694: The ways of the Divine should be properly understood. God exists not for one nation or one community. God incarnates on earth for the benefit of all mankind. Each one gets the reward according to his deserts. As are his actions, so are the fruits thereof. Hence, before doing anything, one should consider whether it is right or wrong. One should see that no harm occurs to anyone on account of one's actions. This is not easy for one who is attached to the pleasures of the body. All sorrow is related to the body and worldly desires.
Sanathana Sarathi, August 1996, p. 219

0695: What we have to safeguard and protect today are Truth and Righteousness and not the nation. When Truth and Righteousness are protected, they will protect the nation.   *Sanathana Sarathi, December 1996, p. 333*

0696: You must acquire the friendship of God. Once you acquire that friendship you can achieve anything. All happiness can be derived therefrom.
Sanathana Sarathi, November 1996, p. 281

0697: Joy and sorrow, profit and loss, light and darkness are pairs of opposites in which the absence of one is the sign of its opposite. For both the root cause is the Atma. All things originate from the Atma. Here is a flower. It has many petals. These petals appear distinct from each other. But all petals have emerged from the same single stem. The stem is the seat of the Atma, from which the petals have emanated. But we view the flower as a single object. The flower is one, but the petals are many. The petals have come out of the one stem.
Sanathana Sarathi, November 1996, p. 290

0698: Students should hold fast to God as the only true friend and supporter. When you have firm faith, the Divine will manifest Himself to you. This is the truth, the truth and nothing but the Truth.   *Sanathana Sarathi, November 1996, p. 299*

0699: If you have a pot with a hole in it, you can never fill it with water. In the same manner, if the pot of our mind has got many holes in the form of sensory desires, then all the work that we do will not fill our mind with sacred thoughts. Only when there are no holes, can your attempts become fruitful and take you to the Divine.   *Summer Showers in Brindavan, 1973, p. 99*

0700: The same God dwells in all beings. There is no justification for differences on the basis of religion. It is attachment to the body which accounts for religious differences. Do not regard the body as permanent. It is a water bubble. The mind is a mad monkey. Don't follow either of them. Follow the conscience.
Sanathana Sarathi, January 1997, p. 2

0701: He who is deluded by this relative reality is the worldly person; he who is aware that it is only relatively real is the spiritual practitioner.
Sathya Sai Speaks, Volume IV, p. 11

0702: Without understanding service and first becoming a servant, one cannot become a leader. Similarly, without being able to destroy, one cannot become a creator.   *Summer Showers in Brindavan, 1973, p. 57*

0703: The names of those who have endeavored to bring about material prosperity in the world without any thought of God will remain only as those inscribed on the surface of water. Such names will gradually be forgotten.
Even if it is a very powerful electric current, it will be no use to you if there

is only the positive aspect and you cannot combine it with the negative. On the contrary, if a machine is only on the negative and is not connected to the positive side of the electric current, the machine will be a lump of metal and no more. The world is like the negative pole. Divinity is like the positive pole. It is only by bringing them together that we can get peace and happiness.

Summer Showers in Brindavan, 1973, p. 101

0704: What are problems? Whatever they are, they are all transient in relation to eternity and of no lasting consequence. What are thoughts? They are creative force within man, and represent the free will given to man by God. Life should be full of joy and it will be, if you live your life in complete harmony with God.

Sathya Sai Speaks, Volume IV, p. 20

0705: Years of rigorous training make the soldier, who can then stand all the rigors of warfare. The heroic fighter is not made in a day. So too, the practicing spiritual aspirant who can win victories, is not made in a day. Restrictions and regulations, drill and techniques have been laid down for him also. Follow them sincerely and steadily and victory is yours.

Sathya Sai Speaks, Volume IV, p. 29

0706: Move forward towards the Light and the shadow falls behind; you move away from it and you have to follow your own shadow.

Go every moment one step nearer to the Lord and then, Maya, the shadow (illusion) will fall back and will not delude you at all.

Sathya Sai Speaks, Volume IV, p. 23

RELATIONSHIPS

0707: There should be an element of reciprocity in all human and personal relations. Love, sympathy, compassion and affection are always mutual. They cannot thrive in isolation. They atrophy and vanish wherever selfishness and jealousy manifest themselves. We must discharge our duties in a spirit of self-surrender, without consideration for wealth or recognition.

Summer Showers, 1979, p. 97

0708: Man should realize that his relationships with his family and friends, and all his worldly attachments, are primarily based on the physical body. A man and his wife are strangers before they get married. The relationship between a husband and his wife does not exist prior to their marriage. Similarly, no filial love could be there between a baby and its mother before the birth of the baby. It is only after the baby is born that the relationship between the child and the mother arises. All mundane bonds are ephemeral. The Atma that you really are knows no parents or other relations. To realize the truth that you are the Atma, you must acquire spiritual knowledge.

Secular knowledge is no doubt necessary to eke out one's living, but spiritual knowledge is essential if the purpose of life is to be fulfilled. Spiritual knowledge is comparable to the infinite ocean whilst the various branches of secular knowledge are like the rivers which ultimately merge in it. Spirituality enables an individual to harmonize the separate elements of his psyche into an integrated experience of the immanent Divinity. Secular knowledge, on the contrary, has brought about the dehumanization and the fragmentation of the human personality.   *Summer Showers, 1979, p. 166*

0709: You must keep the heart hollow so that is will be filled only by Divine thoughts. All human relationships are based on the body, while the relationship with God is from heart to heart. It alone is permanent and unchanging.
                    Sanathana Sarathi, May 1994, p. 125

0710: Consider spiritual life as "sugar" and worldly life, as "tasteless water"; since they are different, you have to mix the two all the time
in your daily routine to enjoy sweetness of life. Worldly wealth will no doubt attract lots of friends and relatives; the moment one loses the richness these friends and relatives will forsake you. Do not labor to amass wealth, but instead engage yourself in selfless service to earn credit in the bank of God.
                    Gems of Wisdom, Sayings of Sai Baba, p. 437

0711: When you associate with anyone, you are affected by the qualities of the other person. That is why it has been said: Through association with the good, develop detachment and solitude. Through seclusion, steady the mind. Through steadiness of the mind, get rid of all delusions. Freedom from delusion is liberation.   *Gems of Wisdom, Significance of Padanamaskar, p. 386*

0712: By developing attachment to persons and possessions, men created causes for their sorrow. By reducing their attachments and developing love in God, they can reduce their misery and increase their happiness. The more they love God, the more the bliss they will experience. Men are plunged in misery because they hanker after the physical instead of yearning for God. If men convert their desire for material objects into the desire for the Supreme, they will enjoy immense happiness. All that is necessary is for them, to see the Divine in everything in the phenomenal world. That will be true devotion. And work will be turned into worship. Make every act holy.   *Sanathana Sarathi, April 1996, p. 88*

RELIGION

0713: The goal of all religions is one. The underlying meaning of all names is the same. You must appreciate this oneness. Whatever name may be used, all are children of one God. All belong to the caste of humanity. The distinctions between religions are the result of historical and geographical factors. People may use diverse names for God, but God is one alone.

Sanathana Sarathi, May 1997, p. 129

0714: The word "religion" contains the prefix "re". "Re" means doing something again. The other part of the word connotes "unifying". Religion may be thus interpreted as reunion, the reunification of two entities separated by time or the restoration of their original organic unity.   *Summer Showers, 1979, p. 55*

0715: Based on their different regional and ethnic differences, people in different regions of the world developed different faiths and cultures. But the essence of all their beliefs is one and the same principle. That is the principle of love. There is no human being in the world without love. However, that love expresses itself in many ways. In a mental asylum there are people with many kinds of delusions. In a sense the entire world may be considered as a mental asylum. There are in the world people crazy about money. There are others who have obsessions regarding their health and sickness. There are others who are crazy about power and position. In this manner every individual is obsessed with some desire or other. There are, again, some who are obsessed with the idea of God. Of all these forms of madness, the madness for God in most commendable.

From birth to death, man is haunted by twelve kinds of worries. By worrying about God all other worries can be got rid of. You must seek to know that, by knowing which, all else can be known, by attaining which, everything else can be attained. The Upanishads have declared: If you knock, the door will open: If you ask, He will answer; If you seek, He will give you what you want.

Every one knocks at the door and asks. What does he ask? He does not knock at the right door. You must knock at the door leading to liberation. Man today knocks at the door leading to hell. Man, who should seek the bliss of the Spirit craves for earthly pleasures. Instead of seeking the Presence of the Lord as the supreme bliss, man is distancing himself from the Divine.

Sanathana Sarathi, March, 1997, p. 66

0716: People consider religion as a bundle of doctrines and of rigorous do's and don'ts prescribed for being followed. This is totally wrong. The sacred aim of religion is to remind man of his divine origin and help to lead him back to God.
Gems of Wisdom, Religion, p. 328

0717: Different religions were established to promote unity, fellow-feeling and devotion, which are the sacred qualities of mankind. Religion is intended to develop human personality and indicate the basic guidelines for right living. It enables man to live in harmony with his fellowmen. It is not restrictive concept. It provides a link between the individual and Divinity. Love, sacrifice, service and righteousness are the four limbs of religion.

It is indeed very unfortunate that religion, which has such high and sacred objectives is construed and practiced in a narrow way and propagated as a narrow creed. All religions propagate unity for promoting the well-being of society. All religions call upon people: 1. to adhere to the path of Truth and; 2. encourage development of good qualities. Thus, the essence of all religions is one and the same.
Gems of Wisdom, Religion, p. 328

0718: Religion is not a restrictive concept. Religion is intended to develop the human personality and indicate basic guide-lines for right living. It provides the link between the individual and the Divine.

All religions propagate unity for promoting the well-being of society. The welfare of the world is bound up with the well-being of society. All religions preached the greatness of spiritual purity. All religions called upon people to adhere to the path of truth. They also teach that good qualities are when all the scriptures proclaim the same truth, when the goal of all human effort in one, where is the basis for any differences? The paths are varied, but the destination is one and the same.
Gems of Wisdom, Religion, p. 331

0719: Religions have come into existence for the purpose of regulating human life. What is common to all of them is the principle of love.
Sanathana Sarathi, March, 1997, p. 58

0720: Love your religion so that you may practice it with greater faith, and when each one practices his religion with faith there will be no hatred in the world because all religions are built on universal love.
Gems of Wisdom, Religion, p. 329

0721: The divine manifests himself in many forms. God is worshipped in many forms for the joy to be derived from it. In ancient Rome many gods were worshipped as in Bharat (Ancient India). At that time there was no belief in one God. Then came Christianity. The concept of unity in diversity came to be accepted. In ancient Grease, Plato, the disciple of Socrates, was the first to point

out the immanence of the Divine in everything in the Universe.
Gems of Wisdom, Religion, p. 329

0722: All Faiths are inter-related and mutually indebted to each other for the principles they teach and the disciplines they recommend. The Vedic Religion was the first in time; Buddhism which appeared about 2500 years age, was its son; Christianity, which was influenced much by the Orient was its grand son. And Islam, which has the Prophets of Christianity as its base, was the great-grandson. All have Love as the Fundamental Discipline of the Mind, in order to chasten it and merge man with the Divine.   *Gems of Wisdom, Religion, p. 329*

0723: It is a mark of ignorance to consider one religion as superior and another as inferior. The teachings of all religions are sacred. The basic doctrines are founded on Truth. The Truth of the Spirit is the essence of religions, the message of all scriptures and the basis of all metaphysics.
Gems of Wisdom, Religion, p. 329

0724: The primary duty of human beings is to recognize that through the paths indicated by different religions are different, the goal or aim is ONE. Love, sacrifice, compassion, morality, integrity, and similar qualities are common to all religions. In different ways, all religions have sought to promote unity in diversity.
Gems of Wisdom, Religion, p. 330

0725: Religion is three fourths character. No person can claim to be religious if he merely observes the sacraments and fails to be upright and compassionate.
Sathya Sai Speaks, Volume II, p. 235

0726: The great saints who worshipped Christ, or Rama or Krishna or Allah were inspired by their profound teachings. But how many of the followers of these faiths live up to these teachings today? If the teachings of the founder of a religion are not followed can it be called a religion? Those who, in the name of religion, further their selfish interests are bringing disrepute to the founder of the religion.
Gems of Wisdom, Religion, p. 333

0727: It is essential to realize and act on the basis that the purpose of religion is to promote unity in diversity, banish divisive tendencies and make human beings lead ideal lives.   *Sanathana Sarathi, January 1997, p. 1*

0728: There is only one religion; the religion of Love. There is only one caste; the caste of humanity. There is only one language; the language of the heart. There is only one God; He is omnipresent.   *Gems of Wisdom, Sai Religion, p. 336*

0729: Love, Sacrifice, Service and Righteousness are the four limbs of religion. Religion brings out the divine and sublime feelings in man and makes him serve society. It evokes all that is great, blissful and good in men and demonstrates the unity of mankind.					*Gems of Wisdom, Religion, p. 334*

0730: All forms of worship and penance are only for control of the mind. They will not give you the realization of God. God is within you, around you, beside you. He is the only true friend. You develop friendship with worldly people, who may desert you when you are bereft of your wealth, power or status. God alone will be with you always.					*Sanathana Sarathi, May 1994, p. 116*

0731: There may be many paths for the same goal. You get confused because many preachers say many different things. You must choose one path, one road. God is one and he can be realized by love. Fill your hearts with love and distribute the love to others considering that all are sparks of the Divine.
					Sanathana Sarathi, May 1994, p. 117

0732: All religions will ultimately teach this aspect of oneness. While the teachings of all religions are one and are sacred, yet those who taught and preached these aspects of different religions, have created some differences because of their attitudes being different. To hate other religions or to look down on them is a very wrong thing to do. Creating differences by stating that one religion is at a lower level and that another is at a higher level, simply shows your ignorance. People who have such ideas, will begin to strengthen their faith in differences between these religions rather than their faith in God.
					Summer Showers in Brindivan, 1977, p. 176

0733: Spirituality means seeking to realize the oneness of all beings. There is only One. All came out of this One only. The entire creation itself came from the One. This truth is proclaimed in all religions. For instance, the name of Yesu (Jesus) itself spells out the truth. "Ye" means one, "su" means good. There is only one good. In the term Allah, "A" stands for Atma, "la" for "layam". Invoking Allah signifies merging in the Atma which is the One God. Names and forms are momentary and transient.					*Sanathana Sarathi, May 1994, p. 126*

0734: To divide man on grounds of religion is a crime against humanity . . . the whole of mankind belongs to one religion . . . the religion of man. All religions proclaim the unity of divinity . . . .for all men, God is the Father. As the children of God, all men are brothers; the basis for a spiritual God-based life is the indwelling spirit.					*Sathya Sai Baba, God as man*

0735: Of course rituals and prayers are necessary in the early stages of spiritual journey. They are the kindergarten of spiritual education. These rules and regulations regarding rites have to be extended and redirected to more socially constructive ends by thought, word and deed which can promote universal reverence, egolessness and equanimity.

Gems of Wisdom, Sins and Repentance, p. 357

0736: Morality and integrity, righteousness and charity, truth and tradition, forbearance and non-violence are basic tenets of all religions. These basic truths are common to all religions. But over the years men have forgotten these truths and have fostered divisive tendencies in the place of unity. As a result, respect for human values has gone. It is essential to recognize the Divine unity that suffuses all the diversity in human existence.   *Sanathana Sarathi, January 1997, p. 1*

0737: When you consider mankind as one species, God is only one, by whatever name you may describe Him, as Allah, Jesus, Rama, Krishna or Buddha. The Bharateeyas hold to the belief that God is one, though the wise may call him by different names. All religious scriptures and godly man have in all ages worshipped God as one. Therefore, no one should have feelings of differences or even entertain ill-will towards others. Cultivate the feeling of Fatherhood of God and brotherhood of Man. Bear no ill-will towards anyone. Help ever; hurt never.

Sanathana Sarathi, June 1994, p. 146

SERVICE

0738: Every man should recognize that the body has been given to him to render service to others. You must use the body for promoting the welfare of society. Of what use is the endless study of books if you do not use your knowledge for the good of others? A mind that is not utilized for imparting joy to others or a body that is not used for the service of others are totally useless. The best way to love God is to love all and serve all. Students should imbibe this ideal.

Sanathana sarathi, February 1997, p. 37

0739: If the individual is deluded into believing that he is serving others, then woe be to him, for there is no other at all. All are One. One man's sorrow is everyone's sorrow. The fundamental flaw is the ignorance of man. If only he was wise, he would have known that all individuals are waves in the surface of the selfsame ocean.   *Sathya Sai Speaks, Volume III, p. 68*

0740: Whatever talent a person has should be dedicated to the service of the rest of humanity, indeed of all living beings. Therein lies fulfillment.
Gems of Wisdom, Service, p. 151

0741: If you cannot pray for the total welfare of the community around you in whom God lives, how is it possible for you to worship an invisible God? The first thing you have to do is look after the welfare of the living community around you.
Summer Showers, 1974, p. 218

0742: Service to man will help your divinity to blossom, for it will gladden your heart and make you feel that life has been worthwhile. Service to man is service to God, for God is in every man, every living being and in every stone and stump.
Sathya Sai Speaks, Volume IV, p. 178

0743: Time moves fast like a whirlwind. The allotted span of life for the body is melting away every moment like a block of ice. However, even before recognizing what is his duty, man departs from this world. What is the aim of human life? What is a man's duty? It is to discover this truth that God has endowed man with a body. This body is given for rendering help to others.
Sanathana Sarathi, September 1994, p. 225

0744: God will not ask you when and where did you do service? He will ask, "with what motive did you do it?" You may boast of its quantity. But God seeks quality, the quality of the heart, the purity of the mind, the holiness of the motive.
Sathya Sai Speaks, Volume XI, p. 195

0745: Investigate, examine, and then you will realize the Self is better served by serving others.   *Gems of Wisdom, Weaknesses of Mankind, p. 135*

0746: Since everyone is of Divine origin, all must take a pledge to serve others. Those who cannot be loving towards others cease to be human. Man should not regard himself as a weak and imbecilic creature.
Gems of Wisdom, Service, p. 150

0747: A good son is one who sets an example by his conduct. One who pursues selfish ends cannot be a good son. A good son is one who reveres and serves his parents, who honors his preceptor, who is humble and respectful towards elders and who earns a good name by his service to society.
Sanathana Sarathi, February 1997, p. 39

0748: If you do not feel the call at the sight of human distress, disease or deviation from the right, how can you muster the determination and dedication necessary to serve the unseen, inscrutable, mysterious God? When you do not love man, your heart will not love God. Despising brother-man, you cannot, at the same time, worship God; if you do, God will not accept that hypocrisy. God is resident in every heart; so, if you serve any one, that service reaches the God within him: it brings to you the Grace of God.
Gems of Wisdom, Bhakthi (Devotion), p. 300

0749: Can one be happy by merely eating four good meals daily or (by) riding (in) prestigious cars or (by) living in many-roomed air conditioned bungalows? No. Happiness consists in helping others. It is brought about by giving up, not by hoarding. Catering to the senses makes man bestial. They will drag him into dirt and disgrace.
Gems of Wisdom, Service, p. 160

0750: The fulfillment of human life consists in the service that man renders without any thought or return, in an attitude of selflessness.
Gems of Wisdom, Service, p. 150

0751: The services to man is more valuable than what you call "services to God". God has no need of your service. Please man; you please God.
Sathya Sai Speaks, Volume V, p. 167

0752: Only that person can be said to lead a full human existence whose speech is adorned by Truth and whose body is dedicated to the service of others. Fullness in life is marked by the harmony of thought, word and deed.
Sanathana Sarathi; October, 1997, p. 26

0753: Every one should realize what one owes to the society in which one is born and from which one derives so many benefits. Young people should reflect on the question what gratitude they can show the society which has given them so much. What service are you doing to society?
Sanathana Sarathi, July 1997, p. 172

0754: Nature is the best teacher for mankind to learn the noble and sacred lesson of selfless sacrifice. Look at the trees which yield fruits for the enjoyment of others, without any trace of selfishness. The rivers flow for the benefit of others, providing water for quenching their thirst and helping them in many ways. Cows give delicious milk to the people without even a trace of selfishness. Similarly, a good person is one who strives ceaselessly to render help to his fellow-beings.
Sanathana Sarathi, May 1994, p. 122

0755: It is the duty of everyone born as a human being to engage himself in service to mankind, which is the only sure way to cross the ocean of worldly life and attain liberation from the cycle of birth and death.

Sanathana Sarathi, March 1994, p. 66

0756: What is the purpose of being a man? It is not for leading an animal existence. Man exists for service. Every man has to return to society by way of service what he has received from it. That service should be rendered selflessly in a spirit of sacrifice. Service is thereby converted to spirituality.

Sanathana Sarathi, March 1994, p.59

0757: You have to engage yourselves in Seva (service). Service does not mean mere rendering help to others of one kind or another. True service means participation in social activities after ridding yourself of egoism and possessiveness and manifesting your qualities of compassion and kindness. The aim is the refinement of your own good nature rather than giving succour to others. There is a Sanskrit saying which declares that greater than penance or pilgrimage, meditation or worship, is service to good people.

Sanathana Sarathi, December 1995, p. 313

0758: Ugaadi teaches man the lesson that he should perfect himself as an embodiment of divinity. You should not waste time, because a moment gone, will not come back. You are only looking after the needs of the body, eager to make it last longer. But you forget that Time is God. There is nothing that can supersede this. So the "Sadhana" you should do is to utilize your time in doing good deeds for the benefit of society at large and not to satisfy your self-interest. Don't waste your energy in unnecessary talk or gossip. God has endowed man with all the organs of perception and action, not for selfish activities, but to do godly deeds and help others. *Sanathana Sarathi, May 1994, p. 124*

0759: God loves those who serve others because He is in all of them. Whomever you may serve, consider it as service to God. Divinise all your actions. Treat every action you perform as God's work.

Sanathana Sarathi, January 199, p. 26

0760: Service involves sacrifice. You should sacrifice that which you consider very dear to you. Sacrifice brings about real communion with the Divine while carnal pleasure results only in disease. Control of the mind alone will lead to union with the Divine. *Sanathana Sarathi, May 1994, p. 126*

0761: Today you pray to a river: Oh river! Overflow with water. Don't pray to the river. Address your prayers to rain. When the rain responds, the rivers will get filled automatically. Likewise, when you serve society as the Divine, automatically your desires will be fulfilled.   *Sanathana Sarathi, December 1995, p. 284*

0762: The fulfillment of man's life on earth consists in filling himself with the love of God and channelising that love into acts of service, service of all who are embodiments of God. There is really no "other" or "neighbor". Everyone is oneself, for all belong to an indivisible whole. Service uplifts us, delights us, satiates our hunger, expands our horizons. Service to man is worship of God, in the one who gives and the one who gets, in the helper and the helped.
Sanathana Sarathi, June 1994, back cover

0763: Every person consumes quantities of food, but does not stop to calculate what he does in return to the society that helped him to live; the food must be transformed into service, either of one's best interest, or of the interests of others. You should not be a burden on others or an enemy of yourself.
Sathya Sai Speaks, Volume IV, p. 19

0764: You should all realize that the human body has been given to you solely to render selfless service. Such service broadens the heart, destroys the ego and generates bliss. Service also helps to promote consciousness of the brotherhood of man and the Fatherhood of God. Your task does not end there. You have at the same time to propagate the idea of the Spiritual oneness of all mankind. Mankind has to be led from dualism to non-dualism.
Sanathana Sarathi, January 1996, p. 25

0765: Service is the supreme aim of life. Everyone should seek to redeem his life by service to his fellow human beings. Render service to the extent of your capacity.   *Sanathana Sarathi, December 1995, p. 331*

0766: Render service to society, without which you cannot exist. Your welfare is bound up with that of society. Develop the feeling of oneness with all, loving all as members of one Divine family.   *Sanathana Sarathi, February 1996, p. 42*

0767: In rendering service, see that you do it for the satisfaction of your conscience and not to impress others. Treating service as an offering to the Divine, do it perfectly. Remember that God is watching every one of your actions. Be your own watchman to scrutinize what you do. When you do everything to satisfy your conscience, you are well on the way to Self-realization.
Sanathana Sarathi, January 1996, p. 26

0768: When we think of service, we seem to think of work which is a lowly kind of work, usually done by a servant. This kind of association of ideas, where service is thought of as something lowly, is not correct. In the context of service, we should realize that God Himself does a lot of service to the world in many ways.

Summer Showers in Brindavan, 1973, p. 58

TIME

0769: Man has been endowed with a body to practice righteousness. Man has to rise above the level of birds and beasts. Dedicate your lives to the service of your fellowmen. Do not lead an idle life. Many are wasting their time. Time is God. Time wasted is life wasted.   *Sanathana Sarathi, April, 1997, p. 95*

0770: It is imperative, therefore, for everyone to introspect and find out how much of his time is being spent in the mad race for fleeting material pleasures, and how much is devoted to the thought of God. The hedonistic man of the present day can spare no time for the contemplation of Divinity. The gates of Heaven shall be open for him only if he can think of God now and then. However, everyone seems to be totally preoccupied with the thoughts of one's children, friends, relations, money and material possessions. Man is thus denying himself the Bliss of spiritual experience, engaged as he is in the pursuit of the transient pleasures of the world. Man must, therefore, divert his vision from the world of temporal joys to the Bliss of the Atma within.   *Summer Showers, 1979, p. 87*

0771: Students must realize that just as a farmer must plough the field day and night, in rain and sun to sow his crop in time, similarly students must study hard during their youth, as that alone will shape their future. They cannot waste any time.   *Gems of Wisdom, The Teacher and Tomorrow, p. 196*

0772: You have to busy yourselves with activity in order to use time and skill to the best advantage. That is your duty, and duty is God. The dull and the inert will hesitate to be active, for fear of exhaustion or failure or loss. The emotional, passionate individuals will plunge headlong and crave for quick results and will be disappointed if they do not come in. The balanced persons will be active, because it is their duty; they will not be agitated by anything- failure or success. The godly will take up activity as a means of worshipping God and they leave the results to God. They know that they are but instruments in the hands of God.

Sanathana Sarathi, March, 1997, back cover

0773: Truth is something which people do not like. They look at if it is inimical to them. Untruth is something which people like. They look at it in a friendly manner. People like to buy intoxicating drinks like toddy and liquor, even if they have to pay a high price. They do not go in for health giving things like buttermilk and curds, even when they are quite cheap. This is what generally happens in most families.

Embodiments of the Divine Self, students! Time is moving away fast like the wind. The duration of our life is melting away like a block of ice. We will drop the body sometime or the other and leave this world without knowing the purpose of life. When life departs, the body will either be buried or cremated. What is distinctive of human life? Man must recognize the sacred task for which he has taken birth and if he spends his time only in fulfilling his sensuous desires he will be wasting his life. The duration of a life is an important factor. Therefore, time should be used properly.

Man is relying very much on his physical and mental strength. He is not making the slightest attempt to fall back on divine strength. Today, in the human heart, there is a huge fire. The fire of anger, the fire of lust, the fire of greed and the fire of attachment are always burning in his heart. He does not seem to realize that all these fires can completely consume him and reduce him to ashes. Unmindful of this, he carries on his life and makes grandiose plans for his future. Mother Veda has been kind to her children - the human race. To sanctify its cravings and to uplift the race, she has position the concept of Time - and its components, the years, months, days, hours, minutes and seconds. Even gods were declared to be bound by Time. The individual is caught in the wheel of Time and Space and rotates with it, unaware of any means of escape.

But, really, he is beyond the reach of Time and Space. The Veda is bent upon the task of making him know this Truth, and liberating him from this narrowness. *Baba, The Breath of Sai, p. 177*

0774: You hail this year as new, but it is not new at all. Nor is man a new arrival on earth. When man himself is not new, how can the year be new? Time is divided into night and day, weeks and years on the basis of the revolutions of the earth and the moon in relation to the sun. In truth, man should regard every moment as new, every day as new. Man is governed by these changes, but God is unaffected, God is changeless. *Sanathana Sarathi, May 1995, p. 131*

0775: Time is Divine, therefore, we must utilize time for performing good action without aspiring for the fruit thereof. The body is meant to enable man to perform sacred actions and spend time in such a manner that Time, the ultimate destroyer, is itself destroyed by him. The translation to the deathless state is brought about by spiritual evolution. Just as the minerals became the tree, the trees gave rise to animate life and the lower animals evolved into man, man too should evolve further and become God.

Man has only a short span of life, here upon earth. But, even in this short life one can, by wisely using the time with care, attain Divine bliss. *Baba, The Breath of Sai, p. 193*

0776: Looking at people who spend their time and wealth in deriving pleasure for themselves in decorating and beautifying their own bodies, we again make the mistake of thinking that they are very intelligent people. As time goes on and as bodies grow older in respect of people who spend their lives and money in fulfilling their sensory desires, we still consider them as men worthy of emulation.

These feelings are all wrong. Even though death is staring in the face of an individual every moment, we see him celebrating his birth anniversary, unmindful of the fact that he may meet his death any moment. How are we to interpret the minds and attitudes of such people who do not seem to bother about what happens to them the next moment?

The frog that has been swallowed by the snake and is shortly to die will itself try to swallow some worms, not realizing that death is ready at hand to snatch it. The snake in its turn does not know when it will be swallowed by the peacock. Unmindful of the fact that the peacock can swallow it any moment, the snake feels proud that it is swallowing the frog. In the same context, the peacock does not know what the hunter will do but in its turn is very proud that it is swallowing a snake. In this world, one person is swallowing another and the other person is swallowing yet another. Each person thinks that he is swallowing another and does not know that yet another person is ready to swallow him.

Baba, The Breath of Sai, p. 179

0777: Time spent in thoughts of God or adoration of the Divine is indeed well spent for it rewards you with a rich harvest on mental peace and courage. Time must be utilized for performing good action, sacred acts. Time is sacred.

The most highly prized article in the world is Time. If even a moment is wasted life is a waste. Time is most important. This body is given to us in order to use it efficiently every minute of its existence.

Human life has been granted to us in order to spend it in Karma as duty. In fact time is to be considered Divine, and adored as such. God is described as He who is Time. He who is beyond Time and He who teaches the principle of time. Time is the Universal Absolute.   *Baba, The Breath of Sai, p. 181*

TRUTH

0778: All real enjoyment of happiness, wealth and comforts is based on Truth. But, for the sake of transient worldly pleasures, sacred Divine Truth is forgotten. The ancients used to shun untruth as a poisonous snake. In the modern age, people are drawn to falsehood and not Truth. They make no effort to realize that they are themselves embodiments of Truth.

Sanathana Sarathi, October 1994, p. 274

0779: Today the number of persons adhering to truth is one in a thousand or so. Most of one's life is spent in untruth. A true human being should lead a life based wholly on truth. Man is in desperate search of bliss in the external world, forgetting that the source of bliss is within him. Ignorance of his inherent Divinity makes a man miserable. When the ignorance goes, his blissful nature reveals itself. Man has to realize this basic truth.

Sanathana Sarathi, August 1996, p. 207

0780: There can be no peace when man forgets the base and concentrates on the superstructure. Man is swayed by the delusion that life is meant only to enjoy, eat, drink and sleep. With this in view, he acquires wealth and increases his possessions. He makes no attempt to understand the purpose for which he is born in this world. Though he attempts to pursue right action, he fails because of his greed, ambition, lust and other temptations. Truth is the foundation on which the character of man is built. When Truth is not respected, the mansion of life collapses like a building that has a weak foundation. Man does not realize this and pursues a life of sensuous pleasures, ignoring Truth which is the Life Force that sustains his entire being.   *Sanathana Sarathi, April 1994, p. 95*

0781: Truth and Righteousness are at the root of human existence. No one should think it is difficult to adhere to truth. In fact, it is easier to speak the truth while it needs a lot of cleverness to tell an untruth and sustain it.

Sanathana Sarathi, April 1994, p. 97

0782: Human life is noble, sacred and precious. The way to realize this truth is to feel that you are a part of the Divine. Only human beings are endowed with the faculty to experience this truth. It is, therefore, the duty of every human being to strive for the realization of this truth.   *Sanathana Sarathi, July 1994, p. 169*

0783: The entire Cosmos is based on the bed rock of truth, wealth and welfare and all comforts and pleasures are dependent on truth. Wherever you turn, truth shines effulgently.   *Sanathana Sarathi, December 1993, p. 309*

0784: Man, it is said, is a combination of Truth and Righteousness. Truth is God. Righteousness is Divine. Verily there is no greater righteousness than adherence to Truth. We must live in the mansion of Peace, whose foundation is Truth, whose walls are Righteousness and whose roof is Love.
Sanathana Sarathi, August 1993, p. 204

0785: There is no greater virtue than Truth. Truth is not limited to one nation or one people. It belongs to all mankind. Truth sustains the cosmos. Therefore Truth is God. Follow the path of Truth. Speak the truth. That is the foremost spiritual exercise.
Sanathana Sarathi, October 1993, p. 257

0786: People feel that adhering to truth is difficult. Actually it is uttering untruth that creates difficult problems. All kinds of plans have to be made to cover up a lie. But to stick to the facts as they are is easy. Men should realize that it is easy to be good. It is going astray that causes difficulties. One cannot always avoid committing a wrong. But one should learn the lesson from it and avoid repeating it. That is sadhana.
Sanathana Sarathi, August 1993, p. 207

0787: Stick to the truth in whatever you do. This may not be easy. But through persistence truth will become a natural habit. Act according to the dictates of your conscience and not the promptings of your senses.
Sanathana Sarathi, January 1996, p. 25

0788: It is not enough to speak about one's ideals. One must live up to them. Today everyone must develop a compassionate heart and be truthful in speech. Truth is means to realize God. God is the very embodiment of Truth. Where there is Truth there is God.
Sanathana Sarathi, April 1996, p. 89

THE UNIVERSE

0789: This is the illusion that deludes mankind. What appears to the eyes, whatever reaches the ears, whatever occurs in the mind, whatever moves the heart. . . all these are capable of deluding the individual. The whole cosmos is an expression of the combination of the seen (drista) and the Seer (drashta). The world that we see is nothing but illusion. Brahman (the Universal Absolute) is the Seer. Creation is a manifestation of the union of the Seer and the seen.
Sanathana Sarathi, October 1991

0790: In the distant past, the world was enveloped in darkness. For millions of years the world was covered by a heavy mass of clouds. Then started a downpour which lasted for thousands of years. This was followed by the formation of oceans, mountains, rivers and forests on the earth. The dissolution of the clouds gradually dispelled the darkness enveloping the world. Then, the sun and the stars became visible from the earth. Man has to learn many things from the phenomena taking place in the universe.
Sanathana Sarathi, April, 1997, p. 93

0791: If we wish to discover the presence of the all-pervading Divine in the universe, we have to recognize the Divine in our daily life. Like the power of sight in the eye and the power of hearing in the ears, God manifests as consciousness in the human body. There is no place in the world where God does not exist. God pervades everything.

Creation is a manifestation of God. It is the form of God. It is called Prakriti (Nature). Hence, man, who is a child of nature, in inherently Divine.

Man is born with Divine qualities. Just as a sapling grows out of a seed, a flower from the sapling and fruit from the flower, God is the seed of the entire cosmos.

Man is intrinsically a combination of morality, righteousness and spirituality. Unfortunately, forgetting these basic qualities, man today is bereft of morality, righteousness and spirituality.

When we consider the sacredness of human birth, it is a shame that man should be so degraded today.

Man is an embodiment of Sath-Chith-Ananda (Being, Awareness and Bliss) which are the attributes of the Divine. But forgetting his humanness, man has descended to the level of the animal and behaves like a demon. People do not respect the words or elders of follow the teachings of the wise.
Sanathana Sarathi, May 1997, p. 120

0792: By developing fondness for the phenomenal world, we are becoming unmindful of our Divinity.
Summer Showers, 1979, p. 39

0793: Seen physically Nature alone is perceived. But seen with the spiritual vision the entire universe is Bhagavan alone. From the perspective of love everything will appear Divine.
Sanathana Sarathi, September, 1996, p. 241

0794: To God all objects in the universe are alike because they are manifestations of the Divine.
Sanathana Sarathi, May 1995, p. 113

0795: When it is realized that the mind is made up of thoughts and doubts, the elimination of thoughts is the means of restraining the mind. Thoughts are associated with desires. As long as desires remain, one cannot have detachment. It is necessary to limit desires.

Today men are subjecting themselves to all kinds of difficulties and problems because they are giving a free rein to the mind. This is where the vital role of the intellect comes in. The intellect enhances the power of man. It is the greatness of the intellect that distinguishes man. The intellect has the potency to comprehend the entire cosmos.   *Gems of Wisdom, Curbing the Mind, p. 46*

0796: Man is a pilgrim set on a long journey: he has started from the stone, moved on to the vegetable and animal and has now come to the human stage. He has still a long way to go to reach the Divine, and so he should not tarry. Every moment is precious; every step must take him further and nearer.
Sathya Sai Speaks, Volume VIII, p. 163

0797: The earth came out of the sun. The moon came from the earth.
Sanathana Sarathi, December 1995, p. 322

0798: People read all kinds of sacred books: the Geeta, the Bible, the Quran, The Granth Saheb and others. All these books confine their teachings to specific subjects. They do not cover other subjects related to the physical, the social etc.... But the cosmos itself constitutes the most comprehensive text-book, covering all subjects, the physical, the mundane, the ethical and the spiritual. The cosmos is therefore the best text. There is nothing you cannot learn from the universe.
Sanathana Sarathi, April, 1997, p. 93

0799: In the vast cosmos, man is like a speck. Essentially, there is no conflict between man and creation. Just as a child is entitled to enjoy the milk from its mother and the bee is entitled to enjoy the honey from flowers, there can be no objection to man enjoying the resources of nature. But as a result of uncontrolled desires and reckless exploitation of natural resources, Nature is exhibiting frightening disorders. Natural calamities like earthquakes, volcanic eruptions, droughts and floods are the result of disturbances in the balance of Nature caused by reckless exploitation of natural resources. Mankind today appears like a foolish man who is wielding the axe at the branch of a tree on which he is sitting.
Sanathana Sarathi, March, 1997, p. 58

0800: Today people think that spirituality has no relation to mundane life and vice versa. This is a big mistake. True Divinity indeed is a combination of spirituality and social obligations. National unity and social harmony are founded upon spirituality. Very few recognize that the Creation is a projection of Creator.
Gems of Wisdom, Where is God? p. 338

0801: The microcosm and the macrocosm are diffused with the same creative energy of 'Paramatma'. This mystical energy is known to the wise. Shut the doors of outward perception and look inwards. Transcend the barriers of thought. Travel along the mountain path of life and reach the peak, and listen to the primordial sound of the 'Pranava'. Come out of the dark night of the soul and divine grace will descend on you.

Summer Showers, 1979, p. 54

0802: If we examine the nature of the human state from the scientific point of view, it is found that the tissues of human body are composed of the four elements; hydrogen, oxygen, nitrogen and carbon. The unified expression of these four elements is the human condition. Ignoring this unity, scientists today are seeking to explore the nature of matter by breaking up the Love principle. The Spirit of Love is spirituality.

Splitting of Love is science. Scientists are exploring matter by dividing Love. They are unaware of the nature of Love. They are ignorant of Purity. Scientists are imbued only with a sense of inquiry into matter. Consequently, today there is a complete divorce between science and spirituality.

Gems of Wisdom, The Scientist and The Saint, p. 254

0803: It is not possible to consider Creation and Creator, Nature and God, as different or separate. Can we see that waves are separate from the Sea? They are of the Sea, with the sea and from the sea. Man too is of God, with and from God. The bubble is born in water, stays in water and is lost in water. The Cosmos too is a bubble born in the Absolute, exists as the Absolute and merges in the absolute or Paramatma. Nara (the human) is the bubble. God is the sea. Recognize this truth as the bubble cannot be conceived without positing water. The Cosmos, this World, cannot be conceived as without God.

Gems of Wisdom, Where is God? p. 341

0804: Scientists today are accomplishing any number of things. But they are unable to recognize the divine potency that exists in the human being.

Although all human bodies are made up of the same elements, hydrogen, oxygen, nitrogen and carbon, individuals vary in their mental and other qualities. What is the reason for these innumerable differences? What is the force that is behind these genetic differences? How do the scientists account for them? When they are able to understand the reason for these infinite differences, the scientists will achieve fullness in their knowledge. The truth is no one can determine the magnitude or range of the power of the Divine.

The fundamental difference between science and spirituality is this: Science is concerned with investigating the external phenomenal universe. Spirituality is engaged in exploring the inner workings if the Divine. The scientist is one who has an external vision. The one who has an internal vision is a saint.

Gems of Wisdom, Power of the Divine, p. 255

0805: The earth is the natural habitat of man. Why should he venture out of the range on the elements of which his body is composed and go places where to he has to take water, air and other essential requisites with him? When he goes to the moon, he does not leave anxiety, fear and falsehood behind. The moon that man has to voyage into is the MIND, not this dead satellite, with no capacity to illumine itself.   *Gems of Wisdom, Serve ever, Hurt Never, p. 403*

0806: There is infinite power within man, power that is beyond comprehension and which is Divine. If man did not have this power, how could he have gone to the moon? What is the power that makes the Earth revolve round itself? The power is within the Earth itself. This energy, present in man and in other objects has been characterized as cosmic energy.

What is this cosmic power? The Sun derives its energy and effulgence from this Cosmic Source. It is the same Cosmic source that accounts for the power of the human mind and the marvelous power of the eye to see the most distant star. With this power of sight, man is able to see the entire creation. There is no greater power than this. This boundless power is being recognized and exercised by each according to the level of his development. Because of man's ability to manifest the Divine boundless Cosmic energy, man is describer as a manifestation of the Divine. Humanness consists in manifestation of what is hidden and invisible to man.   *Gems of Wisdom, How is Man? p. 283*

0807: For the creation of this entire world, the main roots are sounds. If there is no sound, there is no world. If there is no sound, there is no creation. Thus, if the young people who belong to the modern world raise a succession of questions like, "where is God? Is there God? Where is He to be seen?" I get the feeling that they are only displaying a large amount of ignorance. Does this young man who asks a question like that not realize that the answer to his question is contained in the question itself? What is the question? The question is, Is there God or is there no God? The fact that the word God is contained in question asked, namely, "Is there God?" is proof that there is God. If there is no God, then the word God would not have come into existence. Can any of you give a name of something which does not exist?   *Summer Showers: 1972;*
Gems of Wisdom, Where is God? p. 341

0808: Nothing is absolutely real. The waking experience as unreal as the dream experience. When you are in deep sleep, there is no world at all. When you attain the super-conscious fourth stage the "I" alone remains, the universal "I" which was mistaken even in the sleeping stage as limited and particular.
Sathya Sai Speaks, Volume IV, p. 97

0809: The materialist doctrine proceeds on the assumption that consciousness is a product of sensory experiences and that the evolution of Consciousness is dependent on and is based on the evolution of matter. Inanimate matter is the basis for the materialist doctrine. Matter is finite. The Vedic doctrine repudiates the view that consciousness can arise out of physical senses which are limited by their origin in matter which is finite and limited. In total opposition to this materialistic doctrine, the spiritual view was projected to demonstrate the falsity of the concept of the primacy of matter over consciousness.

For the spiritual view, the basis of the Spirit (Atma), the Atma is infinite. The Vidantic doctrine proclaimed the infinite nature of the Self and pointed out that matter is both inert and finite. The Sruti declares: Tripaadasyaamrutam divi. "Consciousness constitutes three-fourths and one-fourth in inert matter." Thus, it is consciousness that animates matter and not matter that gives rise to consciousness. This is the essence of the spiritual concept. Oordhuva moolam Adhah-saakha, says the Gita (the roots are high up, the branches (of the cosmic tree) are below). This is further confirmation of the view that the material universe has emanated from the Universal Consciousness.

It is consciousness that activates matter and not matter that gives rise to consciousness. Modern technology has produced fantastic devices, harnessed new sources of energy, and turned out spacecraft for exploring the moon and other planets in outer space. But can all these instruments operate by themselves? No, behind them lies human ingenuity and intelligence. Greater than all the machines is man.

Man is consciousness incarnate. It is this consciousness that makes the machines move and it is indisputably clear that inert matter cannot create consciousness. Man is the highest object in creation. Man should not be a creature of instinct like the animals, which are subject to Nature, but should become a master of Nature. He should progress from the human to the Divine and be able to rule over Nature. An intelligent human being should not regard himself as bound by worldly attachments. It is not the world that binds man. It has neither eyes to see nor hands to grasp. Man is a prisoner of his own thoughts and desires. In his attachment to the ephemeral and the perishable, man does not realize that everything in the universe has come from the Divine and cannot exist without the power of the Divine.

Gems of Wisdom, Matter and Consciousness, p. 352

0810: Although physically there are on basic differences among human beings, many differences can be seen in their practices, their thoughts and feelings. Every nation is an aggregation of human beings. Differences in the life-styles of human communities in the various nations are quite significant though the natural environment over the globe as a whole is not so varied. This is a significant characteristic of the human predicament.

Truth is one. It is beyond mind and speech. It transcends the categories of time and space. Innumerable seekers have pursued different paths to recognize this truth. There are notable differences among the seekers of Truth. These differences do not affect the nature of the universe. On the contrary, these differences must be viewed as different stages in the understanding of the Cosmic process. It is the existence of these differences that has prompted the continuous search for a unifying principle.

Gems of Wisdom, Why is God not seen? p. 351

0811: There is at the base of everything a power that is continuously at work. It is the will of the Divine that maintains a balance in the universe. For example, during World War II millions of men died in Europe. Two years after the war ended, the children that were born were predominantly males. The Divine Will felt the need for maintaining a balance between the ratio of men and women.
Gems of Wisdom, Sins and Repentance, p. 355

0812: His consciousness can comprehend the cosmos, even as a mirror can reflect the firmament. The heart is a mirror in which one can see the entire universe. Realize from the moment that man is the embodiment of the Divine. Transcend the feeling of smallness. As you think, so you become. Therefore, divinise yourselves by constant reminder of your inherent divinity.
Sanathana Sarathi, July 1993, p. 187

0813: The real and the unreal are not two distinct things; one is the absence of the other, that is all . . . . There is only one appearing as two. . . . the pure mind reflects the Reality clearly - God that is the basis of self as well as the objective world. God is immanent in every particle in the universe. The clear vision can experience Him everywhere at all times, and that vision confers immeasurable inexpressible bliss.   *Gems of Wisdom, Why is God not seen? p. 350*

0814: There is an inner sky also, the sky in the heart. Just as the Sun and the Moon in the outer sky are hidden by clouds, the Sun (intellect) and the Moon (Mind) in the inner sky are also hidden and suppressed by thick clouds of vice and evil. So make all effort to remove these clouds by the strong gale of devotion to God.   *Sathya Sai Speaks; Volume X, p. 23*

0815: Just as there is oil in the sesame seed, butter in milk, fragrance in the flower, tasty juice in the fruit, fire in wood, there is Divinity in this vast Universe. The Divine is all pervasive and is present in every being. It is the Divine Power inside that makes it possible for the eyes to see and ears to hear. The entire creation is the expression of the Will Power of God. Prakriti (Nature) is a manifestation of the Supreme Divine (Paramatma). Man is born to manifest and reflect Divinity. All constituents of Nature reflect their inherent qualities. Man also has to do so but is not reflecting his innate human quality.
Sanathana Sarathi, August 1997, p. 203

0816: Wherever there is smoke, there should be a source in the form of cinders and burning coal; so also for a running train there must be someone called a driver who is responsible for the running of that train. Even for the traffic lights which come up automatically, there must be a source which makes those lights function. While this is so, should there not be one who is responsible for all the creation we see around us?   *Summer Showers in Brindivan, 1977, p. 133*

0817: As soon as the sun rises the day begins, and as soon as the sun sets the night begins. We do not have two suns to demarcate night and day. By rising, the day starts and by setting, the day comes to and end. If we could go deeper, we would know that there is neither a rising, nor setting sun. Because of the revolutions of the earth, we get the impression that the sun is rising or it is setting. In reality, it neither rises nor sets. If we inquire into the duality according to the path of wisdom, we find that beyond the duality there is oneness.

Baba, The Breath of Sai, p. 199

0818: All the diversity you see in creation is a manifestation of the Indivisible One. The cause is the same for both differences and oneness. All the changing entities are based upon the One that is unchanging.

Sanathana Sarathi, February 1995, p. 37

0819: The one and only truth is Brahman. Because it is being projected as this material creation, we see by illusion the world around us. Without milk, you do not get curds. Without curds, you do not get butter. Without Brahman, you do not get the projected world.   *Summer Showers in Brindivan, 1977, p. 151*

0820: Creation posits a Creator; nothing can happen without the Will to make it happen. Before the beginning of things, there must be some Will that willed them to become. It can only be He that has become all this, whatever be the name or form that these have assumed. That Will is Love, It is Wisdom. It is Power, It is Bliss.

If man is valued at his true worth, and treated as a Divine Spark enclosed in the body, then he will rise into new heights of achievement and produce all the necessities of life in profusion. He will cultivate the inner vision and realize that he is not the body or senses or mind or even intellect. He will be full of love and self-confidence.   *Baba, The Breath of Sai, p. 220*

0821: You have to realize that Nature is also a manifestation of God. Hence, Nature should not be ignored. Nature is the effect and God is the cause. Hence you should recognize the immanence of the Divine in the entire cosmos.

Sanathana Sarathi, July 1996, p. 178

0822: Reflections of the sun shining in the sky can be seen in the oceans, rivers, the lakes and in wells. Though the reflections are varied, the sun is one alone. The Divine is present in man like the unseen thread which holds a garland of gems together. The entire cosmos is permeated by the Divine and is the visible manifestation of the Divine.   *Sanathana Sarathi, October 1995, p. 261*

0823: The entire Cosmos, consisting of animate and inanimate objects, is dependent on God. The Divine is governed by Truth. That Truth is governed by noble beings (Uthamaadheenam). The noblest being is Divine. Every human being is inherently noble. It is this nobility that constitutes his divinity. The Divine manifests Himself in human form. There is no need to search for the Divine as a distinct entity somewhere else. Man must strive to realize the Divinity within him.
Sanathana Sarathi, August 1994, p. 214

0824: Why does man get Aananda (bliss) when he contemplates the Cosmic and the Universal? Because he himself is the Cosmic, the Universal!
Sathya Sai Speaks, Volume IV, p. 61

0825: The Divine is omnipresent. All of you are forms of the Divine. All of you are endowed with electro-magnetic energy, atomic power, heat and other forms of energy. The magnetic energy is the most important power in man. From this magnetic energy comes electrical energy. The strength of the electrical is related to the strength of the magnetic energy. When the electrical energy and the magnetic energy come together, the divine power operates. This divine power does not come from outside. It is within human beings. Our very form is divine. That is why I address you all as "Embodiments of the Divine Atma."
Sanathana Sarathi, March 1995, p. 61

0826: The primary requisite for man is to realize the divine potency in him that is the source of all the faculties and talents in him. This is true whether one is an atheist, a theist or an agnostic. No one in the world can get on without this energy. It may be called by different names. Names are not important. The energy is one. It is this divine energy which directs mankind on the right path. Men should strive to recognize the presence of the Divine even in small things.
Sanathana Sarathi, February 1995, p. 31

0827: There is the body. There is the world. There are forests, trees and many other things. In referring to all these, we use the word "is" - that it exists. This term "is", signifying existence, proclaims the fundamental fact about man. There is only one thing that exists. But man forgets this Divine Reality because of his selfishness and self-centeredness. The latter reflect his egoism and ostentatiousness. It is only when the last two are extinguished, will man's inner Divinity manifest itself.   *Sanathana Sarathi, December 1993, p. 312*

0828: Creation has to be viewed as a Cosmic Stage. God is the director and dramatis personae in this play. He assigns all the roles of the characters in the play. All creatures in the world are manifestations of the Divine. The good and evil in the world are expressions of the Divine consciousness. Man should not be misled by these expressions. Behind all the various actions of the actors, the

Divine director is at work. It should be realized that though names and forms may vary, languages and nationalities may bedifferent, the human race is one in its divine essence. All are sparks of the Divine- The Lord declared in the Gita: "All beings in the world of the living are aspects of my Eternal Self."

Sanathana Sarathi, February 1995, p. 37

0829: Words originate in the mind. But, when it comes to the tongue (body), it appears different under different situations. When it goes beyond the mind, the word becomes Truth itself. Vedas call this Truth as "Bhur". It is the radiation. In the materialization of body, this truth is all pervasive and is the vibration of that truth which is the conscience. Hence from Radiation comes Vibration: from Vibration comes Materialization.   *Sanathana Sarathi, October 1993, p. 270*

0830: We light many candles with the flame of a single candle. But remember, only a burning candle can light other candles. An unlit candle cannot light other unlit candles. Only one who has earned wisdom can enlighten others who are in ignorance. One who is himself unilluminated cannot illumine others dwelling in darkness, Maya. One must light his own lamp from the universal light of love and thence forward he can transmit illumination to all who seek and strive. All lamps shine alike since they are all sparks of the Param Hyothi, the Universal Luminosity that is God.   *Sanathana Sarathi, February 1995, back cover*

0831: How can man realize the Truth? Only when he experiences non-dualism. As long as he is steeped in dualism (that he and the Divine are different), he is bound to be racked by the opposites: joy and sorrow, the real and the unreal.

All that exists in the cosmos belongs to God. But man imagines that he is the owner of various things and is a prisoner of the conception of "mine and thine". In reality all are only trustees of the property belonging to the Divine. This means that everyone has to consider himself as a trustee for the world's goods. A bank cashier handles an enormous amount of money. None of it belongs to him. He cannot use it for himself, but has to ensure its safety and right use. Likewise, all are trustees responsible for the proper use of the goods entrusted to them. No one can claim ownership.   *Sanathana Sarathi, January 1995, p. 13*

0832: If you want to transform the world, to promote all-round prosperity in the country, to make the prayer that "all people should become happy" become reality. Develop faith in the Self. Never forget God. Without God there is no universe. Let the non-believers have their way. But they have no right to question the beliefs of others. To ask for physical proofs of the existence of experience like bliss or love or for subtle things like the fragrance of a flower is impracticable. To deny the reality of love on the grounds that it has no recognizable form is meaningless. Love may have no form, but the mother who exhibits love has a form.

All beings are manifestations of the Cosmic Divine. The forms are different but the spirit that animates them all is One; like the current that illumines bulbs of different colors and wattage. Cultivate this feeling of oneness and do not be critical of any faith or religion. Dedicate your lives to the service of your fellow beings. Thereby you will be redeeming your lives.

Sanathana Sarathi, August 1995, p. 222

0833: If a piece of charcoal is kept apart from fire, it cannot burn. Both must be brought close together and you must use a fan to make the charcoal catch fire. Love is the fan which will make you glow with divine effulgence. This is the truth proclaimed by the Upanishads, which say: "You are God". You think you are only the body. The body is inert without the soul which is the Life Force.

You need not go anywhere searching for God. Divinity is within you. Just as there are many limbs in the body which are activated by one heart inside, the same God is the Life Force for all beings. The entire Universe is a reflection of the Supreme Being.   *Sanathana Sarathi, May 1994, p. 115*

0834: All that you see, hear, think and do are due to the power of Brahman (the Absolute). The feeling that you are the doer and the possessor is the source of all troubles. It is only when man realizes that everything is permeated by the Divine bliss. The phenomenal world enables man to participate in mundane activities related to the physical, the social and the natural. But human life should not be confined to these alone. The sensory life is based on the inner life. Life and the world are lifes two sides. The world is external and life is internal. The phenomenal universe is based on the inner subtle entity.

Sanathana Sarathi, June 1994, p. 147

0835: Remember that the cosmos is changing constantly. The minutes that have passed cannot be ever retrieved. So the past is not ours anymore; the present slips from our grasp; the future is unknown! The world is a caravan inn where man can rest a while during his pilgrimage to his source- the Divine. It is a "bridge, wide and strongly built; but no one can build a house thereon for his permanent residence".   *Sathya Sai Speaks: volume X, p. 212*

0836: In the cosmic context, nature is the mirror. God is the viewer. All that is reflected in nature is Divine. The One alone exists. The object and the image appear because of the presence of the mirror. When there is no mirror, there is no image. This is the mystery relating to nature and the wonders of the Lord. The glories of the Lord are multifarious and marvelous beyond words.

God's arithmetic is different from mans. For instance, when a mirror is placed before you, you have three entities. Yourself, the mirror and your image. When you take away the mirror, according to ordinary arithmetic, three minus one should be two. But when the mirror is removed only you remain. Three minus one becomes one.   *Sanathana Sarathi, October 1996, p. 277*

0837: Deeming the physical body alone as real, man goes after worldly objects and ultimately ends up in misery. Man must take the spiritual path. This means that one should recognize the entire cosmos as an image of the Divine. Once one has this conviction, evil can never approach him. He experiences bliss at all times and everywhere. He desires that all should be happy.

Unfortunately, most people today do not cultivate such a broad feeling. They are immersed in concerns about themselves and their family. They should transcend these narrow feelings and have regard of society as a whole. They should deem service to society as service to God.

Sanathana Sarathi, August 1995, p. 200

0838: It is purity of mind that helps to sublimate mankind, directs it towards God and enables it to manifest the inherent divinity in man. "What is perceived is liable to perish" (says an aphorism). That which is seen, that which appears to be real, is bound to pass away in the stream of time. All that is apparent is the phenomenal world is bound to disappear sometime or other. We should make every effort to know that which is invisible but imperishable. All external objects seen with the eye are bound to disappear.

Sanathana Sarathi, December 1995, p. 319

0839: Do not divorce yourself from nature. The cosmos is permeated by the Divine. Hence recognize the Divine even in your enemy. His heart is bound to change when you love even the one who has harmed you, he is also bound to change. Do not allow your love to be affected in any way.

Sanathana Sarathi, December 1996, p. 313

0840: Human life is immensely precious. But this sacred life is haunted by troubles of various kinds in daily living. Like is like an ocean carrying waves of pleasure and pain. In his ordinary life man is driven by innumerable desires to seek worldly pleasures of various kinds. This precious life is rendered meaningless and worthless by the pursuit of these mundane desires.

The body is essential for living. Without it man cannot accomplish anything. Human life is a composite of body, mind and spirit. But man today ignores the mind and spirit and wastes his life by preoccupation with the body alone.

The mind is the most important organ in the body. It is vital for doing anything. Man's life is based on the mind. The universe is filled with mental consciousness. The cosmos is rooted in the mind. The mind is a bundle of thoughts. Hence man has to purify the mind by sacred thoughts. Only when he has noble thoughts he can lead an ideal life. Out of thoughts are born the desires. Desires activate the mind. Hence it is necessary to keep desires under control.

Sanathana Sarathi, December 1995, p. 330

0841: All that one sees in the entire universe is a manifestation of the Brahman.

Some people declare: "Where is Brahman, and what are we, petty human beings? How can we be equal to the all encompassing Brahman?" This is not correct. You are that omnipotent, all-pervading Brahman. Because of your worldly attitude, you are not recognizing the Reality. You are separating yourself from the Divine. All that you see is Brahman. To search for God as something different from you is a delusion. But this truth is not easily recognized by man.

When you look at the ocean, its endless series of waves and the foam from the waves, they all appear separate from each other. But the truth is they are all one. The water in the waves and in the foam comes from the same ocean and has the same qualities.   *Sanathana Sarathi, August 1996, p. 200*

0842: You are the formless come in the form of man, the Infinite, come in the role of the Finite, the formless Infinite appearing as the formful Infinitesimal, the Absolute pretending to be the Relative, the Atma behaving as the Body, the Metaphysical masquerading as the merely Physical. The Universal Atma (Self) is the basis of all being. The sky was there before houses were built under it. It penetrated and pervaded them for some time; then, the houses crumbled and became heaps and mounds; but, the sky was not affected at all. So too, the Atma pervades the body and subsists even when the body is reduced to dust.
              Sathya Sai Speaks, Volume IV, p. 44

0843: This vast cosmos, consisting of moving and unmoving objects, is permeated with truth. All names and forms are founded on Dharma (Righteousness). Dharma is the form of God. The Spirit (Atma) which is present in the subtlest of the subtle and vastest of the vast as a witness, is verily the Brahmam (the all- pervading Consciousness).

All the objects in the universe are made up of atoms. The atom is the embodiment of the Spirit (Atma). Hence there is no place in the universe without the Atma or Brahmam.   *Sanathana Sarathi, June 1996, p. 153*

0844: The whole cosmos is associated with plurality based on the distinction between "I" and "this". "This" refers to the seer. Without the seer, the seen cannot exist.

This is a cloth. The reference to the cloth cannot be made without using the term "this".

This is a glass. Here, again we cannot refer to the tumbler without using the term "this". The term "this" has to be used to refer to a specific object. When I say, "this is a hall", the statement points to a specific object that is perceived.

All names and forms are associated with objects of perception. It is the seer who testifies to the existence of what is perceived.
              Sanathana Sarathi, December 1997, p. 310

0845: Human beings are different in form and name. Oneness amongst them can be achieved only by a feeling of oneness in thought, by a recognition that the whole cosmos is permeated by the Divine.

God is the cause, the world is the effect. In this marvelous universe, why is man unable to recognize his true nature. Divinity is present in every atom of the cosmos. You have to realize that you are that Divinity.

Sanathana Sarathi, October 1996, p. 259

0846: The basis of the Advaitic doctrine is the spiritual oneness of the entire cosmos. It is the Spirit that is common to all beings. The Spirit is the source of all beings and their ultimate destination.

The Atmic principle resides in the heart of every being. Hence there is no need to go in search of God. You are the Divine.

Sanathana Sarathi, October 1996, p. 273

0847: The cosmos is a creation of the Divine. It is surcharged with energy. This energy is not localized at a particular point in space or in time. Though this energy is all-pervading, man is not able to recognize its divine nature. As he cannot recognize it, he presumes that it does not exist. Electrical energy is present all the time (in electrical installations). But its presence is recognized only when a bulb is switched on. Likewise, though God is omnipresent, His divine effulgence will shine only in those who adore Him with a pure heart.

Sanathana Sarathi, September 1995, p. 226

0848: Recognize the fact that the whole universe is within you. You have all the powers in you. They are derived from the Divine Spirit within you. It is the Divinity which endows you with a free will. Forgetting the supreme power of the Spirit, people place their reliance on the powers of the body, the mind and the intellect.

Sanathana Sarathi, January 1997, p. 3

0849: Forgetting the spiritual basis of the universe man gets entangled in misery through his worldly attachments. It was out of a recognition of this truth that Buddha declared: "Everywhere there is sorrow. Everything is momentary and everything is perishable." To consider worldly things as permanent is the cause of sorrow. If man recognizes that the world is permeated by the Brahmam, which is all bliss, he will free himself from the cause of sorrow.

Sanathana Sarathi, June 1996, p. 153

0850: Above everything, if one has firm faith in God, one can face the future with confidence. There is no room for doubts as to who is God and where He is to be found. God is the Cosmic Form (Viraata-Swarupa). The whole universe is the manifestation of God. What does God teach? The lessons are given through Nature (Prakriti) which conveys lessons to mankind. The earth, for instance, is revolving round itself at a speed of 1000 miles an hour. This is going without rest. This revolution of earth produces night and day. This enables man to have a time for work and time for rest. In addition, the earth is going round the sun at a speed of 66,000 miles per hour. This motion of the earth is responsible for the changes in seasons. The changes in seasons cause rainfall, enable the cultivation of crops and help people to live in comfort. The earth thus is a visible manifestation of God. The ancients hailed the earth as "Bhoomaatha" (Holy Mother Earth) for this reason. All the essential necessaries of life come from the earth. The earth thus teaches man that he should do his duty even as the earth itself is performing its duties.   *Sanathana Sarathi, April 1996, p. 86*

0851: Nature in its myriad forms is the effect. God is the cause. The entire cosmos is a manifestation of cause and effect. Hence the universe is a manifestation of the Divine.   *Sanathana Sarathi, June 1996, p. 153*

0852: From the infinite ocean of Sath-Chith-Ananda (Being-Awareness-Bliss), innumerable living creatures emerge like waves. While the Divine is in the state of Sathyam-Jnanam-Anantham (Truth-Wisdom-Infinity) man is in the state of Sath-Chith-Ananda. Embodiments of Divine Atma! When you fill your vision with love, the whole creation will appear divine to you.

  The cosmos appears to you as a manifestation of diversity, but in reality there is no diversity. No one makes any effort to discover the Divine unity that underlies the diversity.   *Sanathana Sarathi, August 1996, p. 200*

0853: How many realize the wonders in God's creation. There is a chick inside the egg. A huge tree comes out of a small seed. A human being is born from a human being. Who is responsible for all this? Only the Divine will. Without recognition these miraculous powers of the Divine, people make much of human achievements.   *Sanathana Sarathi, October 1996, p. 264*

WEALTH

0854: People in the world today are taking to evil ways and cherishing evil thoughts the like of which have never before prevailed. Men are consumed by a limitless passion for wealth and power. No doubt money is necessary for meeting one's daily needs. But even here there should be a limit. The vast ocean, when it swells beyond its bounds, causes disaster. The food that is required for sustaining the body is conductive to health only when it is consumed within limits. Over-eating poisons the physical system. Food may give satisfaction or cause illness. By his food habits man is becoming a prey to disease. Food is essential, but it must be taken within limits for it to be wholesome. Likewise, health is essential but within limits. When there is excessive wealth, many dangers ensue. With excessive wealth man turns arrogant and loses the sense of discrimination between right and wrong.   *Sanathana Sarathi, December 1994, p. 310*

0855: Together with the growth of one's wealth, one's spirit of sacrifice should grow commensurably. Increase in wealth should bring about an increase in generosity. *Sanathana Sarathi, December 1994, p. 31*

0856: When money earned by honest means does not always confer happiness, how can you get happiness through money earned by dishonest means? Hence, it should be realized that excessive wealth can never confer peace of happiness. When you have large wealth, offer it for good causes to help others. Thereby you will derive satisfaction. *Sanathana Sarathi, December 1994, p. 311*

0857: What is the wealth that one should really seek? It is the wealth of Divine Wisdom. Pursuit of this knowledge is the real quest for wealth, not the pursuit of money and possessions. It is "Jnana Aiswarya" that one must seek. Only that knowledge will lead man to the goal of human life. *Sanathana Sarathi, April 1994, p. 96*

0858: People should regard all wealth as coming from God to be used for sacred proposes. No one brings anything with him at birth and carries anything with him at death. All relationships in between are transient. Treat all alike. Even bad people will be transformed if you treat them with love. *Sanathana Sarathi, January 1996, p. 4*

0859: You know from the experience of the Cauvery River floods that nothing can save a man from drowning in the floods, neither status, nor caste, nor wealth nor even health, unless he knows the simple art of swimming. Need I say that crossing the ocean of worldly life, reaching the other shore of the sea of Birth-Death, is similarly possible only for those who know the art of spiritual discipline? Those who are trying to build the human community on a foundation of wealth, are building on sand; those who seek to build it on the rock of righteousness are the wise. *Sathya Sai Speaks, Volume IV, p. 17*

WISDOM

0860: In all that man does with a view to love himself, it is not possible for him to ignore loving others. Without cultivating love for others, you can never cultivate love for yourself. Sorrow for yourself is gained by hurting others. *Summer Showers, 1973, p. 2*

0861: Remember always that it is easy to do what is pleasant, but it is difficult to be engaged in what is beneficial. Not all that is pleasant is profitable. Success comes to those who give up the path strewn with roses and brave the hammer blows and sword- thrusts of the path fraught with danger. As a matter of fact, no road is strewn with rose petals. Life is a battlefield, where duties and desires are always in conflict. Smother the fiery fumes of desire, hatred and anger that rise up in your heart. It is sheer cowardice to yield to those enemies that turn you into beasts.   *Sanathana Sarathi, May 1997, p. 139*

0862: A mans strength is considerably reduced by his anger. The Lord is not visible to the non-believer. No one can expect to receive whatever he prays for, because in his ignorance he may ask for what is not good for him. The wise man will not seek anything from God, but leave everything to God.
                    Sanathana Sarathi, September, 1993

0863: Wisdom lies in the practical application of theoretical knowledge to life and its problems. You may memorize all the seven hundred verses of the Bhagavad Gita, recite the Vedas or read the puranas, but there will be of no avail unless you put into practice the sacred teachings contained in them. The assiduous study of the scriptures will be a futile exercise if the truths propounded in them are not translated into action.   *Summer Showers, 1979, p. 106*

0864: It is disingenuous on the part of people to plead that in their busy preoccupation's they have no time to think of God. Persons who waste their time watching T.V. or playing cards in clubs cannot pretend that they cannot spare a few moments for God. Make proper use of time. Time is sacred. Time is Divine. Dedicate every activity to God.

Seek to serve society and your fellow beings. There is no need to worship anyone. People worship inanimate idols, but ignore the needs of living beings around them. What kind of worship is it which ignores the needs of fellow human beings? God comes in human form. Human beings are Divine.
                    Sanathana Sarathi, May 1997, p. 123

0865: When you see the world with the eye of divine bliss, you will find bliss everywhere. If there is hatred in your vision, you will see hatred everywhere. Hence, change your vision to start with. Look at the world with the vision of peace, love and compassion. Then the whole world will appear loving and peaceful. When your heart is filled with love, you will experience the Divine in the entire cosmos. See the Divine in everyone. Eschew hatred and ill-will.
                    Sanathana Sarathi, May 1997, p. 125

0866: From today try to cleanse the heart of whatever impurities there may be in it. How is this to be done? One, by meditation on God. Secondly, by service to society. By these two alone is purity of the heart achieved. If you secure the love of God, you can secure anything. There is love in you. Use it to win the love of God.   *Sanathana Sarathi, May 1997, p. 125*

0867: Wisdom resides in every heart like an effulgent beam of light. In the modern age, it is described as superconsciousness. Our consciousness is the wakeful state. The dream state is called subconsciousness and the state of deep sleep is unconsciousness. Beyond these, there is the Turiya or the fourth state, that of superconsciousness.

You should strive to manifest the divinity latent in you and realize that the superconsciousness in you is your real Master. You must follow that Master, face the Devil or the evil tendencies in you, fight them to the end and finish the game of life with success.   *Summer Showers, 1979, p. 50- 51*

0868: People greet the new year as if it is going to confer on them some new benefits. The good or evil, gains or losses, the renown or infamy experienced by people are not the outcome of the passage of years. They are the consequences of their own actions. We should not consider the Lord, who is the Spirit of Time, as likely to cause good or ill to us. Our actions, good or bad, bear fruits according to their nature.

Many are wondering what troubles and losses the new year will bring. For all our troubles and difficulties the year is not responsible. Our conduct alone is responsible. If our actions are good the results will be good. Bad actions will lead to bad consequences. People think that good and bad are related to bad time. Not at all. Their thoughts are the cause. Hence, they should develop good thoughts and do good deeds. They should cherish good feelings and associate with good persons.

People should realize the preciousness of time. Most of the time available is wasted by people. This is utterly wrong. Time should be used always for right purposes. That is the foremost duty of every man. Waste of time is waste of life. The Lord of Time protects those who take refuge in Him, even against the Lord of Death ("Kaala"). Time takes its revenge on those who misuse it. A nations' prosperity is dependent on how people use their time in the performance of good actions.   *Sanathana Sarathi, May 1997, p. 121*

0869: As long as people adhere to truth, prosperity will descend on them. Truth is that which is valid for all the three categories of time: past, present, and the future. Truth is Divine. The one who adheres to Truth will lack nothing in the world.

Fame will follow the man who has the spirit of sacrifice.

In the world today both truth and sacrifice are rare. These two are the proper goals for human existence.

Knowledge is gained by the extent to which it is diligently pursued. Diligent study is essential for the acquisition of knowledge. The Geeta has declared that earnest practice leads to success in meditation. Meditation helps to promote the spirit of sacrifice. Peace is secured from sacrifice. Hence, diligence is essential for achieving anything. All actions in ones life are performed well through constant practice. *Sanathana Sarathi, April, 1997, p. 92*

0870: Today the world is afflicted with seven kinds of diseases. First: business without morality. This is a major malady afflicting the world. Second: Politics without principles. Third: Education without character. Fourth: Sustenance without sacrifice. Fifth: A harvest without labor. Sixth: Humanness without virtue. Seventh: Devotion without faith.

What is the use of devotion without faith? What is the use of claiming to be a man without human qualities? How can you expect a crop without cultivation? What is the use of education without character?
Sanathana Sarathi, April, 1997, p. 89

0871: To worship God as immanent in every atom or cell in the body is the highest form of worship. *Sanathana Sarathi, April, 1997, p. 89*

0872: Young people should realize the superiority of spiritual power over the power of technology. *Sanathana Sarathi, April 1997, p. 85*

0873: Men should understand the true relationship between the external phenomenal world and the world of the Spirit inside. The external world is a reflection of the inner being. All the happiness that he seeks from external objects is within himself. *Sanathana Sarathi, April 1997, p. 86*

0874: People should realize the impermanence of worldly pleasures and the transient nature of youth, wealth and progeny. People should turn their minds towards the eternal Divine.

It may be asked if the Divine is present in all things, is there no difference between good and bad, truth and falsehood? For the person who has the conviction that the Divine is present in everything there is no good or bad. He sees the Divine equally in all things. Good and evil exist for the one who looks at these things in terms of these differences.

In the Geeta, Krishna pointed out to Arjuna how he was the active force behind all events and Arjuna should consider himself as an instrument of the Divine. When anyone acts out of the firm conviction that he is an instrument of the Divine and dedicates all his actions to the Divine, he will see no distinction between right and wrong. It is attachment to the body that produces the illusion of individual doership. When that attachment goes, there is realization of oneness with the Divine.

No doubt the body is necessary for certain purposes; but it should be regarded as an instrument and all actions should be performed as offerings to the Divine.

Divinity is present equally in all, irrespective of their beliefs. The believers should conduct themselves on the basis that the Divine is present in them and redeem their lives by action up to the injunctions of the Divine.

Some scientists may deny God, but they do not realize that the powers of the electron and proton are derived from the Divine. God may be called by any name, but God is one. The atheists may adore something without calling it God, but nonetheless the Divine is present in it. *Sanathana Sarathi, April 1997, p. 87*

0875: When silence is practiced, bliss will manifest itself. The one who talks much will do little. One who acts will talk little.
Sanathana Sarathi, April, 1997, p. 96

0876: If you wish to change the world, these two principles are the recipe. Truth purifies the heart. Sacrifice transforms the physical environment. By this double transformation the entire world is divinised.
Sanathana Sarathi, April, 1997, p. 94

0877: Where there is divergence between thought, word and deed, Vedanta declares that it is evil. The triple harmony is the mark of high souled beings. The wicked revel in disharmony.   *Sanathana Sarathi, March, 1997, p. 67*

0878: Some believe that Rama, Krishna and Sai Baba are God. This can only be attributed to sheer ignorance. You are also God. In order to make you realize that all beings are Divine, that all are embodiments of the Supreme Being, God comes as an Avatar. I have assumed this Form to make you all realize your innate Divinity. Recognizing this purpose to fulfill which Avatars come, you should take to the spiritual life with ardor and zest.   *Summer Showers, 1979, p. 83*

0879: Born in water and momentarily floating on it, the water bubble disappears into the water; Nara (man), likewise, emerges from Narayana (God) and merges back into Him.   *Summer Showers, 1979, p. 124*

0880: In daily life, when someone commits a mistake, we scold him as being devoid of intelligence. When we come across a good man, we remark, "he is one having intelligence". Buddhi (intelligence) develops the Divine Nature which is within us. Therefore, it is necessary for man to follow the intelligence which offers permanent, supreme delight and which continues from birth to birth, displaying Divine Attributes. The mind is indestructible, but the intelligence cannot be destroyed. The intelligence guides and leads man to the Atma. We should follow

the intelligence which seeks the eternal delight of the Atma, and not the mind which hankers after the pleasures of the senses.
Summer Showers, 1979, p. 78

0881: The negative effect of sinful actions can be neutralized only by the positive effect of meritorious actions.   *Summer Showers, 1979, p. 106*

0882: Just as there is divine nature behind the phenomenal nature, there is also the divine mind behind the phenomenal mind. True spirituality lies in the recognition and apprehension of the Divinity underlying the phenomenal world of mind and matter.   *Summer Showers, 1979, p. 122*

0883: There is an intimate relationship between jnana (wisdom) and vidya (education). Education can become an aid to wisdom. Education imparts information which is formally known as knowledge. Wisdom is the spiritualization and sublimation of this knowledge. Real education should not end with the acquisition of knowledge alone, but should transform it into wisdom. True education should lead to liberation from the world of sorrow. But modern education has, instead, a paradoxical effect on the individual. It has led to the increase of sorrow and not its elimination. As modern education has advanced sorrow has increased. With the explosion of education, the totality of misery in the world has increased enormously. Modern education is thus not conductive to redemption from "dukha" or world-sorrow. The cause for this multiplication of human sorrow may be traced to man's lack of faith in the essential unity underlying the phenomenal multiplicity. Selfishness, the source of human sorrow, is a concommitant of ahamkara, or egoism. Mamakara is extended egoism or selfishness extended to kith and kin and to personal belongings.

The combination of ahamkara and mamakara results in moha, or attachment to the evanescent objects of the world.
Summer Showers, 1979, p. 129

0884: A little forbearance and patience on our part will make the abusive epithets of our enemies boomerang on themselves just as a registered letter goes back to its sender if it is returned unaccepted by the addressee.
Summer Showers, 1979, p. 154

0885: Man's greatness is not revealed in the mighty tasks that he undertakes ostentatiously. It is displayed rather in the little acts executed with absolute sincerity and largeness of heart. We must seek to sanctify every little work we perform with a sense of dedication to God.

What is the cause of man's misery? Is sorrow natural to man or is it a mere artifact? Ignorance is the ultimate cause of sorrow. Attachment arises from ignorance and leads to birth, which may be called the immediate cause of sorrow.

We must, therefore, strive to remove our ignorance and avoid sorrow. Sorrow is not natural to man. Were it so, its elimination would have led to the extinction of the human nature. The baby bubbling over with joy in its cradle points to the fact that joy is natural to man. With the child playing happily in its cradle, the mother nonchalantly carries on with the household chores. But, a sudden cry from the baby makes the mother give up her work and rush to it, and she searches for an insect or ant that could possibly have made the baby cry.

Summer Showers, 1979, p. 117

0886: When Buddha was going round begging for alms as a mendicant, his father, Suddhodana, called him and said: "Son! Why are you going about as a beggar? I am a king and are leading the life of a beggar. This is not proper at all". Buddha gave him a fitting reply. "Sire, you are Brahman and I am Brahman. You are not father and I am not son. Both of us are Brahman. In the phenomenal world, you belong to the lineage of rulers. I belong to the lineage on renunciants. All those who follow my ideals are all renunciants. Your lineage is based on attachment. My lineage is based on renunciation. To those who have attachment, it becomes a disease. To the renunciants, detachment becomes the means to Nirvana (liberation from bondage)".   *Sanathana Sarathi, June, 1997, p. 148*

0887: If there were no clouds in man's life, it would be difficult to discern the true value of light. So too, there can be nothing extraordinary about happiness which does not arise out of genuine exertion.

Without truth, righteousness, peace and love, the education that one would have acquired would be meaningless. Charity would bring no merit and the results of all good deeds would verily become naught if man lacks these four virtues. Even so, no heavenly good would accrue to those who wield power in the world, yet lack these cardinal virtues. Truth, righteousness, peace and love are the four foundation-walls in which the edifice of the grand mansion of Sanathana Dharma (Eternal, Universal Religion) stands. What else can I make known unto you, O assembly of good and gentle persons!   *Summer Showers, 1979, p. 155*

0888: There are three reasons for man to be born. One is sin, the second is an unfulfilled desire for some experience and the third is lack of knowledge of ignorance. The feeling that he has not fulfilled a desire and his wanting to take birth again to fulfill such a desire is one main reason. Man does several bad things and commits a sin; he has to be reborn to experience the consequences. Ignorance makes you seek a rebirth under these circumstances. These three constitute the basis for our rebirth.

If God, the goal is not cherished in the memory, one has to wander through many births and arrive home late.

Gems of Wisdom, Law of Karma, p. 106

0889: The body is meant to enable man to perform sacred actions and spend his time in such a manner that Time, the ultimate destroyer, is itself destroyed by him. This transition to the deathless state is brought about by spiritual evolution. Just as the minerals became the tree, the trees gave rise to animate life and the lower animals evolved into man, man too should evolve further and become God.
Summer Showers, 1979, p. 164

0890: Thus you must know where you have come from, what you are and where you are going. In other words, you should comprehend your divine antecedents, your divine nature and your divine destiny. You must strive
to get back to the spiritual haven from which you have come. You have come from the Atma, you are essentially the Atma and you must realize your identity with the Atma. Dedicate you faculties for the realization of the sublime truth of your divinity.
Summer Showers, 1979, p. 165

0891: Remember your great ancient heritage and revere your parents as the embodiments of God. Your mother and father are God for you. Do not cause them anguish now, for your children will surely cause you pain in your later life, as for everything in this world there is a reaction and a reflection. For the sacrifices they undertake for you, and for your own future well-being, love your parents and serve them with devotion. Be good, do good and see good-that is the way to God!
Summer Showers, 1979, p. 168

0892: Everyone should realize that the same Universal Divine Spirit is the Indweller in every being. All are embodiments of the Divine. When this sacred feeling fills everyone there will be no room for conflict or chaos.
Sanathana Sarathi, September, 1996, p. 229

0893: When a man declares that "I am a man", the reference to "man" is finite and impermanent. The "I" is permanent, everlasting.
Sanathana Sarathi, September, 1996, p. 230

0894: Man has to realize how much he owes to God who has provided so many things for his life and comfort. Prayer is the expression of man's gratitude to God. It is also the eternal Divine within him. The Upanishads beckon man to realize the bliss within him. Prayer is essential for developing love for God.
Sanathana Sarathi, September, 1996, p. 236

0895: Man's primary aim should be to recognize the unity that underlies the diversity in the phenomenal world. To break up what is one into many pieces is easy. But it is difficult to bring them together into a meaningful unit. It is in the unifying process that the utility of things can be understood. The role of both

diversity and unity in life has to be properly understood.
Sanathana Sarathi, September, 1996, p. 237

0896: Awareness consists in the conscious remembrance of God on all
occasions.   *Sanathana Sarathi, September, 1996, p. 240*

0897: Students should realize that the body is made up of materials coming from
the earth and will go back to the earth when life is extinct. The body is like a mud
pot which serves its purpose for a time and when it is broken it becomes in
course of time one with the mud from which it was made. A seed sown in the
ground grows into a tree with branches, flowers and fruits. All the things in the
tree have come out of the earth. Likewise the body is made up of the five
elements. It must be used properly.
Sanathana Sarathi, September, 1996, p. 243

0898: It is easy to conquer anger through love, attachment through reasoning,
falsehood through truth, bad thoughts through good, and greed through charity.
Sanathana Sarathi, June, 1997, p. 166

0899: Happiness consists in helping others. It is acquired by giving up, not by
hoarding.   *Gems of Wisdom, Sense Control and Detachment, p. 69*

0900: Struggle to realize Atma, to visualize God; even failure in this struggle is
nobler than the success on other worldly affairs.
Sanathana Sarathi, June, 1997, p. 166

0901: The equipment each of you have brought from previous lives may be
different. Spiritual strength will be less in one, more in another in proportion to the
efforts of each now and in the past.   *Gems of Wisdom, Gunas, p. 55*

0902: You know only the present, what is happening before your eyes; you do not
know that the present is related to the past and is preparing the course of the
future. It is like the headlines and titles of a firm on the screen: as the letters
gleam one after the other, you read them and pass on to the next that comes to
view. Each new letter or word wipes out the one already before your eye, just as
each birth wipes out the memory of the one already experienced.
Sathya Sai Speaks, Volume III, p. 161

0903: The exaggerated outward show of wealth creates jealousy in others not in
possession of the same, resulting in hatred and violence. The pride generated in

the possessor is fatal to his spiritual progress. When such pride overtakes entire groups of people, it leads to the general decline in spiritual values. The capability of producing a colossal amount of material goods is gaining more respect than the leading of a righteous life and the result is loneliness, dissatisfaction, disappointment, fear, insecurity, helplessness, anger hatred.
Gems of Wisdom, Weaknesses of Mankind, p. 135

0904: Through deep detachment, the craving for sensual pleasure must disappear. Be like a trustee so far as family, riches, status and knowledge is concerned. Leave them gladly when the call of death comes.
Gems of Wisdom, Sense Control and Detachment, p. 69

0905: Grief is caused, as joy is caused, by the attachment of the senses to objects; once you know that you are not the senses or the mind, but "He" who operates the senses and wields the mind, you cross the bounds of pleasure and pain.
Gems of Wisdom, Senses, p. 63

0906: The senses, by maintaining contact with the world, provide the feeling of joy and grief. To avoid being buffeted between joy and grief, we have to develop an attitude of unconcern and consider both as a gift from God.
Gems of Wisdom, Sense Control and Detachment, p. 71

0907: You do not see the foundations of a multi-storied skyscraper. Can you, therefore, argue that it simply sits on the ground? The foundations of this life are laid deep in the past, in lives already lived by you. This structure has been shaped by the ground plan of those lives. The unseen decides the bends and the ends: the number of floors, the height and weight.
Sathya Sai Speaks, Volume VII, p. 46

0908: Adore man, the adoration reaches Me. Neglect man, you neglect Me. Of what avail is it to worship the Lord and to suppress man, His counterpart? Love for God must be manifested as Love for man, and Love must express itself as service.
Gems of Wisdom, Shanthi, p. 130

0909: Overcome by inner foes, how can man succeed in over-whelming the outer foes? Burdened with sloth and dullness, how can he achieve wisdom? Prompted by passion, how can he cultivate devotion? Balance and equanimity, these alone can confer peace and harmony.
Sathya Sai Speaks, Volume X, p. 138

0910: What is it that gives each individual this special ability to develop talents? Is it not what he is carrying with him from his previous birth? You may argue that it is

the effort that the individual puts in that is responsible for his become either a poet or a singer. This is not the case. You will have to think how, without any special training, these individuals are sometimes exhibiting such special skills.
Summer Showers, 1973, p. 37

0911: Truth is the mother; wisdom is the father; right conduct is the brother; compassion is the friend; peace is the spouse; forgiveness is the son; these six alone are the real relations for everyone.
Sanathana Sarathi, September, 1996, p. 225

0912: Man is perpetually in search of peace, which is to be first established with oneself, then it is extended to the family, society and the country. Santhi (Peace) comes from within; contentment is a mental condition.
Sathya Sai Speaks, Volume V, p. 281

0913: Happiness is the nature of Atma.
      The Atma is unaffected by any subject or object. Even if the senses, mind, intelligence are inactive, that will not affect the Atma. They have nothing to so with the Atma, which you really are. To know the Atma as such an entity, unaffected and un-attached, is the secret of Wisdom.
Gems of Wisdom, Happiness, p. 162

0914: No one has the right to advise others unless he is already practicing what he preaches. First, establish the reign of love between the various members in your own home. Let the family become a center of harmonious living, sympathetic understanding and mutual faith. The holy duty of man is to be ever aware of the Atman that is installed in every living being. This will make him conscious of the kinship he has with all. This is the basis of the brotherhood of man and the Fatherhood of God.   *Gems of Wisdom, Doubt, p. 124*

0915: I would like to tell you that it is not what you hear that is beneficial, but what you put into daily practice.   *Sathya Sai Speaks, Volume V, p. 327*

0916: Truth does not mean merely telling the facts as one sees or knows them. Truth is that which does not change with time. It must be spoken with complete purity of mind, speech and body. *Gems of Wisdom, Values by Example, p. 203*

0917: Many people think of God only when grief overtakes them; of course, it is good to do so; it is better than seeking the help of those who are also equally liable to grief. But, man should think of God in grief and in joy, in peace and in strife, in all weathers.

God first; world next; myself last. This is the legitimate sequence for the devotee. But man has reversed it and has made it "Myself first, the world next and God last"! Hold fast to God then you will be safe.

Gems of Wisdom, Bhakthi (Devotion), p. 309

0918: Man should not consider that happiness consists in having a houseful of children equipped with all the amenities for comfortable living. Nor can peace be realized through wealth, power or position. Peace, indeed, is the outcome or our actions and thoughts. *Gems of Wisdom, Shanthi, p. 131*

0919: Discriminate before you develop attachment. If you have attachment towards wife and children, land and buildings, bank accounts and balances, when these decline you will come to grief. Develop attachment towards the Universal, and you too, will grow in love and splendor.

Gems of Wisdom, Attachment, p. 139

0920: Lust stands out as the predominant leader of all bad qualities. The other three, anger, attachment and greed, follow the leader. In fact, desire (kama), the lord of lust, is responsible for our death, It increases our attachment and thereby weakens our intelligence and we become inhuman.

Gems of Wisdom, Attachment, p. 141

0921: Man has been enslaved by money. He lives a superficial, hollow, artificial life. This is indeed a great pity. Man should seek to possess only as much money as is most essential for his living. The quantity of riches one must earn can be compared to the shoes one wears; if too small, they cause pain; if too big, they are a hindrance to physical and mental comfort. When we have more, it breeds pride, sloth and contempt for others. In pursuit of money, man descends to the level of the beast. Money is of the nature of manure. Piled up in one place, it pollutes the air, Spread it wide; scatter it over fields; it rewards you with a bumper harvest. So too, when money is spent in all four quarters for promotion good works, it yields contentment and happiness in plenty.

The end of wisdom is freedom. The end of culture is perfection. The end of knowledge in love. The end of education is character.

Gems of Wisdom, Degradation, p. 147

0922: We think of wealth as consisting of buildings, property, material goods and we have lost ourselves in the mad pursuit of temporal values. These do not constitute real wealth which is capable of giving us abounding joy. Character is our wealth and good conduct is our treasure. Knowledge of God is the foundation for both. We should not lose the abiding, precious and eternal wealth, which is knowledge of God, for fleeting and temporary things which are like the passing clouds. *Gems of Wisdom, Degradation, p. 148*

0923: Whatever one learns or does not learn, one must, after being born as man, learn about the Atman, for that alone can confer Bliss and Immortality.
Sathya Sai Speaks, Volume X, p. 184

0924: Nourish your aged parents; revere them. If you honor your mother, the Mother of the Universe will guard you against harm. If you honor your father, the Father of all beings will guard you. This is as true as the fact that if you honor your parents, your children will honor you.   *Gems of Wisdom, Happiness, p. 161*

0925: Believing that the world as cognised during the waking state is real and that the highest goal is the attainment of happiness in that world, man accumulates the instruments and symbols of that happiness; he fashions after his own taste and inclination according to the dictates of his own reason, the laws, ideals, institutions and principles that would bolster that happiness. This attempt leads to a philosophy which can be named "western".

But can the goal of Life be just this - to struggle amidst the waves of joy and grief that rise and fall in this visible objective world, to be carried along the current of desire, gathering food, shelter, comfort and pleasure, and finally, to flounder into the jaws of death? Consider what is happening now: in the name of progress, art is degraded into immoral and sensuous entertainment; educational advance results, not in advance of humility and reverence, but in rampant indiscipline, arrogance and irreverence. The emphasis long place on the development of character and the promotion of virtue through education has now been dropped. In this place enthroned as ideals worldly success, self-aggrandizement and high standard of living. Greed is growing out of control. Scientific development is not resulting in peace and happiness, but increase in terror, unrest, and anxiety. Man is analyzing and utilizing the outer world; but the inner world which is basic is ignored and forgotten.
Gems of Wisdom, Education, p. 188

0926: The powers of man are limited by the experience and his knowledge.
Gems of Wisdom, Practice and Precept, p. 242

0927: The company of bad men is the prelude to the disappearance of wisdom. The company of good men makes wisdom blossom.
Ram Katha Rasavahini, p. 367

0928: Dharma is bound up with a great many variety of meanings and does not mean only duty, which pertains to one individual. Dharma is eternal, same for everyone, everywhere. The birth place of dharma is the heart. What emanates from the heart as a pure idea, when translated into action, is dharma, or you can, say, act in a manner that you want others to act towards you. Do unto others as you want them to do unto you.

Every single thing has its dharma; Water has its dharma, the obligation to move; Fire the dharma to burn; the Magnet to attract. And everyone of these is keeping up its Dharma undamaged, including the Solar System. Among the things endowed with consciousness, the plants and trees, the insects and birds born out of eggs or the mammals- all have retained their specific Dharma unaffected by the passage of time. But man is the only living thing that has slipped and is sliding down. The experience of many generations of seekers, who, sought the means of contentment and Joy, embodied in the precepts of practical living, collectively called Sastras in neglected and new-tangled nostrums are recommended and tried on a vast scale. No wonder, contentment and joy are far, far away from human grasp.   *Gems of Wisdom, Dharma, p. 233*

0929: The secret of happiness is not in doing what one likes, but in liking what one has to do. Whatever work you have to do, you should do it with pleasure and liking.   *Summer Showers, 1977, p. 100*

0930: What exactly is Peace? It is the stage in which the senses are mastered and held in balance.   *Santhana Sarathi, January 1985, p. 11*

0931: The human being is a composite of man and beast and God, and in the inevitable struggle among the three for ascending, you must ensure that God wins.   *Sathya Sai Speaks; Volume V, p. 104*

0932: Observe the four F's:
     -Follow the master: the inner voice of conscience.
     -Face the devil: the antisocial urges.
     -Fight to the end: until one is able to overcome the six inner foes.
     -Finish the game: life on earth.
                                    Sathya Sai Speaks, Volume X, p. 28

0933: If there is righteousness in the heart, there will be beauty in character. If there is beauty in character, there will be harmony in the home. When there is harmony in the home, there will be order in the Nation. When there is order in the Nations, there will be peace in the world.
                        Gems of Wisdom, Practice and Precept, p. 241

0934: Life sustained by food is short; life sustained by the Atma is eternal. Do not claim to long life, but to Divine life. Do not live for more years on earth, but for more virtues in the heart.   *Sathya Sai Speaks; Volume XI, p. 40*

0935: Spirituality is fundamental for man to reveal to him the means for the blossoming of his qualities. It, however, does not mean leading a solitary ascetic life. Spirituality means looking upon the whole of mankind as one family and realizing the unity in diversity.

Gems of Wisdom, Spiritual Quality is Essential, p. 279

0936: What is spirituality? It is the resolute pursuit of cosmic consciousness. It aims at enabling man to manifest, in all its fullness, the Divine Cosmic Consciousness that is present within and outside him. It means getting rid of the animal nature in man. It means breaking down the barriers between God and nature and establishing their essential oneness.

Gems of Wisdom, Spirituality, p. 273

0937: Many are content with their dealings with the objective world. Their ideal is only to amass material wealth and satisfy material needs. Examine yourselves and discover at what level you are by analyzing your desires and activities. In this way you can yourselves sublimate your thoughts and urges.

Activity causes birth and death and fills up the years of one's life. It supports good and evil, joy and grief.

However, man is willfully unaware of the activities that will lighten the burden of his life and also illumine the Atman. It is the Atman that illumines all, but man is in the dark about its existence. Just as everything sweet is sweet on account of the sugar it contains, all things and objects are cognized because the Atman is behind the cognition. It is the Universal Witness. It is the sun that activates all but never gets activated itself. You, too must establish yourself in the position of a witness. *Gems of Wisdom, Spiritual Level, p. 263*

0938: Spiritual life does not mean leaving the home and living in a solitary place. True spiritual life is that which teaches us unity or oneness and makes us lead a life of selflessness and love. *Gems of Wisdom, Spirituality, p. 273*

0939: The higher life which makes man human, depends on the cultivation of the six cardinal values: Truth, Right Conduct, Love, Equanimity, Peace, Nonviolence.

Sathya Sai Speaks, Volume V, p. 304

0940: When one refers to social life, it is asked what connection is has with spiritual pursuits. Similarly when one refers to spiritual life, it is assumed that it has no connection with social activities of any kind. Both these views are wrong. Spiritual life contributes not only to the Divine unfolding of society and the divinization of mankind, but it makes society itself a manifestation of the Cosmic Being. The divinity that is the basis of society is reflected through the divinity of the individual. *Gems of Wisdom, Spiritual Quality is Essential, p. 277*

0941: It must be understood that the root cause of suffering is due to the lack of wisdom which enables you to realize the indwelling unity amongst apparent diversity, and the safest and surest means of uprooting this sufferance is by removing ignorance, resulting in the realization of the real.
Gems of Wisdom, Spiritual Quality is Essential, p. 276

0942: Even to place one foot forward, man needs an inner urge, a purpose, a prompting. His will is moved by his wish. Therefore, man should endeavor to wish for higher and holier goals.
Gems of Wisdom, Spiritual Quality is Essential, p. 277

0943: Many feel that it is human to err and the Lord should forgive them. In fact, if they are truly human they should not commit mistakes at all. Should a mistake be committed, it should not be repeated. It is a grievous error to think that it is natural for man to err.

Such a feeling should not be entertained by anyone. To follow the directives of the senses is a mark of the animal. To be guided always by the Atma is the sign of the human. No one has the right to justify his weakness and lapses as natural to a human being. They can at best be regarded as signs of mental debility. Man must continually strive to master his senses.

Only through the spiritual path can man achieve this. If there is real faith and devotion in a man, the senses will be powerless against him. When you dive deep into a problem and inquire from your heart whether your proposed action is good for your society, your conscience shall give you the right answer.

Man must first decide, after vigorous self-examination, the path that he wishes to traverse. Life should not be spent in just eating.
Gems of Wisdom, Spiritual Quality is Essential, p. 278

0944: A tongue of a human that does not pronounce the Name of God, a hand that has no charity, the years of life which did not taste the bliss of peace, talents which yield no fruit of success, a life that has not accumulated wisdom, a religious place where there is no atmosphere of reverence, talk that does not communicate sense- all these are of no worth.
Gems of Wisdom, Spiritual Quality is Essential, p. 279

0945: Man's vision, which is now turned outward towards the phenomenal universe, should be turned inwards towards the Indwelling Spirit. One should manifest the divine consciousness inherent in him. He should submit himself to that Consciousness as a Spiritual discipline. This is called "Conscious Realization of the Inner Divine".

The first task is to develop awareness of the Divinity within. The next stage is the realization of the truth that the divinity that is within one's self is equally present in all others. One must recognize that the veil barrier that appears to separate him from others is born of delusion and every effort should be made to remove it. Only then will it be possible to experience the oneness of all living things. Atam eva idam Sarvam says the Sruti. "I am indeed all this. " The realization dawns: "All this is contained in me." And then there is the consciousness, I am Divine; the Divine is in me. I am Brahman, Brahman is myself. There is no distinction between Brahman and me.

Gems of Wisdom, Awareness of Divinity, p. 281

0946: The inextricable connection between the phenomenal world outside and the world of consciousness inside eludes the understanding of ordinary people. Immersed in the desire for enjoying worldly pleasures, they do not attempt to discover the boundless joy to be derived from the inner Spirit. This is because all the sense organs are open only to experiences from outside. It is surprising that the common man is subject to the outward vision. Only a few develop the inner vision and enjoy spiritual bliss.

Is it the body that derives joy from looking at a thing of beauty? Or is it the Atma? What is it that relishes the good that is consumed? The body or the Spirit? What is it that enjoys fragrance of is moved by companionship? Inquiring in this manner, it will be found that it is the Atma that is the enjoyer and not the physical body. The body by itself is gross and is incapable of experiencing joy. It must be realized that the Spirit transcends the mind and the intellect and pervades the entire cosmos. The Spirit is the basis for the cognition of the external world and experiencing the inner world.

Gems of Wisdom, p. 282

0947: Each one has come embodied into this world of Joy and grief, of growth and decay, of hope and despair in order to discover the way home, to get back to the source from which he has strayed into this wilderness. This has to be done within the allotted time of sojourn, from each day the sun steals a fraction away. But, man is attracted by the phantom lights and he ignores the call of destiny. His senses lead him on and on, deeper and deeper into the maze, until he dies with a moan instead of with a smile. The years between birth and death are wasted in wasteful acquisition and worthless achievements. The Maya that has been shadowing the Divinity that is his essence.

Gems of Wisdom, What is this Cosmic Power? p. 284

0948: Two different characteristics are to be found among men. One characteristic, which is rather common, is for one to delude himself that he is a good man, with many virtues, intelligence and talents. The other quality, which is rare, is recognition of the good quality in others, their merits, abilities and good deeds and to appreciate their ideals. Jesus belonged to the second category, He saw the good qualities in others, rejoiced over virtues and shared his joy with others.

Gems of Wisdom, Love- The Key to Human Unity, p. 290

0949: If God, the goal is not cherished in the memory, one has to wander through many births and arrive home late.

Sathya Sai Speaks; Volume III, p. 308

0950: Ideally, therefore, when one prays, one should in complete resignation say, "Thy will be done," and ought not to ask for this or that, for he has neither the wisdom nor the foresight to know what is best for him.

Sathya Sai Speaks; Volume X, p. 200

0951: If you give up all and surrender to the Lord, He will guard you and guide you. When you complain "O He has not guarded me", I reply "you have not surrendered. The Lord has come just for this very task.

Sathya Sai Speaks; Volume IV, p. 16

0952: You can get the feeling for the Divine only if you have a taste of the prema (LOVE) of the Divine. That is why I have come to give you a taste of that prema so that the yearning for God will be planted in your hearts. Mastery over mountains of information has been attained by man now, but wisdom has lagged behind. Hence, man's capacity to probe and progress into the realm of the universal and Absolute has to be developed.

Gems of Wisdom, Sins and Repentance, p. 354

0953: Yearning for God and constant contemplation of the Divine arises from innate urges derived from past lives.

Gems of Wisdom, Why is God not seen?, p. 344

0954: How can God shine in the heart that is darkened by bad thoughts and intentions? *Gems of Wisdom, Why is God not seen?, p. 344*

0955: In the world there are four categories of persons:
1. Those who are aware of their own faults and excellencies of others.
2. Those who broadcast their own good qualification as well as of others.
3. Those who talk of their excellencies and refer only to the faults of others.
4. Those who project their own faults as excellencies and the good qualifications of others as faults.

Should you desire to become aware of the Divine, the Sacred, the Atma, the Bhagavaan, then try to be in the first category.

Sathya Sai Speaks, Volume X, p. 183

0956: Human effort is essential. Efforts are in human hands; success or defeat rests with the Divine. Gems of Wisdom, Bhakthi (Devotion), p. 315

0957: It is God's word that if you have devotion to God, He will look after all your future. He will look after all the welfare that is due you.

Gems of Wisdom, Why is God not seen?, p. 347

0958: People must pray to God with love for God and not for petty favors or material benefits. People must seek the Divine internally not in external objects.

Devotees should strive for transformation in their hearts and minds so that they totally give up their attachments to worldly objects and get immersed in God. God values your feelings and not your physical performances. Make the Lord's name the goad for controlling the mind, which tends to behave like an elephant in a rut.   *Sanathana Sarathi; October, 1997, p. 262*

0959: When you travel towards God, whoever objects has to be bypassed.

Gems of Wisdom, Why is God not seen?, p. 346

0960: God does not shower Grace on people because they sing His praises. Nor does He come down upon them because they do not deify Him. Recitation of the Divine attributes only enables us to dwell on elevating ideals and approximate ourselves more and more of the Divinity that is our nature. We become what we contemplate.   *Sathya Sai Speaks, Volume X, p. 157*

0961: How are all equal? Because they have all the same consciousness within them. When the sun rises, not all lotuses in the lake bloom; only the grown buds open their petals. The others await their chance. It is the same with men. Differences do exist because of unripeness, though all fruits have to ripen and fall someday. Every being has to reach the goal however slow they walk or however curved their road.

To act according to the dictates of the senses is the code of animals. What man should have is the Divine consciousness.

Gems of Wisdom, Behavior (Conduct), p. 401

0962: If one thinks that God is separate from him, it may be so for him, but if anyone totally gives up his thoughts, he then becomes God himself. All thoughts are illusions, so, if you give them up, you yourself become God. Therefore, you all of you - give up all thoughts. Come forward and enjoy the Divinity that you are

Gems of Wisdom, Sins and Repentance, p. 354

0963: The tear glands have been provided to you not for weeping helplessly before others with hands extended for alms, but to shed tears of joy, of thankfulness, at the feet of the Lord.

Gems of Wisdom, Significance of Padanamaskar, p. 386

0964: Forget and forgive all that has happened amongst you from this very moment and start a new chapter of love and brotherhood from now on.
Sathya Sai Speaks, Volume X, p. 24

0965: If a devotee has dedicated his all..... body, mind and existence .... to the Lord, the Lord will himself look after everything, for He will always be with the bhakta under such conditions, there is no need for prayer.. But have you so dedicated yourself and surrendered every thing to the Lord?
Prasantha Vahini, p. 14

0966: There is a great deal of talk about freedom. Language of heart, refinement of sensibilities and purity of the mind constitute true freedom, self-control, self-satisfaction and self-knowledge constitutes together the supreme expression of freedom. Freedom today has been equated to animal behavior. This a travesty of freedom. Real freedom consists in submitting to the will of the Divine.
Gems of Wisdom, Freedom, p. 407

0967: Do not think that only those who worship a picture or image with pompous paraphernalia are devotees. Whoever treads the moral path, whoever acts as he speaks and specks as he has seen, whoever melts at another's misery and exalts at another's joy is a devotee, perhaps a greater devotee.
Gems of Wisdom, Quality of a Devotee, p. 390

0968: You must realize that greatness related to power, position of wealth is transient. It is lost when power and position go. But goodness is respected always. Therefore dedicate your lives to goodness. What is goodness? It is living according to Dharma (the code of right conduct) and justice, to love all and cherish faith in God. To help the needy and raise the lowly-all these constitute goodness.   *Sanathana Sarathi, August 1997, p. 209*

0969: Love lives by giving and forgiving. Self lives by getting and forgetting.
Summer Showers in Brindivan, 1977, p. 80

0970: Discipline is essential for the success of every endeavor of man, whatever the field, whether it be economic, social, education, or merely material and worldly. It is even more essential to success in spiritual effort.
Sathya Sai Speaks; Volume VII, p. 328

0971: Men are eager to get happiness and when there is a possibility of acquiring indivisible happiness, they jump at the idea; but, soon get tired. They seek short cuts, lean on others to carry their weight and aspire for much fruit in return for the little cultivation. But, rigorous discipline and steady faith are absolutely necessary for success in the spiritual struggle. Mere listening to discourses will not be of any use. To have that discipline, one has to control the senses which drag the mind towards the pleasurable attractions of the external world; to have steady faith, one must be able to control the wayward mind, that paints attractive pictures in false colors to lure you on from birth to birth.   *Gems of Wisdom, Self Control, p. 412*

0972: Everyone today is seeking comfort and pleasure; that is the be-all and the end-all. If you tell a man that he can eat whatever he likes in whatever quantity he wants, he is delighted. But, if you add that he might develop, as a consequence, some illness, he will treat you as an enemy. No regime or control is popular. But strength is derived only from controls, from restraint, from regulation. Man becomes tough and capable of endurance only if he welcomes hardships. Struggle and you get strength to succeed.
Gems of Wisdom, Self Control, p. 414

0973: In money there is no evil. In scholarship there is no evil. In knowledge and intelligence there is no evil. Evil arises from the activities which man carries on with their help.   *Gems of Wisdom, The Sai Phenomenon, p. 447*

0974: Long ago a person had three friends. When he wanted them to help him, the first said I can help you from within the house; the second said, I will not enter the witness box and the third said, I will not speak for you, wherever you want me to.
The first is the property and possessions. The second is the Kinsmen, who will come as far as the cemetery. The third friend is the fair name earned by one's virtues and service, they persist even after the death.
Gems of Wisdom, Sayings of Sai Baba, p. 438

0975: The pilgrim must traverse and over step the vast wastes of worldly desires (kama) and overcome the thick slushy growths of anger and hate (krodha) and negotiate the cliffs of hatred and malice (dwesha), so that he might relax on the green pastures of concord and love.(prema).
Gems of Wisdom, Pilgrimage, p. 418

0976: Many blame God for their poverty. God is the magnet and man is the iron. If the iron rusted covered with dust and mud (laziness, lust, greed, immorality) how can the magnet (God) attract? Examine your own actions sincerely and purify the heart, so that God can help you.
Gems of Wisdom, The Sai Phenomenon, p. 446

0977: Intelligence without gratitude is valueless. Every man should be grateful to those who have helped him.   *Sanathana Sarathi, September 1997, p. 238*

0978: Every child bears the imprint of its parents. As all human beings have come from God, they should carry the marks of the creator. Man has taken birth to manifest the Divine in him.   *Sanathana Sarathi, August 1997, p. 200*

0979: Well-prepared and properly cooked food today will become poison after three days. We need not go so far. We can take an example which we see in our daily life. If we eat fresh food today, by tomorrow it gets changed into excreted matter. We may think that the food that we are eating is good. What we excrete tomorrow is bad. Both good and bad are different. In this manner, by change of time, we are calling things good and bad, but there is no intrinsic difference.
Summer Showers in Brindivan, 1977, p. 210

0980: In ancient times, the sages and saints sacrificed everything for the sake of the welfare of humanity. Even the youth of those times followed suit. They are remembered even today because of their spirit of selfless sacrifice. On the contrary, the youth of today are becoming exceedingly greedy and totally selfish and harboring feelings of hatred and jealousy, while those in the ancient times were leading a life of Thyaaga and Yoga (sacrifice and sense control). The present day youth want to lead a life of Bhoga (enjoying worldly and carnal pleasures) which results in Roga (disease).
Sanathana Sarathi, August 1997, p. 210

0981: We are now neither here nor there. We are in the middle. We are living in the Bhuloka along with human beings. On one side there is the Divine world. If we develop qualities like lust and anger, we will move closer and closer to the lower world and we will become more and more distant from the Divine world. But if we travel towards the Divine world, then we will become more and more distant from the lower world. To attach importance to the transient pleasures in the same as moving away from divinity.   *Summer Showers in Brindivan, 1977, p. 21*

0982: Some persons consider small defects in others as huge mistakes and criticize them while they ignore even great drawbacks in themselves. This is highly improper. The correct method is to magnify your own small mistakes and consider them as big mistakes and the big mistakes of others as small mistakes as small ones of no consequence. That is how you can control the commission of errors. With this attitude, you will be able to realize the Divine. The love of humans is earthly and selfish while Divine Love is spiritual and selfless. It is pure love. The ancients described the Divine as eternal, immortal, pure and unsullied. In order to experience Love of God, you should give up petty minded selfishness and expand your love.   *Sanathana Sarathi, August 1997, p. 212*

0983: If a piece of salt went into the ocean to find the ocean, it gets dissolved in the ocean and cannot come back in its original form. So also, we learn that the jeeva which wants to learn the nature of atma, when it goes there, it will get completely merged in the atma and cannot come back.
Summer Showers in Brindivan, 1977, p. 144

0984: The non-recognition or recognition of one's own self, can be the cause of sorrow or of happiness as the case may be. Here it is also established that this happiness which we experience in one's own form or one's own self. The permanent bliss that one gets by the knowledge of atma has been described by several people by saying that atma is all-knowing and atma is above duality. Atma is one and not two, atma is permanent, atma is unwavering, atma is above description and above suffering. There is different ways of describing atma but these words cannot undertake to tell us the form of atma. It is not possible for anyone to establish its form. One can only experience this for oneself. It is not possible for others to give a description which enables another person to experience this. Here the bliss or the happiness which can be got out of demonstration or description will not be as good as that obtained form direct experience. Thus, knowledge of this atma can come only out of experience and cannot come out of reading books.   *Summer Showers in Brindivan, 1977, p. 78*

0985: Truth is God, It is only through Truth you can get peace, plenty and prosperity. Truth only bears the wealth of the whole world. There is no greater Dharma (virtue) than Truth. The mansion of Dharma is raised on the foundation of Truth. Though people may follow several spiritual paths, Truth is the most important of all. Any where and at any time, for any individual Truth is absolutely essential. Because Truth is forgotten, the whole world is in turmoil. It is only from Truth that all creation has originated, including human beings, the whole creation merges back into Truth. One who follows Truth and Righteousness will always be successful. Mere strength of armory, valor, skill and ability will not do. These are only worldly and external powers. The power of Truth is supreme. To foster Truth and Righteousness is the bounden duty of man. He should recognize the importance of harmony in thought, word and deed.

You may think that relating exactly what you saw is Truth. It is not so. Suppose you see a person taking the role of king in a drama. You see him on the stage with the royal robe and after the drama is all over, he may be in his usual dress. Which is true? Is it his role on the stage or is it his role outside? If you analyze this,
it becomes obvious that what is subject to change may be termed as fact but not Truth. Truth remains true at all points in time.
Sanathana Sarathi, August 1997, p. 215

0986: For every action of yours, there is always a reaction, there is resound and reflection. If in the future you want to have a life of peace and of happiness, that will depend upon the kind of action which you take at the present time only. If you respect your parents today, your children will respect you in the future. The kind of seed, which you plant today, will determine the kind of tree which will grow. So, if you want to be near God, see good, do good, be good; this is the way, the royal way for you to go near God. To be good, to do good and to see good is the primary duty of every human being.

The wealth which we may earn, the prosperity which we may acquire, the mansions which we may build are all transient and temporary. Our conduct is the most important thing in our life. It is only when we can shape our present conduct along a proper path, that our future can hopefully be peaceful and happy.
Summer Showers in Brindivan, 1977, p. 20

0987: Whatever form of worship one may adopt, it has to be done whole-heartedly. There must be complete harmony between thought, word and deed. True humanness consists in the combination of three H's- Heart, Head and Hand.
Sanathana Sarathi; October, 1997, p. 256

0988: The final result of the work will depend on the attitude with which the work is done.   *Summer Showers in Brindivan, 1977, p. 94*

0989: One's actions will reflect the kind of ideas which one has in one's mind.
Summer Showers in Brindivan, 1977, p. 95

0990: The secret of happiness is not doing what one likes but in doing what one has to do.   *Summer Showers in Brindivan, 1977, p. 100*

0991: God or the devil, good and bad, are denizens of one's own heart. Where God is, there the devil cannot be. It is like the game of "musical chairs", only one person can occupy one chair. Seat God for ever in the heart, after ridding it of other occupants. Let this inert body be activated by Divine Consciousness.
Baba, The Breath of Sai, p. 238

0992: What arises out of untruth can be got rid of by listening to truth.
Summer Showers in Brindivan, 1977, p. 197

0993: Take the troubles that come to you as tests and opportunities to learn non-attachment. It is the hot summer that sends you to air-conditioning. Grief sends you to God.   *Baba, The Breath of Sai, p. 281*

0994: It is more important for people to be good rather than being great. Most parents these days desire that their children should become great in various ways: in scholarship, wealth and position. This is totally misconceived. They should really desire that their children should be good. Greatness signifies quantity. Goodness is an index of quality.

Sanathana Sarathi; October, 1997, p. 269

0995: The kind of sadhana which we should do is to elevate things from a low level to a high level. You must worship a picture as God but not worship God as a picture. This means that this piece of paper is God, this tumbler is God, this microphone is God; everything is God. You must attempt to take these things from a low level to the status of God. Unfortunately, today, people regard God as patter, regard God as a tumbler and so on. Thereby we are bringing God from a high position to the position of these trivial things.

Summer Showers in Brindivan, 1977, p. 209

0996: Every event will give us some pleasure and happiness and sorrow. Pain and pleasure always come together. It is not possible for anyone to separate them from each other. Pleasure alone, isolated from pain, is never possible. When pain fructifies and gives its fruit, it becomes pleasure. Pleasure has no separate form on its own. We should promote the strength in us by which we can accept both pain and pleasure with an equal mind.

Summer Showers in Brindivan, 1977, p. 210

0997: Man does not live only by food. He lives by the experience of Self. Modernized people, who cannot recognize this truth, are under the illusion that the material world is important. The body is made up of the five material elements and it is inevitable that the body will fall one day or the other. The one who lives within the body is eternal. The divinity in the body has neither birth nor death. What resides in the body in the form of Self is God.

Baba, The Breath of Sai, p. 226

0998: These days India is advancing fast in science and technology. No wonder that there are many who lay excessive faith by the conclusions of physical sciences and ridicule the science of the spirit. These science-minded people would answer the question, "Who are you?" by saying "I am the body which contains about 10 gallons of water, one gallon of lime, lead enough for making 9,000 pencils, phosphorus enough for making 11,000 matches and as much iron as there is in a nail two inches long". All this stuff would seem to cost only about a hundred rupees, but actually even if you spend ten million rupees, you cannot make a human body. For as spiritualists would put it, the human body has risen out of Divine Will, is alive on account of Divine Power, and is able to act as a result of Divine Grace.   *Baba, The Breath of Sai, p. 219*

0999: People imagine that this bliss is to be found in jobs, marriage, property or progeny. That is not the case. You hope for happiness in one thing after another: education, jobs, marriage, children and so on. But happiness eludes you. The only enduring happiness is got by oneness with the Divine. The answer to the question, "Where is happiness?" is: "Happiness is union with God". Students tend to forget this, in the pursuit of worldly pleasures. It is only through the ripeness of experience that this realization can come. For instance, you see a barren field in the summer. After a night's rain, you find grass coming up. Wherefrom did it come? It is from the field. What was present in the form of seeds in the earth came up as grass after the rain. Likewise the bliss within you will sprout when you water your parched heart with the rain of divine love.

Sanathana Sarathi, March 1996, p. 73

1000: Man has to pay attention to three basic duties in his quest for happiness. 1. He should forget what he has to forget, namely, the world around him and its tantalizing pleasures. 2. He has to reach where he has to reach, namely, the goal of the Divine, the Presence of the Almighty. And 3. He has to give up what he has to give up, namely, material desires and pursuits. When the mind is turned towards God or goodness, it becomes human. If it is turned towards evil thoughts and wicked egoism, it becomes demonic. It is not good for man to be constantly engaged in exciting things, exciting food, talk, books, films, games, sights, sound. They are passionate things that disturb and agitate the mind.

Baba, The Breath of Sai, p. 221

1001: Why is man today afflicted with fear and anxiety? Are we to search for the reasons outside us or do they lie within us? The reason lies in the false emphasis we have laid on things of the material world, ignoring things of the spirit. The body that man bears is essentially the receptacle of God. It is a temple, where God is installed and where God is the Master.

The Divine is the core, the essence of your being. God is everywhere. When He is recognized and adored as the Indweller of your body. it becomes a Temple, and it is no more a burden. God is shining, announcing Himself through you; He is expressing Himself through every thought, word and deed that emanates from you.

Baba, The Breath of Sai

1002: Man is the victim of many a pain; to those who identify themselves with the body, life is a series of trouble and misery. But, to those who know that the body is but a vehicle, these cannot cause anxiety. I must emphasize bodily health is important, for ill health affects mental poise and concentration. When the body is fit, mental functions too run smooth; when the body suffers, the mind too gets unsettled. So, the raft called body which is the only means of getting across the sea of change has to be kept in good trim.

Untruth, injustice, anxiety - all cause leaks and loosen the knots of that raft. With such a poor raft, it is foolish to attempt the crossing. The raft has to be cast aside when the crossing has been effected; there is no more use for it. The human raft is the most efficient, for it is built out of Discrimination, Keenness of

Intellect and Renunciation, hard timber that can stand the beat of wave and the sway of current. If one does not make the best use of this chance, it may not come again for a long, long time.   *Baba, The Breath of Sai, p. 230*

1003: The awareness that the world is one family dawns when one recognizes the truth of the indwelling spirit. The messages of Christ and the other world prophets must be practiced earnestly by man; all men must share in the precious heritage of selfless and universal love and develop it by practice in daily life. Be the harbingers of the new age. . . be free from selfishness and greed, hatred and violence. Be a light unto yourselves; may you become worthy instruments for the revival of the religion of love and the resurgence of human values.
                              Sathya Sai Baba, God as man

1004: Delusion has to die; then only does the cycle of change end. Then only is man liberated form the bonds of birth, life and death. Call it "Reaching the goal," or "Merging in the Absolute or Universal", or "Becoming one with Infinite" -- the names may differ, but the finish is the same. Every mortal must attain immortality; for he is a child of Immortality. That is why I dislike people condemning themselves as sinners, "born in sin, living in sin, fundamentally sin itself, etc.! I always remind such people that it is treason to their inner reality to heap such stark falsehoods upon their own heads.   *Baba, The Breath of Sai, p. 264*

1005: Even when speaking the truth, one should not inflame passion, diminish enthusiasm or inflict injury. Speak the truth, speak pleasantly; if unpleasant, do not speak the Truth, is a modifying factor. Also, because it is pleasant, do not speak falsehood.   *Baba, The Breath of Sai, p. 239*

1006: Animals like cattle and birds cannot change the qualities which they acquire with their birth. The lion, for instance, is born as a cruel animal. The cat is born with the quality of trapping the rats and of killing them. It lives with these qualities. Try as they may, these animals cannot change their bad and cruel qualities. You can make a cat sit on the chair and give it good food like milk, curd and so on, and try to convert the cat, but the moment it sees a rat, it jumps to kill the rat. Thus the animal, which is born with cruel qualities, cannot change in spite of our best efforts. However, man is not like that.

Man may be born with cruel qualities but such a person, by contact with good people, by living with good people in a good environment, can change his qualities. It is in this context that it has been said that of all the living things that are born on a mother's womb, to have a human birth is the most difficult thing. Even if bad qualities come to man by birth, there are ample opportunities for him to get rid of such bad qualities by contact with good people.
                              Baba, The Breath of Sai, p. 242

1007: He who has greatest satisfaction in life is the richest man. He who has much desires is the poorest man. To be free from all desires is the mark of greatness.   *Sanathana Sarathi, November 1997, p. 298*

1008: Struggle to realize the Self, to visualize God; even failure in this struggle is noble, than success in other worldly attempts. The buffalo has horns, the elephant has tusks, but what a difference. To live in the body, with the body, with God, for God is the life of man.   *Baba, The Breath of Sai, p. 288*

1009: What has to be gained is not money, but virtue. The means of sustenance are sought after and collected by birds and beasts; there is nothing especially human in this pursuit. When intelligence is used for the acquisition of food and physical comforts, man is lost in animal pursuits.
Baba, The Breath of Sai, p. 242

1010: What is needed today in the world is the diverting of the mind from preoccupation with the external world of Nature to the Divinity within. This is the sadhana (spiritual discipline) you have to do. In this way you see the Divine in everything instead of seeing Nature as a physical phenomenon. When you see the external world as a manifestation of God, you will not notice the phenomenal aspect of Nature (Prakriti). View Nature as a manifestation on God.
Sanathana Sarathi, November 1997, p. 302

1011: You are going on adding to your objects of attachment from the moment you are born in the world. First, you have mother and father, then brothers, sisters, relatives and friends. After marriage, another set of relatives and friends are added through your spouse. Thus attachment goes on multiplying.

On the other hand, if you go on detaching yourself from various relationships one after other, your attachments get reduced and you develop detachment leading to liberation. Attachment and detachment relate to external objects. Divinity is in closest proximity to you, but it takes time to understand Divinity.   *Sanathana Sarathi, July 1994, p. 174*

1012: Embodiments of Love! Purify your minds. Shed jealousy and hatred. Chanting God's name will confer bliss on you. You are unable to understand the inner feelings of joy that the chanting of the Divine name will yield. You should identify yourself with the Divine vibrations which are like electric waves creating boundless energy.   *Sanathana Sarathi, April 1994, p. 99*

1013: People should understand that the Self (Atma) is one only. There are so many in this hall. Each one of you may consider that everyone has a separate and distinct Atma. This is totally wrong. Like the reflection of the Sun in a myriad different vessels filled with water, the same Cosmic Self is dwelling in everyone. The reflection is one and the same, though the vessels might be different but the indwelling Atma is one.   *Sanathana Sarathi, November 1997, p. 297*

1014: Does one need a lamp to see the light from another lamp? And yet, man who has the light of wisdom in his heart goes in search of wisdom elsewhere. This search, born of ignorance, leads him to seek gurus. To acquire knowledge of the Self (Atma-Jnana), man needs no guru (preceptor). No preceptor can give this knowledge because Mother Nature (Prakriti) has herself conferred on her children the keys to this knowledge for their protection.
                    Sanathana Sarathi, November 1997, p. 295

1015: Any human being who has compassion for others, who adheres to Truth and who dedicates his body to the good of others will experience no serious trouble. The primary reason is one's devotion to God.
                    Sanathana Sarathi, September 1994, p. 225

1016: I am the embodiment of love: love is My instrument. There is no creature without love; the lowest loves itself, at least and its "Self is God". So there are no atheists, though some might dislike Him or refuse Him, as malarial patients dislike sweets or diabetic patients refuse to have anything to do with sweet. Those who preen themselves as atheists will one day, when their illness is gone, relish God and revere Him.   *Sanathana Sarathi, August 1994, back cover*

1017: The constant integrated awareness which is in everyone, is covered by the ash of worldly desires. When the ash is blown off, the fire of Brahman reveals itself.   *Sanathana Sarathi, May 1996, p. 128*

1018: Without being able to control the senses, what is the use of learning every kind of knowledge? All knowledge is useless, if one has not acquired Self-knowledge. Such a person may be regarded as intellectually clever, but cannot be called intelligent. The first step, therefore, is to know one's self. Spirituality is the means to acquire knowledge of yourself. Hence, as much importance should be assigned to the promotion of good qualities in the educational process as is given to academic studies.   *Sanathana Sarathi, April 1993, p. 92*

1019: Education confers humility. Humility does not mean mere bending of the head. Only an attitude of mind free from egoism, ostentation and attachment can be called humility. Today neither teachers nor parents are able to teach such humility to the children because they themselves have not cultivated that attitude. The water you can draw from a tap depends on the nature of the water in the tank. Today teachers and parents have not filled their minds with sacred feelings.

How can they be expected to infuse the children with such feelings? Here is a piece of burning charcoal. If you take proper care of it, it will soon get covered up with ashes. In the heart of every human being, there is the fire of wisdom (Jnaana-Agni). That fire signifies a pure heart. Today we are not able to see that fire because the heart is enveloped by the ash of worldly desires. When the ash is blown away, the fire will be visible. Men tend to forget the noble and ideal sentiments in their hearts because they are covered by worldly material and sensual desires.   *Sanathana Sarathi, August 1994, p. 210*

1020: Because we have trained ourselves on seeing only the external world, we have lost our capacity to develop inner vision.
Summer Showers in Brindavan, 1973, p. 44

1021: The ripe fruit of devotion confers the wisdom which eliminates differences. Devotion is a fragment of the Divine. Without devotion, awareness of the Divine cannot be experienced. Equally, devotion without consciousness of the Divine can only breed egoism.   *Sanathana Sarathi, September 1994, p. 226*

1022: To see an effulgent light you do not need another lamp. Likewise to know the self-luminous Atmic Knowledge there is no need for any other knowledge. Every human being has in him the knowledge of his true form. Owing to his failure to know this stupendous fact, man pursues all kinds of worldly knowledge.
Sanathana Sarathi, February 1995, p. 37

1023: For one who lacks Intelligence and wisdom, detachment becomes a burden. For one who lacks knowledge, the body becomes a burden. For one who lacks love, the mind becomes a burden.
Sanathana Sarathi, October 1993, p. 272

1024: Men are wasting their precious lives in the pursuit of fleeting and petty pleasures. Make the best use of the opportunity you have now got. That is true devotion. You alone are responsible for your condition because of the way your mind works. Do your duty, recognize the truth of your being, and you will be able to experience your divinity. You have to purify your heart to experience the Divine. You may have desires, aspirations and yearning for happiness. But there is nothing equal to the bliss of experiencing the Divine and you will secure this bliss, wherever God may be.   *Sanathana Sarathi, April 1994, p. 91*

1025: The Vedas have declared that man can attain immortality by renunciation and not by any other means, actions, wealth or progeny. What is it that has to be renounced? One has to renounce one's bad qualities. Men today are only human in form, but are filled with beastly qualities. To manifest their inherent divine

nature, men have to cultivate love of God and fear of sin, and adhere to social morality. When people have fear of sin and love of God, they will not indulge in immoral acts. Thereby morality in society will be automatically ensured. It is meaningless to be born as a human being and lead an animal existence.
Sanathana Sarathi, July 1994, p. 169

1026: You are the "Seer". Everything that you see is the "seen". When the vision is concentrated on the Atma within, both are one. When you get the feeling "I am you" there is no scope for any worry. This is the easiest royal path to comprehend the Reality. Without understanding this, people waste their lives in the process of meditation and other futile pursuits.   *Sanathana Sarathi, July 1994, p. 173*

1027: Happiness is a attribute of the mind. Joy is your birthright. Happiness is only an interval between two miseries; misery is gap between two moments of happiness. You must equate both happiness and misery and transcend both, teaching the mind to dive deeper into the realms of Bliss. Bliss is the nature of the Self, your own innermost Reality.

Discover the fountain of joy within; that is a never-failing, ever-full, ever-cool fountain; for it rises from God.   *Baba, The Breath of Sai, p. 287*

1028: A man seeking to harm others nourishes many evil thoughts is his mind. But these thoughts cause him ten times the harm they do to others. He is not aware of this truth. Consequently, he indulges in abuse of others and on doing harm to them. But there are no "others", but only manifestations of the Divine. Not realizing the divinity in others, man tries to harm them. But whoever wields the sword against others, will perish by the sword. The harm which he does to others will be the undoing of himself. Whoever abuses others, will also be the target of abuse by others. As are the thoughts, so is the outcome. The entire human existence is based upon thoughts and their results.
Sanathana Sarathi, August 1993, p. 212

1029: If the heart is pure, everything else will be pure. The Atma is like a flame in the body. When it is covered by the ten senses, its light filters through ten holes, as it were. And when it is covered, in addition, with the blanket of Abhimaana (Attachment to worldly objects), the effulgence of the Atma (Self) is not visible. When attachment is given up and the body consciousness goes, the Self is revealed in all its brightness.   *Sanathana Sarathi, June 1994, p. 150*

1030: When the heart is filled with compassion, the hands are dedicated to the service of others, the body is engaged in constant help to others; the life of such a person is sacred, purposeful and noble.
Sanathana Sarathi, December 1993, p. 309

1031: The love of God can arise only from loving thoughts. There must be yearning for God, just as one has to experience hunger to think of food. There is hunger for God in every one, but the disease of self-pride prevents one from feeling that hunger. The denial of God is a kind of disease. The unbeliever is afflicted by a variety of diseases like pride, envy, anger and greed.

Sanathana Sarathi, January 1995, p. 26

1032: All organs in the human body should be kept functioning properly. Only then it would be possible to rise from the human to the divine level. How is this to be accomplished? By dedicating every action to the Lord. When every action is done with the consciousness that it is done for the pleasure of the Lord, life gets divinised. There is no need for anyone to give up any of his duties or actions in daily life. All that is needed is to perform every one of them in a spirit of dedication to the Lord. *Sanathana Sarathi, March 1996, p. 60*

1033: Devotees are generally confused about meditation. Just as you can't receive the radio program broadcast from any station clearly unless you tune to the appropriate wavelength perfectly, even in meditation you will not get the desired communion with God until you attune yourself to the divine perfectly. Some aspirants mistake concentration for meditation. Concentration is needed in reading, writing, walking, talking, eating, etc.. Concentration is below the senses, contemplation is in the middle and meditation is above the senses. Meditation, in fact, is transcending the senses and the mind. During meditation, the mind is actively thinking of several things of the past, the present and the future. The thoughts are running fast. Scarcely does any one concentrate on the Divine even though one sits in the lotus pose and closes his eyes. There is no need for sitting for meditation and wasting time in this manner. One can transform every act in daily chores like making chappathis can be transformed into acts of worship of the Divine. Since the body is an instrument, you can make God happy through this instrument and enjoy happiness yourself in the process. In this way you practice meditation in your daily duties. *Sanathana Sarathi, May, 1993, p. 123*

1034: After long searches here and there, in temples and in churches, in earths and in heavens, at last you come back. Completing the circle from where you started, to your own soul, and find that He, for whom you have been seeking all over the world, for whom you have been weeping and praying in churches and temples, on whom you were looking as the mystery of all mysteries, shrouded in the clouds, is the nearest of the near, is your ownself, the reality of your life, body and soul. *Sathya Sai Speaks, Volume IV, p. 192*

1035: Everyone wants to achieve happiness and makes all sorts of efforts for this purpose without knowing where to find it. He thinks he can get happiness when he gets a job to earn his livelihood and pursues his studies only with this end in view. After he gets a job, he is still not happy. He wants to get married. He marries and sets up a family. Even then there is no happiness. He wants progeny. He gets a child. Still he is not happy. He wants promotion so that he can earn more to maintain his family. He gets it. Even then he is not happy. And he goes on like that in quest of happiness that eludes him. Happiness is not there in all these attainments of possessions. It is only in the heart within. He is himself the embodiment of happiness. Yet, without realizing this, he goes on seeking happiness elsewhere.   *Sanathana Sarathi, May 1994, p. 123*

1036: The world today is filled with two kinds of intoxication. One is intoxication arising from wealth. The other is the intoxication of power. These two are not different from each other. They are like the two parts of a seed. Through wealth, one secures positions of power and power is used to acquire wealth. Man's life today is based on these two: power and pelf. Man's conceit grows beyond bounds when he has only one of these two. The state of those who have both needs no description. Forgetting humanness, cherishing animal qualities, man develops a demonic nature. Man today makes no effort to realize the greatness and power of the mind. Instead, he is submerged in worldly activities and wastes his life.
                    Sanathana Sarathi, June 1994, p. 148

1037: Permanent bliss is only within and once you realize that you are the blissful Atma and not the transient body, you will always be happy. Some people raise the question "Where is God?" God cannot be seen outside. You must direct your vision inside. Then you will realize that the entire world is a reflection of the Atma within you.   *Sanathana Sarathi, May 1994, p. 124*

1038: Man has to realize his divinity and look at all Nature from the Divine point of view. Instead, man looks at everything only from the mundane point of view. The body is indeed perishable, but it is also the means for realizing the imperishable Truth.   *Sanathana Sarathi, May 1995, p. 114*

1039: What is the purpose of life? It is not eating or sleeping. It is to lead an ideal life. Every human being has to accomplish certain aims in life which are in tune with humanness. You have to realize that the Lord is the indweller in all beings and experience unity in diversity. The entire creation is present within the human body. This is the mystery of creation. The human body is a marvelous creation. Every organ in the body discharges its specific function and nothing else. Only the Divine can create such a wonderful organism. The Atma is the Master within the body. Never betray the Master. Be grateful to God for endowing you with such a marvelous body.   *Sanathana Sarathi, May 1995, p. 127*

1040: For the proper utilization of time, which is Divine, the Vedic texts laid down basic injunctions for mankind. Among these, foremost are "Sathyam Vada;

Dharmam Chara" ("Speak the Truth; Follow Righteousness").
Sanathana Sarathi, May 1995, p. 130

1041: The quest for Truth is linked with the pursuit of wisdom. For the acquisition of wisdom, purity of the intellect is essential. If the intellect is not pure, the senses are likely to go haywire. Purity of the intellect is in fact, essential for every purpose.   *Sanathana Sarathi, May 1995, p. 130*

1042: Some teachers declare: Give up the world and take hold of God. Do these teachers follow what they preach? No. They are very much in the world and still preach in this manner. It is not possible to give up the world. The world also is a manifestation of God. Unfortunately, people go on looking at this Divine manifestation but do not see it as such. All that you see is a form of the Divine. Do not see it as different from God.   *Sanathana Sarathi, May 1995, p. 133*

1043: Only those teachings which you retain and put into practice will remain with you and all others will go out of you.
Summer Showers in Brindavan, 1973, p. 83

1044: The one who pursues the spiritual path not only benefits himself but promotes the well-being of others. He is like the incense stick which consumes itself in the process of spreading its fragrance while burning.
Sanathana Sarathi, April 1995, p. 98

1045: Consider the body as a vessel, wisdom as a rope and use the vessel to draw the nectar of divinity from the well of spirituality. Not otherwise can immortality be attained.   *Sanathana Sarathi, April 1995, p. 98*

1046: In running a race only one runner comes first. Similarly, there may be thousands of flowers on the branches of a tree, but very few become fruits. People are of different sorts. There are the theists, the atheists, the agnostics, the slothful people, the yogis, the hedonists, the stoics, the cynics, the saints and the sinners. Each individual occupies a particular position in the world in accordance with his samskaras or the physical and spiritual characteristics acquired during previous lives.   *Summer Showers, 1979, p. 104*

1047: All of you who are here have come from different parts of India and the world. After your stay here, you have to go back to your native places. Likewise human beings have come to the planet earth as pilgrims. They have to return to their original home. You have come from the Atma. You have to go back to the

Atma. You have come from the Brahman (Supreme Self). You have to merge in the Brahman. You have to become the Brahman. That is the ideal. That is the goal. In between there may be many impediments. You should ignore them. Have unshakable faith. That is true devotion.

Sanathana Sarathi, September 1995, p. 229

1048: A nation's well being or troubles are dependent on the actions of the people. Actions are related to men's thoughts. If the country's condition is not what it should be, what is the reason? Men's thoughts and actions are not what they should be.

Sanathana Sarathi, December 1995, p. 286

1049: The most important element in man's existence is thought (sankalpa). As are the thoughts, so is the speech. As is the speech so are the actions. The harmony of these three will lead to the experience of Divinity.

Sanathana Sarathi, August 1995, p. 220

1050: It is not right that man, who is endowed with immense potencies, should be content with what is seen by the physical eyes. Such eyes are possessed equally by beasts and birds, as well as insects and germs. What, then is the uniqueness of the sight given to man? It must be realized that it is difficult to secure human birth. Having acquired this privilege, human beings should not be content with what is seen by the physical eyes. Man should acquire the eyes of wisdom.

It may be argued that even the physical eyes help man to acquire knowledge. The eyes see everything but cannot see themselves, how can they see the mind or see Maadhava (the Divine Lord)? To have a vision of the Lord, the physical eyes are not competent. One must acquire the eyes of wisdom for this purpose.

The eyes are there, but when they develop a disease, the eyes are not aware of it. When the ears lose the power of hearing, they are not aware of the loss. The senses which cannot know their own state, how can they know God? The physical eyes can only serve to see external objects in nature and examine their properties and explain them, but cannot recognize the Divine.

Sanathana Sarathi, December 1995, p. 319

1051: Where is the need to search for God, when He is omnipresent? It is a ludicrous exercise. When you are yourself Divine, where is the need for a quest? A man who goes inquiring about where he is will be deemed crazy.

Sanathana Sarathi, December 1997, p. 311

1052: Thoughts and desires are not the same. There are many thoughts that are not desires. If thoughts go too deeply into objects, desires arise. If there is a desire, there is a thought. But not all thoughts are desires. Dark clouds bring rain. God's grace is in drops like rain, they accumulate and then there is a torrent. If there is a very strong desire for God, even bad thoughts just pass through the mind and are not held. Desire directed to God brings discrimination. Intelligence, which is discrimination, is not the mind, nor is it thoughts. Intelligence is the direct Atma Shakti, a direct force of the Atma.

Sanathana Sarathi, November 1996, back cover

1053: When men begin to recognize the omnipresence of God they will be transformed. All their thoughts and actions will get divinised. It may be asked: "Who is responsible for the evil in the world? The persons indulging in the evil deeds are responsible. God is only a witness. The rewards of punishments people receive in life are fruits of their own actions and not conferred by God.

When all actions are done in a spirit of dedication to the Divine and with a recognition of one's own divinity, all actions become sanctified. Identification of the 'I' with the body is the cause of all troubles. It turns the "I" into the ego. The ego is at the root of all troubles. There is nothing wrong in looking after the body, but life should not be based on attachment to the body.

Sanathana Sarathi, December 1997, p. 312

1054: There are many evidences to demonstrate the Divinity that is inherent in man. But few men are ready to make the sacrifice that is required to experience this Divinity. *Sanathana Sarathi, October 1995, p. 262*

1055: Man will be happy only when he is struggling along the path to God, just as a fish is happy while swimming in water. Work; wisdom; worship are the three paths to God, but because of desire (Kama), Karma is warped through anger. Wisdom is befogged, and due to greed, worship is ruined; but by developing love, man can conquer all these weaknesses.   *Sanathana Sarathi, December 1995*

1056: Man is a reservoir of all potencies. The eternal principle of divinity is present in man, but he is not able to recognize it as he is deluded by the external world. A man produces a brilliant diamond out of a piece of rugged rock, but more value is given to the diamond than to the man who fashioned it.

Sanathana Sarathi, June 1996, p. 151

1057: Make your lives simple. Execute the daily tasks in a spirit of love and mutual co-operation. Be tolerant towards the errors and failings of others. Look upon them with sympathy and equanimity. Be calm and without agitations under all conditions. Then your sentiments will be tender and unselfish. Envy, hatred and vindictiveness will not be able to gain entrance in the strong hold of your mind. You will have peace and happiness.

Sanathana Sarathi, March 1996, p. 79

1058: Divine love is the only panacea for all your troubles and miseries arising from insatiable desires and frustrated ambitions. God's love is like a lighthouse beacon. It shows you the right path. Divert the bost of your life towards the lighthouse of Divine love. You are then bound to gain the shore of bliss.
Sanathana Sarathi, December 1996, p. 313

1059: Removal of immorality is the only way to immortality. If you get rid of evil qualities like attachment, hatred and envy, you will realize immortality. These bad traits make you remote from God. When you get rid of them, God becomes close to you.

Hence, gradually you have to give up the animal qualities and develop godly qualities such as truth, righteousness, justice and morality. By a process of self-inquiry you can get rid of your animal qualities like anger. How long are you going to remain in the same round of birth and death without realizing the goal of human existence? All pujas, rituals and penances are performed for this realization. You have secured as extremely precious gift by your present birth. Do not waste it. Utilize every available moment for a worthwhile purpose.
Sanathana Sarathi, November 1996, p. 288

1060: Divinity is not easily perceived or realized. It is easy to talk about the Divine. It is easy to comment on the miracles and sports of the Divine. But to understand them in their fullness is very difficult. To look at something evil and shout about it like crows is not a good thing. It is better to sing like the cuckoo over something good. Tastes differ from person to person. One man's sweet is another man's poison. With such diverse tendencies, how can men recognize the Divine? The ancient sages of Bharat carried out many spiritual investigations and though the study of the scriptures proclaimed their experience of the Divine. The Upanishads declared: "Raso vai saha". That is, the Divine is present in all things as their essence like sugar in sugarcane and butter in milk. God is present both in the good and the bad, in truth and untruth, in merit and sin. That being the case, how is one to determine what is false and what is unrighteous? The Gita declares: "My Spirit is the indwelling spirit in all beings". The individual who realizes this truth will experience equal mindedness. *Sanathana Sarathi, March 1996, p. 63*

1061: Bear in mind four dicta to be observed: Run away from bad company. Welcome association with good people. Do meritorious acts continually. Remember what is transient and what is permanent. Be with God, think with God, see with God and dedicate all actions to God. Consider all as members of one Divine family. Regard yourself as a trustee and use your wealth and talents for the good of others. Be compassionate at all times. Students in particular should always be ready to go to the help of people in distress. God today is in search of good men. Everyone should strive to be sincere in thought, word and deed. Then you need not go in search of God. God will discover you.
Sanathana Sarathi, March 1996, p. 67

1062: Understand that there is no free will for individuals. They are constrained by various limitations. God alone has total free will. All others are bound in one way or another.

Whatever one's efforts, the ultimate outcome lies with Providence. Therefore, place your faith in God and do your duty, wherever you may be. Do not cause any harm to others. Observe continence, avoid covetousness and lead a good, righteous life. A bad habit, which may seem trivial in the beginning, may develop into a menace in later life. Correct such faults in the initial stages. Pursue spiritual exercises with the same enthusiasm you have for sports and studies.
Sanathana Sarathi, March 1996, p. 74

1063: Only through devotion does man attain the supreme Truth. Through devotion alone, does man get release from the disease of birth and death. Through devotion man seeks to realize God. Through devotion alone he achieves liberation.   *Sanathana Sarathi, February 1996, p. 37*

1064: At one time we are joyous, and at another time we are sorrowful. The one and the same object which is a source of happiness turns out to be a source of agony with the interval of time. Therefore, joy and grief are only states of mind, and the objects which are themselves subject to change cannot give us lasting happiness. Change is not real. Whatever can be changed basically cannot be real. Knowing that the life of placid enjoyment is naturally inimical to serious spiritual effort, the good people consider difficulties as stepping stones to a higher life.   *Summer Showers in Brindavan, 1973, p. 208*

1065: The essence of all creeds is one and the same thing. Man's primary duty is to surrender to God. "Surrender" means attaining the state in which the devotee feels he is one with God. This feeling arises out of the conviction that the same divinity is present in all. Bodies of human beings are varied like bulbs, but the current passing through them is the same. The color of the bulbs or their wattage may vary; but the current activating them is the same
Sanathana Sarathi, January 1997, p. 2

1066: The Divine is not anywhere else. It is enshrined in one's heart. Hence, the man who seeks the Divine within his heart redeems himself. He then attains liberation. All external spiritual exercises are of temporary value. They should be internalized to experience lasting bliss. All mental exercises also leave the heart unaffected. In the nine paths of devotion, beginning with listening to sacred things and ending with total surrender of the self, the last is the most important. After total surrender, there is no need for any other effort.
Sanathana Sarathi, February 1996, page 44

1067: Man should be dedicated to action. Today he does not adhere to this principle. How, then, can he expect the fruits? Men must work. They must perform good deeds and realize good results. They must share the fruits of their labors with others. This is the foremost duty of man. If everyone does his duty, there will be no room for conflict in the world. This is the lesson taught by the earth.

"Karthavyam" (Duty) is most important. The lawyer should do his duty. The doctor, the farmer, the administrator, the businessman, each should discharge his respective duty. If this is done, the world will have no problems. Everyone should aim at excellence in the performance of one's duties. Then the nation will be prosperous and happy. Today very few discharge their duties properly. Instead of doing their work, they interfere in other people's work. They fail to do their work and spoil that of others.

Sanathana Sarathi, April 1996, p. 87

1068: The Divine that the human really is, has been forgotten. It was once glowing and shining in the experience, but, it no longer inspires the individual with sublime confidence. The Veda maatha has been deserted; spurious guardians and sham caretakers have won the hearts of the people.

Sathya Sai Speaks, Volume IV, p.92

1069: Today all spiritual exercises are ostensibly undertaken for realizing God. But there is no need for undertaking them. Human birth itself is a mark of Divinity. What is essential is to recognize the indwelling Divinity and live on that basis.

Where is God? Not in temples or pilgrim centers or other places. He dwells in the heart of everyone. To experience the Divinity within, one has to see the Divine in all others and render them service in that spirit.

Sanathana Sarathi, November 1996, p. 285

1070: Man has evolved from the animal to the human and he must progress towards the Divine. Unfortunately, today he tends to revert to animality. Man should realize the infinite preciousness of human birth.

Sanathana Sarathi, August 1996, p. 207

1071: Giving up attachment to the body, the scriptures call men to surrender to God. What is meant by "surrender"? Forgetting the body and thinking of God, that is surrender. Surrender does not mean offering to God your worthless body and your perishable possessions. Such offerings have no meaning for the Divine. People going to Tirumala make all kinds of promises to God if their desires are fulfilled. Does God need any of their offerings? No. Why should God be commercialized? You should seek oneness with God. God will be pleased if you realize your true self. Your happiness is His bliss.

Develop therefore, this sense of spiritual unity (Ekaatma bhaavam). It is the loss of this sense of unity that is at the root of all the differences and divisions in the world today. You have no need to search for God. God is truth. Adhere to truth; follow Dharma. What is Dharma? It is not charity or gifts of earthly goods that constitute Dharma. Dharma means purity and unity in thought, word and deed. Turn your mind towards God. All will be well with you. If you turn the mind towards the phenomenal world, you will experience only misery. The mind is man's most precious possession. Without is man ceases to be human. The human birth has been given to man for practicing Dharma.

Sanathana Sarathi, April 1996, p. 96

1072: Develop greater love in your heart. As your love grows, the Spirit in you will shine brighter. Spiritual growth calls for restraint on desires. In addition, you have also to get rid of bad qualities like attachment and aversion. The three great enemies of man are desire, anger and greed. Desire destroys devotion. Anger annihilates wisdom, greed poisons every action. These three vices are destructive of Karma (good deeds), devotion and wisdom. All the three have to be totally given up. The only cure for them is to burn them in the fire of Divine love.

Sanathana Sarathi, July 1996, p. 172

1073: Without cultivating love for others, you can never cultivate love for yourself. Sorrow for yourself is gained by hurting others. In the same manner, victory in every war will result in another war. So also, any happiness that you can give to others will result in happiness for yourself in the end. Man must realize that he cannot get anything without sharing it with humanity around him. So, you must believe that happiness of the people around you will lead to your own happiness in due course. *Summer Showers in Brindavan, 1973, p. 2*

1074: We have friends and foes, likes and dislikes, whereas Vendanta teaches us to develop equal mindedness. Just as we do not punish our teeth for accidentally biting our tongue because we consider both the organs as parts of our body. So also, we have to bear in mind that the eternal and universal Atma resides in everyone and everywhere.

We should not accentuate differences, but concentrate upon unity. If we attach importance to the bodily relationship than the individual variation will come to the fore. On the other hand, we should remember that a teacher, a friend, an actor,a guru, and a disciple are different from each other only in a name and form. The Atma which is the witnessing consciousness in all of them is the same. The presence of atma in all these names and forms establishes the oneness of all of them. *Summer Showers in Brindavan, 1973, p. 112*

1075: Freedom is independence from externals. Perfect freedom in not given to any man on earth. Lesser the number of wants, the greater is the freedom. Hence, perfect freedom is absolute desirelessness.

Sathya Sai Speaks, Volume IV, p. 15

1076: This microphone before me must have been made by someone, is it not? He is not seen or known by you, but of his existence, there can be no doubt. Besides, it is certain he must be knowing all about this microphone which he has made. So too, there must be a creator for this universe and He must be knowing all about it. This universe is composed of the five elements and He is the master of all the five, their manipulator, aware of their subtle characteristics and properties. He is the Kshetrajna, he who knows this kshetra or field. When I speak into the mike, all of you can hear me clearly; but the tape recorder here, the fan, the bulbs, the tube-lights, all operate on account of the self-same unseen electric current that animates each of them.
Sathya Sai Speaks, Volume IV, p. 139

1077: While eating and sleeping are common to all living beings, man is distinguished by two qualities. One is dharma or right conduct and the other is Jnana or wisdom. If this Jnana and dharma are not present in man, he will also have to be classed along with all other living things.
Summer Showers in Brindavan, 1973, p. 157

1078: When delusion is shed, grief gets destroyed; joy is established: dukha nivritti and aananda prapti both happen at the same time. The mind is the villain; it is another name for desire; the texture of the mind is just desire; both warp and woof are desire and nothing else. If desire goes, the mind disappears. When you pull out all the yarn from a piece of cloth, you have no more cloth. So too, pull out desires from the mind, it disappears, and you are free. Grief and joy are the obverse and reverse of the same experience. Joy is when grief ends; grief is when joy ends. When you invite a blind man for dinner, you must set on the table two plates, for he comes along with another man who will lead him in. Grief and joy are inseparable companions.   *Sathya Sai Speaks, Volume IV, p. 153*

1079: Don't rely on the body. It is a water bubble. Don't rely on the mind, which is like a mad monkey. Follow the conscience. When you follow the conscience with full self-confidence, you can accomplish anything. For one who lacks intelligence and wisdom; detachment becomes a burden. For one who lacks knowledge, the body becomes a burden. For one who lacks love, the mind becomes a burden. Man must develop discrimination to be free from all these burdens.
Sanathana Sarathi, October, 1993, p. 257

CLOSING STATEMENTS

1080: The awareness that the world is one family dawns when one recognizes the truth of the indwelling spirit. The messages of Christ and the other world prophets must be practiced earnestly by man; all men must share in the precious heritage of selfless and universal love and develop it by practice in daily life. Be the harbingers of the new age. . . be free from selfishness and greed, hatred and violence. Be a light unto yourselves; may you become worthy instruments for the revival of the religion of love and the resurgence of human values.

Sathya Sai Baba, God as man

1081: God's Grace is as the shower of rain, as the sunlight. You have to do some spiritual discipline to acquire it; the spiritual discipline of keeping a pot upright to receive the rain, the spiritual discipline of opening the door of your heart, so that the sun may illumine it. Like the music that is broadcast over the radio, it is all round you; but you must switch on your receiver and tune the identical wavelength so that you can hear it and enjoy it. Pray for Grace; but do at least this little spiritual discipline. Grace will set everything right. Its main consequence is "self-realization" but there are other incidental benefits too, like a happy contented life here below, and a cool courageous temper, established in unruffled equanimity or peace. The main benefit from a jewel is personal joy; but when one has come to the last coin in the purse, one can sell it and start life again! That is an incidental advantage. The plantain tree has the bunch of fruits as its main gift! But the leaves, the soft core of the trunk- the flower bud- these are subsidiary items that can also be put into profitable use. This is the nature of Grace. It fulfills a variety of wants.

When you have no faith in God, you cannot gauge the efficacy of Grace.

You have won this human body, this human life, as the reward for many lives spent in acquiring merit. You have reward for many lives spent in acquiring merit. You have won this chance, this unique good fortune of being able to get darsan of Sai. Plunging deep into the waters of this tumultuous ocean of change you have heroically emerged from its depths again. Hold on firmly to it. Pray that you may have it for ever and be filled with the joy that it confers. That is the way by which you can render this life fruitful.   *Baba, The Breath of Sai, p. 295*

1082: I am hoping that you will not forget what you have learned here, that you will recapitulate them and keep on thinking of them. Animals have no inner vision. They have only external or outward vision. But we are not animals. We should develop the inner vision. Even an animal, which has no inward vision, comes back to its resting place and begins to ruminate and digest its food after it has taken its food. If we human beings, who have both inward and outward vision, do not recapitulate and digest what we have listened to, we will become worse than animals. What you have learned should enter into your blood vessels and all the time it should manifest itself from your interior. I am hoping that you will remember all the good things that you have listened to during your stay here and put them into practice in your daily life and enjoy the bliss thereof and be of some service and help to the community around you.

Summer Showers in Brindivan, 1977, p. 254

END OF BOOK

<u>**Books Referenced for the Selected Statements Used In This Book:**</u>

- ALL **SANATHANA SARATHI** publications noted were English versions.

-**SUMMER SHOWERS IN BRINDAVAN 1973**,
      Published by BHAGAVAN SRI SAI SEVA SAMITHI,
      GULAB BHAWAN, Second Edition, 1975

-**SUMMER SHOWERS IN BRINDAVAN 1977**,
      Published in India by SRI SATHYA BOOKS AND
      PUBLICATIONS TRUST (Ananthapur Dist.) A.P. 51534.

-**SUMMER SHOWERS IN BRINDAVAN 1979**,
      Published in India by SRI SATHYA BOOKS AND
      PUBLICATIONS TRUST (Ananthapur Dist.) A.P. 51534.

-**GEMS OF WISDOM**, Compiled and Published by
      C.M. SAHNI, 4 SAI DEEP COMPLEX, Puttaparthi 51534,
      INDIA

-**BABA, THE BREATH OF SAI**, Compiled by
      GRACE T. McMARTIN

-**SATHYA SAI SPEAKS, VOLUME IV (1964)**,
      (Revised and Enlarged Edition), Published in India by
      SRI SATHYA BOOKS AND PUBLICATIONS TRUST
      (Ananthapur Dist.) A.P. 51534.

- **SATHYA SAI BABA, GOD AS MAN**

It is my sincere hope that this is not the end of the readers' desire for this type of knowledge, for as the title of this book denotes, this is just **the beginning of wisdom**.

You can find many similar books already in print, and many books about Sai Baba at:

SATHYA SAI BOOK CENTER OF AMERICA
305 WEST FIRST STREET
TUSTIN, CALIFORNIA
92780

PH: (714) 669-0522
FAX: (714) 669-9138

OR

SRI SATHYA SAI BOOKS AND PUBLICATIONS TRUST
ANANTAPUR DISTRICT,
ANDHRA PRADESH, INDIA
PIN CODE: 515 134